BEYOND REALISM AND IDEALISM

By Wilbur Marshall Urban

THE INTELLIGIBLE WORLD

VALUATION

FUNDAMENTALS OF ETHICS

LANGUAGE AND REALITY

BEYOND REALISM AND IDEALISM

by

WILBUR MARSHALL
URBAN

London
GEORGE ALLEN & UNWIN LTD
Ruskin House   Museum Street

PRINTED IN GREAT BRITAIN
in 11-Point Baskerville Type
BY W. S. COWELL LIMITED
IPSWICH

PREFACE

As A beginner in philosophy I read in Hegel's *Philosophy of Religion*[1] these striking words: 'The contrast of idealistic and realistic philosophy is of no importance; such expressions as subjectivity and objectivity, reality and ideality, are simply bare abstractions.' At the time I was impressed both by the insight and the essential truth of the statement and, since that time, can truly say I have never willingly allowed myself to be called either an exclusive realist or an exclusive idealist.

The idea expressed in the title of this book, *Beyond Realism and Idealism*, has for many years been in the background of all my thoughts. More and more I became convinced of the fatal character of this division among philosophers. It has seemed little less than tragic that preoccupation with this debate should divert the energies of many first-rate minds from the more magnificent problems of philosophy, and should blind them to that which from time immemorial has made philosophy the significant thing it is in human culture. To see so many philosophers who, in contrast to the unphilosophical have so much in common, caught in this endless strife of systems has at times filled me with a profound melancholy—a melancholy but slightly tempered by the element of humour which this curious situation must arouse in any but the most academic mind.

Twenty-five years ago I published an article in *The Philosophical Review* entitled 'Beyond Realism and Idealism' in which was presented in preliminary form a thesis which has become one of the main elements in the present argument.[2] I there maintained that the issue between epistemological realism and idealism is not an issue of fact or of logic but of cognitive meanings and values, and tried to show that this problem, which is insoluble on the factual or logical levels, is capable of solution when transferred to this higher court. I argued for a consistency of idealism with realism, or synthesis of the two positions, which should retain the essential cognitive meanings

[1] *The Philosophy of Religion*, III, p. 169.

[2] "Beyond Realism and Idealism," *The Philosophical Review*, Vol. XXIV, No. 2, 1917. This was followed by a discussion between Professor Creighton and the present writer, entitled "Beyond Realism and Idealism vs. Two Types of Idealism," *The Philosophical Review*, Vol. XXVII, No. 1, January 1918.

and values of both. This paper inaugurated a discussion with J. E. Creighton in which he accepted my main contention but argued that objective idealism, properly understood, actually achieves this synthesis. For reasons into which I need not enter here, I was unable to accept his emendation, but his important distinction between 'two types of idealism' led me to further study and to a deeper understanding of the problem. As I look back on that discussion now, I find much in my own argument which was at once crude and ununderstanding, but so far as the position as a whole is concerned I do not find it necessary to change it at any really significant point.

In the quarter century following the publication of this article further study has but confirmed me in my original insight. During these years I have continually asked myself two questions which, I believe, every philosopher should seriously ponder. The first of these is heart-searching enough. How is it possible that an opposition of this sort—so fatal to philosophical advance, and in a way so unnecessary, should have arisen? The second is no less heart-searching. Why is it that if it is a problem capable of solution—like other problems of matter of fact and logic—that the debate is interminable and neither convinces the other? Surely this is an extraordinary situation and must have some special reason.

To the first question I finally found an answer which is satisfactory to myself if not to others. Briefly it is that the conflict, as we now understand it, is a wholly modern phenomenon —the product of the sensationalistic empiricism which came into being with the psychological analysis of knowledge of Locke and Hume; that the opposition, as we now know it, did not exist in classical European philosophy; and that *philosophia perennis* is in very truth above the battle. The fact that the issue, as we now understand it, is conditioned both in form and content by local and temporal cultural conditions at least suggests the possibility, that with the understanding of the sources of the opposition, the opposition itself may be transcended.

The second question, it seems to me, also has an answer—one also which if not satisfactory to others is at least satisfactory to me. The interminable character of the debate does indeed exhibit a most extraordinary situation and must accordingly have an extraordinary reason. The days of splendid debate between idealists and realists which characterized the early decades of the twentieth century were followed by a 'peace without victory,' a peace of exhaustion in which each side could only wonder at the perversity if not stupidity of the other. Why this stale-mate? I think there is a reason and the development of this reason constitutes also an important phase of my argument.

Meinong recognized the anomolous character of this situation. Speaking of the idealistic train of thought, he once wrote that it constitutes a curious exception to the usual run of things in science in that the old knowledge (realism) is not supplanted by the new. The idealistic argument may for a time convince, but the old realistic conviction returns with all its pristine vigour. This is indeed true, but the same holds true of the realistic argument and it is strange that so keen a thinker as Meinong did not recognize this fact. Just as little can the realist refute the idealist. The latter may also be convinced for a time but the old idealistic conviction returns with all its pristine force. This anomalous position suggests, I believe, the reason for the stale-mate. Neither can refute the other and neither can prove his own position. The reason for this is that neither position is knowledge in the ordinary sense of the word.

The argument of the book falls into two main parts. Chapters I to VI are concerned with the argument for the transcendence of the opposition; chapters VII to X with an attempt to develop in detail a position which can be described as beyond realism and idealism. The method of the first part of the study is dialectical in the broad sense of the term. As the problem itself is dialectical, the solution of the problem is dialectical also. The working out of the argument consists in showing that neither position can be either proved or disproved factually and logically, and, secondly, that when the nature of the opposition is properly understood, the two positions are found to be not contradictory but complementary. The development of the argument in its two aspects requires a study of the entire problem of the place of dialectic in philosophy.

Chapters VII to X are of a different character. Chapters VII and VIII attempt to show that a study of the actual presuppositions of knowledge in the different sciences, physical and social, indicates that science itself is beyond the distinction of realism and idealism, and actually presupposes both. They thus serve as a sort of empirical confirmation of the main thesis of the entire study. Chapter IX seeks to formulate a philosophy which can in very truth be described as beyond realism and idealism and discusses the relation of this epistemological opposition to the conflict between idealism and naturalism, with which it is often identified. This latter conflict is believed to be irreconcilable and an attempt is made to develop 'an idealistic philosophy on realistic lines.' The final chapter, the Epilogue, discusses the significance of such a transcendence of realism and idealism for modern culture and philosophy.

The present work bears a definite relation to my preceding studies in philosophy. The standpoint of *The Intelligible World* was described as beyond realism and idealism in its epistemology and in Chapter III, entitled 'Genuine Knowledge and *Bona Fide* Logic,' I interpreted both realism and idealism in this sense. In my article 'Metaphysics and Value' in *Contemporary American Philosophers*, I stated in a preliminary way the position now to be developed and indicated that it is fundamental to my entire philosophical outlook. Again in *Language and Reality* I stated the same position from another angle in the chapter on 'Intelligible Communication.' The present work may therefore be viewed as a development of the epistemological presuppositions of my entire philosophy which can be understood rightly only as occupying a position beyond realism and idealism. If despite all these preceding statements, my position is still described as exclusively idealistic, it can only be because the issues involved are not really understood. In contrast with naturalism my view is indeed idealistic in the metaphysical sense, as all traditional philosophy has been, but so far as the epistemological issue is concerned, it is neither an exclusive idealism nor an exclusive realism.

It goes without saying that a proposal, seemingly so radical as this, is not the product of one erratic mind but has received impetus from many sources. It has been surprising as well as heartening to discover how many philosophers, of otherwise very diverse views, had come to feel very much as I did about this fatal division in philosophy. Of these I shall speak as occasion arises, but I should like to refer to one in the present context. It was a book by Bosanquet, *The Meeting of Extremes in*

Modern Philosophy, which perhaps most influenced my thought, at least in the beginning. He was right, I felt, in holding that these two extremes had come together at many points, that the developments of modern thought had more or less outmoded the terms realism and idealism, and that, if possible, they should be dropped from our philosophical vocabulary. I have no desire to call upon any of these distinguished philosophers either for support or justification—my argument is my own and for it I am alone responsible—I wish only to express my appreciation of what I have learned from them, and especially in confirming me in the belief that the issue with which I was concerned was not wholly unreal.

I am under no illusions as to the probable fate of this book. It may be taken for granted that a position such as this will scarcely commend itself to the majority of philosophers. From those in whom the opposition is so hardened that defence of their chosen position has become a large part of their intellectual life, the response is likely to be one of indignant repudiation or at least of amused contempt. And yet I can not escape the conviction that the time is ripe for just such an enterprise as this— certainly much more propitious than the quarter century in which Bosanquet's proposal fell on deaf ears. If I am not greatly mistaken, the logic of history is increasingly outmoding this old conflict and a growing impatience with these old problems is joined with a renewed interest in the more significant problems of metaphysics and speculative philosophy. If so, it is high time. If ever philosophy needed the freeing of its energies for the larger problems that concern our peace, it is now. Something of this I have sought to suggest in the Epilogue of the book.

CONTENTS

INTRODUCTION

*The Epistemological Problem in General and the Opposition
of Realism and Idealism.*

I — A

THERE are some philosophers who deprecate the epistemological problem as such. We have knowledge, they tell us,
and no theory of knowledge can either create or destroy
it. We have thought, intellect, reason: why all this continual
sharpening of the instrument without ever using it? Like Goethe
they are more or less contemptuous of all this 'thinking about
thought'.

With much of this, every sane philospher will agree. There is
much activity—in both epistemology and logic—which exem-
plifies the fanaticism of which it is said that it redoubles its
activity when it has forgotten its end. With the main contention
there can, however, be no sympathy. Unfortunately, we must
think about thought—if the products of our thought, knowledge, science itself, are to have any meaning for us other than
that which the products of any other unthinking instinct have—
if the will to know is not to be merely one of many transmutations or disguises of the will to life itself. 'We must know,' cries
Lossky, accepting thereby all the painful reflection upon
thought and knowledge which this necessity inevitably implies.
We must know—and any metaphysical theory that leaves knowledge impossible stands self-condemned from the beginning. In
this sense the central and ultimate philosophical problem is that
of epistemology, not metaphysics.

This is why the problem of knowledge—somewhat to the
bewilderment of the non-philosophical—has bulked so large in
all significant philosophical discussion. The fact that knowledge,
science, exists at all, that the human mind has proved capable
of acquiring it, when taken together with the other acquire-
ments of the human spirit, itself outweighs in philosophical
significance all other facts, whether about man or nature
acquired through the study of the physical sciences. That, for
instance, 'the human mind should possess the power of com-
prehending its own natural origins, of ranging in thought over

13

and the justification of those two great antithetic movements in philosophic thought which we call idealism and realism. Both represent insistent and critical thinking about thought. Both represent two great theories of human knowledge—but still more fundamentally, they represent two great contrasting evaluations of knowledge. It is only as such that they can be understood.

Both realist and idealist are philosophers, which means that they feel the insistence and the real import of the cry: We must know! The tragedy of the situation—or is it, perhaps, still more the humour?—is that each thinks that the other has a theory of knowledge which makes genuine knowledge impossible. Each thinks that the other's theory denatures knowledge *ab initio*. To the realist it is scarcely understandable how one can call that knowledge at all in which knowing makes any difference to the thing known—in which the thing known is not wholly other than the knower. To the idealist it seems inconceivable that any one should talk of knowledge in any intelligible sense if the supposed object of knowledge is wholly independent of the knower—in which there is not in some way and in some degree mutual involvement of mind and object. Neither denies that we have the thing called knowledge—that is indeed an empirical fact; what they are concerned with is the question whether it is genuine knowledge, and what are the conditions of such knowledge. It is not my purpose here to define epistemological realism and idealism except in so far as it is necessary in order to talk about them in this most general way; the problem of definition comes later. Still less it is my purpose to consider now any of the arguments by which either realist or idealist arrives at his theory of knowledge, or seeks to defend it; this also is a problem for later consideration. All that we have here in mind is to show the place of both in the general theory of knowledge.

The problem of knowledge, it has been said, is 'part of the problem of values at large,' and, properly understood this is not only true, but the only way in which the problem of knowledge can be understood. The very fact that we must know, and that we recognize and acknowledge that 'must,' indicates that prior to the activity of knowledge, that which constitutes its very driving force, is the acknowledgment of truth as a value and of the obligation to seek it as one of the supreme goods of life. But the problem of knowledge is part of the problem of values in a still more significant way, and it is at this point that the opposition of idealism and realism arises. For both idealist and realist the problem is not merely that of the nature of *knowledge*, but of *genuine knowledge*. For the realist 'the peculiar significance' of knowledge—its inmost value—is conceived to be lost if the object of knowledge is not held to be independent of the knower, however that independence be conceived. For the idealist, on the other hand, the real significance of knowledge is lost if the object of knowledge is not in some sense mind-dependent, however that mind-dependence may be conceived. In both cases it is this prior assumption, this prior evaluation of knowledge, which at once determines the theory and constitutes the drive of the argument. The point I am making may be stated in the following way, and this form of statement will have increasing significance as the argument proceeds. Both idealism and realism —as theories of knowledge—are constituted, so to speak, by certain empirically and logically unsupported judgments of value, and it is the acknowledgment of these values which constitutes the driving force of idealism and the resistance of realism.

II
Realism and Idealism in The History of Philosophy.
The Problem Ancient and Modern.

A

In a sense, of course, the problem of knowledge is as old as philosophic thought. In a sense also, the opposition embodied in the terms 'realism and idealism' has also been present from the beginning. In another sense—and a very important sense—both the general problem and the specific opposition are products of the modern era.

The inquiries into human knowledge, and the critiques of human reason which characterized the seventeenth and eighteenth centuries, stand out in marked contrast to any discussions of knowledge, of reason, and of truth, during the classical and Christian eras. In the case of the latter discussions of 'knowledge' and reason are, so to speak, appendixes to metaphysics and part of metaphysics. In the case of the former they are the propeaedutic or the prolegomena to all philosophy and metaphysics.[1]

It is easy to see how this came about. The underlying assumption of the entire European tradition was trust in human reason—*ratio est capabilis*. Despite lapses into scepticism—whether the intellectual scepticism of the Greek Pyrrho or the more moral and emotional scepticism of a Christian Tertullian, the main tendency was trust in reason and knowledge. Even the method of doubt of Descartes—with the problematical idealism which it entailed—was, in a sense, but a secondary strain in the general movement of European rationalism. It was not until the physiology of knowledge of Locke, with the devastating scepticism to which it led, appeared, that the problem of knowledge in the modern sense arose.

If this was true for the problem of knowledge in general, it is *a fortiori* true for the opposition in theories of knowledge known as realism and idealism. In the sense that Plato has been called an idealist and Aristotle a realist, the opposition has, indeed, always been with us. But in another sense—and for the purposes of this study a very important sense—the opposition, as we now know it, is wholly modern and arose out of specific historic conditions. The very use of the terms realism and idealism is, as we shall see, wholly modern, and this in itself suggests that the problem itself is modern.

For the underlying assumption of the entire European tradition—whether idealistic or realistic in its tendencies—was the assumption of antecedent being, the division in philosophies concerning the question merely of the nature of this antecedent being, whether ultimately ideal or material, matter or spirit. In the sense of the modern opposition, traditional philosophy was in a very real sense 'above the battle'. The opposition, as we know it, arose out of precisely the same conditions which gave rise to the inquiries into knowledge and the critiques of reason

[1] The writing of the history of philosophy differs in no essential way from the writing of any history: it must be rewritten with every significant change in intellectual climate. Histories of philosophy, as we know them, were written largely in the modern period, after the epistemological issue became dominant. In telling the story of the ancient philosophers, it is only natural that the historian should emphasize this aspect and should read into the earlier thinkers problems which were not natural to them or at least largely secondary.

themselves, namely, the sensationalism of the modern physiology of knowledge. Once the origin of knowledge was found exclusively in sensation, and the objective ideas of traditional thought became the subjective ideas of the mind, all the peculiar issues of the modern debate came into being. It was inevitable that Berkeley should appear, but it was equally inevitable that the issue of realism should arise in a form unknown to philosophy hitherto.

I shall maintain, therefore, that, like the epistemological problem in general, as we now understand it, the specific problem of realism and idealism, as now formulated, is a wholly modern problem. It arises out of an historically local situation and it is only when we recognize this fact that the significance of the opposition can be understood. The fact that the terms realism and idealism, as now understood, were not known prior to this modern situation is, if not a proof, at least a significant indication of the modernity of the problem. It is one of the main theses of this essay that traditional philosophy is beyond realism and idealism in this sense. The 'proof' of this thesis belongs to a later context but sufficient has been said to indicate the general grounds for this position.[1]

B

The use of the terms idealism and realism is, as we have said, itself wholly modern. In all probability they appeared first about the end of the seventeenth century. Leibniz used the term idealist in contrast to the materialist, apparently in no other sense than as a designation of form as opposed to matter. This meaning of the term went back, of course, to the Platonic sense of idea as form. Thus Leibniz in a letter of 1714 accuses the Platonists of neglecting efficient and material causes. 'The Idealists, like Plato and Aristotle,' he writes, 'are right when they find the source of all things in final and formal causes, but they are wrong when they neglect efficient and material causes and conclude, as Henry More and other Platonists have done, that there are phenomena incapable of mechanical explanation. The materialists are wrong, on the other hand, in engaging themselves simply with the mechanical philosophy, neglecting the metaphysical view and trying to explain everything by what

[1] See chapter x.

affects the senses only.' He goes on to claim that he has himself 'penetrated to the harmony of the two realms.'[1]

The word idealism thus applied merely to a metaphysical view and to a method of explanation. But at this very time this meaning of the word was fast disappearing. It had to adjust itself to the changes brought about by the philosophies of Descartes and Locke. It became now the characterization for the system which admitted no reality other than the world of thought, and since Berkeley was held to be the chief representative of this belief, it was chiefly with reference to him and his followers that the term was used. In this sense the term was apparently first used by Wolff, who included the idealists with the materialists and sceptics as three evil sects. Against the charge of idealism Wolff protects the name of Plato with all energy. It was against idealism as thus understood that in the course of the century both the term and the party of realism appeared, as the assumption of an outer world independent of thought. In the middle ages, as is well known, it had, in contrast to nominalism, almost the opposite sense. The essence of mediaeval realism is the insistence upon the reality of universals or essences which, according to Otto Willman, constitutes the true idealism in contrast to the false idealism of the present.[2]

The situation was completely transformed through Kant, and with it the meaning of idealism. He accepts, in the first instance, the usage of Wolff, his definition of idealism in the *Prolegomena* being framed with Berkeley in view, such idealism 'consisting in the assertion that there are no other than thinking beings, that the other things which we believe ourselves to perceive are only ideas in thinking beings.' But idealism in this sense he attempts to refute and idealism in this sense is now degraded to empirical or psychological idealism, over against which he sets his own system as critical or transcendental idealism.

But this which was characteristic of Kant's own special form of idealism soon became, despite many opposing voices, identified with the concept of idealism itself. For most of his followers idealism has almost an opposite meaning from that which it had in Berkeley. The fact that Kant's formulation of his own critical idealism presupposed the 'refutation' both of the dogmatic

---

[1] Letter to Christian Wolff, 1714.

[2] Otto Willman, *Geschichte des Idealismus*.

idealism of Berkeley and the problematical idealism of Descartes —however convincing or unconvincing that refutation may be felt to be, is determinative for the entire history of the notion since Kant. Historically, we find in the movement that followed not only an attempt to escape the consequences of Locke's 'physiology of knowledge,' but also to reinstate in a new form the essentially realistic element in all traditional philosophy.[1]

Since the time of Kant and Hegel equally far-reaching changes in the meanings of these terms have taken place. These include changes in the meanings of idealism, some of which will be considered later, but chiefly in the meanings of realism. To the older motives embodied in the historic opposition of realism, new motives of an entirely different kind have been added.

In the seventeenth and eighteenth centuries, as we have seen, the term idealism was used only in opposition to materialism and mechanism, and when one spoke of realism one meant merely the realism of universals. But the term realism had also to adjust itself to changing conditons. Not only did later idealisms react against the subjectivism of the 'physiology of knowledge', but later realisms also. Realism, as now understood —new realism and the various critical realisms—are as much a reaction against psychologism as are the later idealisms. Thus epistemological realism itself has taken on new forms and come to have entirely different meanings. All realists are, to be sure, concerned with establishing the independent reality of sense data and the physical object in some sense—and some of them are almost exclusively concerned with this task—but others are equally interested in establishing the independent reality of values and of various sorts of universals and complexes. Nearly every conceivable kind of 'entity' has received the realistic baptism at somebody's hands and the different types of realism are almost as opposed as are realism and idealism.[2]

---

[1] See chapter x, pp. 257 f.

[2] The phenomenological movement is in this later sense realistic. Husserl tells us that his theory of objects aims to establish a kind of realism lying between platonic realism, on the one hand, resulting from metaphysical hypostatization, and psychological realism, on the other, produced by the sort of psychological hypostatizing that Berkeley criticized in Locke.

C

The conclusions to be drawn from this historical sketch are fairly obvious and, as it seems to me, quite significant. The changing meanings of the terms idealism and realism suggest that, as it has been said, the difficulty is not with their lack of meaning, but with their extreme richness of meaning—an embarrassment of riches which, as Bosanquet maintains, makes them almost worthless for philosophical discussion. Certainly we must conclude that they have no fixed meanings—that no logical definition is possible. There is no 'cardinal principle' of either realism or idealism to which these varying forms can be reduced. In other words no definitions are possible which do not include the historical background or the specific universe of discourse in which the terms are used. From this general fact certain corollaries follow which I will seek to develop. But first let us examine the extent of these changes.

The transmutations and transformations of this pair of concepts, idealism and realism, constitute one of the outstanding phenomena of modern thought. The terms have in many cases, so to speak, entirely changed places. If, to use a mathematical figure, we think of realism and idealism as representing a certain polarity of thought, the entire movement of thought in the modern world represents a complete movement of the system of co-ordinates through 360 degrees. Epistemological idealism passes from mentalism to transcendental idealism, and from this to objective idealism which may be viewed as a form of spiritual realism. On the other hand, realism passes from naïve physical realism, through various types of critical realism, to forms of logical realism which differ little from idealism. The meeting of extremes has been so patent that it is not strange that idealism and realism in some of their modern forms have been said to be 'separated only by a word.'

From this situation follow, as I have said, certain corollaries. The first of these is the impossibility of logical definition.

Before this succession of different phases a logic of fixed concepts stands helpless. With the dialectic of the historical movement of thought, as we have described it, ordinary logic can do nothing. The point I am here making is of the utmost importance. The attempt to fix the meanings of these terms, idealism and realism, in logical definition has been made over and over again, but it is always as fruitless in practice as it is fallacious in theory. The attempt, for instance, to define idealism by reducing it to mentalism or the subjective idealism of a Berkeley—to determine in this way the 'cardinal principle of idealism' is a case in point. The attempt of the modern 'realists' to analyze out of the many idealisms their essential form has wholly miscarried and the indignation of the idealists when it is sought to force them into this procrustean bed wholly justified. The similar attempt to reduce the various realisms to their 'simplest terms' is equally fallacious. When such attempts are made, not only does it become fatally easy for each to convict the other of trivial ambiguities and fallacious absurdities; it becomes equally easy to make the whole of epistemology, if not philosophy itself, a futile revolving about meaningless questions. Any philosophical tendency, when reduced to its essential elements does, as Paulhan insists, 'lose its colour, fade away and die.' By the very process of reduction and abstraction is eliminated all that gives the driving force to idealism and the power of resistance to realism.

A second corollary of even more significance follows from this situation, namely, the dialectical character of the opposition between realism and idealism.

The changing meanings which follow upon the changing backgrounds of thought are indeed historically conditioned. It is possible to define them only within an historical context or within a system of concepts. But the changes which are thus historical from one point of view display, on closer examination, an inner determinism which can be described only as dialectical. Nothing is clearer in the history of modern philosophy than precisely this dialectical movement—and nothing perhaps is more significant for our problem. The changes in the meaning of one of the poles begets inevitably changes in the meaning of the other. As we shall see more particularly later, the critical realism which follows upon Berkeley's devastating analysis of perception is a different realism than the newer forms which follow upon the idealist's equally devastating criticism of the doctrine of externality of relations. The same is true of the different forms of idealism: they are dialectical reactions to changing forms of realism.

III

The Identity and Continuity of Epistemological Intentions:
The Driving Force of Idealism and the Resistance of Realism.

A

We have seen why fixed definitions of the terms realism and idealism are impossible. We have also seen why the opposition is dialectical and not logical. But it does not follow from these facts that there is no continuity of meaning in these positions. It is easy to fail to see this continuity—to see in these changes merely a succession of entirely different phases, and to overlook the identity of epistemological intention which runs through them all. It is this that we must now seek to show, but first let me make clear what I mean by epistemological intention.

The term intention is used in two ways, the one subjective, as when we speak of the intentions of persons, the other objective, as when we speak of the intention or intent of a law. Now it is beyond question, of course, that every philosophy is the expression of a philosopher, that the kind of philosophy he holds depends in a sense on the kind of man he is. We may thus speak of the intent of his philosophizing in this psychological or sub-jective sense. But this is only one aspect of the situation. There are also movements in philosophy—movements which transcend individuals and which have a unity and continuity of intention which also transcend the intentions of individuals.

These general considerations apply especially to the relatively permanent opposition between realism and idealism. There is a sense, I suppose, in which every one is 'born' an idealist or a realist, just as he is born a conservative or a liberal. There is ground also for the view that the sources of the opposition are psychological, and a certain justification also for the thesis that the problem, being psychological in origin, its solution must be psychological also—no logical or speculative solution being possible.[1] Here we shall merely contend that the opposition is more than this—that it represents two contrasting ideals of knowledge—of what genuine knowledge is, and of what the conditions of such knowledge necessarily must be. These ideals,

---

[1] This position is maintained by C. G. Jung in *Psychological Types*. It will be examined critically later, chapter v, pp. 119 f.

embodying, as they do, ultimate cognitive values, constitute the underlying epistemological intentions which persist throughout the changing forms which constitute the history of idealism and realism respectively.

B

In such fashion then we may characterize the unity and continuity of epistemological intention which permeates both idealism and realism, despite the historical changes in the meanings of the terms. We shall describe these intentions as 'the driving force of idealism' and 'the resistance of realism,' and it is under these headings that the developments of idealism and realism will be described in the two ensuing chapters. Certain comments on the choice of these terms are, however, here in order.

I have used these terms in the first instance to bring out the close relations of these perennial philosophies to life. Idealism is the driving force of all vital culture—that which creates, but also that which revives and reforms. Realism, and its resistances, are the stabilizing elements in culture—that which restrains and conserves. It is not different when these terms are transferred to the realm of knowledge. Realism and idealism are both necessary *life forms* of the human reason. In a sense they are intellectual transmutations of the will to life itself. The cry we must know is a form of the cry we must live. Moreover, the cry we must know has, as we have seen, no meaning except as certain ideals of genuine knowledge are presupposed, certain cognitive values implicit or explicit in the knowing activity itself. Both idealism and realism are life forms of reason in this sense. But while both are equally necessary, both are not equally significant or important. In this respect there is a difference which is of great significance for our entire position.

We have spoken of the driving force of idealism. As it is the driving force of life, so also is it the driving force of all knowledge and philosophy. It is the primary and creative motive. This, as we shall see in the next chapter, the history of European philosophy makes abundantly clear. There is a natural idealism as well as a natural realism, and this natural idealism is the life form in which the human spirit first 'makes its immortal claim.' The feeling that reality does not belong to the ever-changing world of the senses but that true being is found in the incorporeal world of ideas or essences which communicate to phenomena whatever permanent existence and knowability they have, may have found its first logical and speculative expression in Plato, but is as old as thought itself and native to the human as such.

This is the driving force of idealism, but opposed to it has always been the resistance of realism. It, too, is natural, for it arises out of a primary, even 'biological', adaptation to the world, and is thus also a necessary life form of thought. There *is* a natural realism, but because it is thus original and necessary it is a mistake to consider it the only primary attitude. In fact, the resistance of realism, it is safe to say, is in a sense secondary and parasitic. Were it not for the original driving force of idealism there would be no self-conscious realism as metaphysical and epistemological theory.[1]

IV

Realism vs. Idealism: The Dialectical Nature of the Problem.

A

A problem properly formulated, it is often said, is a problem half solved. It was with a view to the proper formulation of our problem that we attempted the preceding historical sketch. One thing stands out clearly I think, namely that, since the opposition of realism and idealism is dialectical in character, the problem created by it is dialectical also, and, we may perhaps add, if it is solvable at all it must be solved dialectically. Let us see then first, in what sense the problem is dialectical.

It has been frequently pointed out—and I think that it is becoming more and more realized—that all epistemological discussion involves passing from the sphere of existence to the sphere of discourse. Of this professed idealists have, on the whole, been more aware than professed realists, namely, that epistemology involves this 'radical shift from the world of things to the world of discourse and meanings.'[2] Now this fact of radical shift is of the utmost significance. We shall first state this significance in a general form and then apply it to our specific problem.

[1] For a fuller development of this thesis see chapter ii.

[2] John Dewey, *Experience and Nature*, p. 140.

In general we may say that any debate about knowledge, its nature, its conditions and its possibility, is not a debate about things at all—the world of things already presupposes such knowledge—but about the meaning and value of what we call knowledge. This general fact becomes obvious in the case of the debate between realism and idealism. Such debate is never about the existence or non-existence of 'things', or about the truth or falsity of hypotheses for the explanation of things, but always a debate about the meaning of knowledge and the beliefs or postulates necessary for the significance of knowledge. The realist thinks genuine knowledge is impossible unless the thing known is independent of the knower, and the idealist thinks that genuine knowledge is impossible if it is wholly independent—unless there be mutual implication of knower and known. It is this debate that, in one form or another, they are constantly carrying on, and this belongs, as we shall see more specifically presently, wholly to the world of discourse and dialectic.

It is the implicit, if not always the explicit, recognition of the above facts which has led many to call the whole problem meaningless. The very fact that this radical shift has taken place —that it does not concern the world of things at all—leads them to suppose that the entire question is a meaningless one. The latest attempt to show this is that of the logical positivists, who hope thereby to eliminate the entire discussion as meaningless. Since I believe that they have a good deal to say for themselves on this point I shall start with this theme. I shall state their argument in the form given by A. J. Ayer.[1]

As is well known, the argument begins by distinguishing between two meanings of real and realism; the first of these is meaningful; the second is not. There is one form of the question as to what is real or not real which is meaningful. In the ordinary sense of the term real—in the sense in which 'being real' is opposed to 'being illusory', there are definite empirical tests for determining whether the object is real or not. Let us suppose that a picture is discovered and the suggestion made that it was painted by Goya. There is a definite procedure for dealing with such a question. The experts examine the picture to see in what way it resembles the accredited works of Goya

---

[1] A. J. Ayer, *Language, Truth and Logic*, Chapter VIII, pp. 218 ff.

and to see whether it bears any marks which are characteristic of forgery; they look up contemporary records for evidence of the existence of such a picture. In the end they may still disagree but each one knows what empirical evidence would go to confirm or discredit his opinion. Now in a similar manner, in any question of the real or unreal in history or in physical science the empirical criteria are in general known and the meaning of the real here is the way in which it may be verified. This is a genuine meaning of reality and unreality. But now the expert or the historian, or the physical scientist, may also unhappily be a philosopher and may ask whether the picture or the historical happening, or the entity with which the physicist deals, is real in another and more subtle sense, namely, whether they are wholly independent of the mind or wholly or partly dependent upon it. This is the metaphysical question—and this form of the question is, it is held, meaningless.

Thus is the 'metaphysical'—or better epistemological—question of realism and idealism declared meaningless, and it is proposed to eliminate the perennial opposition from human culture and from philosophical discourse. Let us examine this proposal with care, for I think we shall find it not without important suggestions for our own study.

With one phase of this argument I find myself in complete agreement—namely, that there is no empirical criterion for the determination of this metaphysical or epistemological question. 'What possible experience,' Mr Ayer asks, 'could any of the disputants have which would be relevant to the solution of this dispute one way or another?' In the first sense of the word real, he points out, the disputants have satisfied themselves that the picture is real by obtaining a correlated series of sensations of touch. Is there any similar process by which they could discover that the picture is real as opposed to ideal? With him, I answer, none, and I shall seek to make good my contention in the sequel. But with the second phase of the argument I am not in agreement. There is, then, no empirical criterion for determining this metaphysical question and the recognition of this fact becomes of determinative importance in connection with the question of empirical refutations of realism and idealism respectively. But does it follow that the problem is fictitious and meaningless? By no means. The problem is, as we have seen, not within the realm of *things* at all—of pictures, of historical happenings or of physical entities—it is within the realm of discourse and meaning and here, as we shall see, the problem has genuine significance.

For the disputants are, as we have seen, disputing, not over facts but over meanings—over two meanings of knowledge. For the one, the very significance of knowledge is lost if the postulate of independent entities is denied; such denial 'strikes at the very roots of the intelligence and degrades knowledge in that it affects to exalt it.' For the other the significance of knowledge is just as truly lost if the object of knowledge is conceived as wholly unrelated to mind, 'the absolute existence of unthinking things,' without any relation to mind, being as Berkeley said, 'perfectly unintelligible.' The issue here raised is wholly meaningful and, as I believe, capable of solution. It is precisely because it belongs to the world of meanings and not of things that it is the meaningful problem it is. But it is equally certain that if the problem itself is thus meaningful, there must be procedures relevant to the solution of the dispute. It is also clear that since the problem has no meaning from the empirical or purely logical point of view, and cannot be solved by their methods, other procedures must be employed. There must be a change of venue and the issue taken to another court. That there is such a higher court is, of course, one of the main theses of this book. Here only a preliminary indication of its character is possible.

B

A problem properly formulated is, as we have said, half solved; but it is only half solved and it is with the second part of the solution that we shall now be concerned. The formulation of the problem showed it to be dialectical in character; the solution we shall now maintain must be dialectical also. It is not my intention to go fully into the nature of dialectic at this point, but merely to suggest in a preliminary way its relation to the present problem.

Let us assume then, for the sake of the argument, that in the present dispute neither realist nor idealist can find any empirical criterion relevant to its solution—an assumption which will, I think, be justified in the sequel. Let us further assume that, despite this fact, the dispute is meaningful, otherwise it would not be constantly carried on. What then, we may well ask, are they disputing about and how could the dispute be conceivably resolved?

I think there can be little question what the dispute is really about. It concerns the meaning and value of knowledge—more particularly the necessary presuppositions of genuine knowledge. Both idealist and realist are philosophers and, as such, echo the essentially philosophic cry, We must know! Knowledge must be possible! Each insists, however, that the other, in the very enunciation of his theory, has thereby denied the significance of all knowledge. Each has, therefore, as the major premise of his argument, some empirically and logically unsupported judgment of cognitive value—namely, as to what the nature and presuppositions of genuine knowledge are. This being the character of the dispute, it seems also reasonably clear what the character of the solution must be. The only way to solve it is to make explicit these implicit presuppositions—together with the cognitive values implied; to determine whether they are actually in contradiction as the dispute assumes, or whether we are really concerned, not with a contradiction, but rather with an opposition which can be ultimately resolved; and finally whether, instead of saying 'either-or', it is possible to say 'both-and'—in short, to show that both postulates may be necessary for genuine knowledge, and thus both idealistic and realistic theories contain necessary elements of truth.

Dialectic in the historic sense has always been concerned with issues of this general type. It consists, in the first place, in developing the underivable first principles or presuppositions upon which our opinions or beliefs rest and making them explicit. It consists, further, in comparing these antithetical, that is apparently contradictory doctrines, with the view to determining whether they are true or false alternatives, and thus leading the way through what are natural and perhaps inevitable preliminary errors, to some larger truth which includes them both. It seeks to exhibit a complex truth in its various aspects by looking at it first from one side and then from another, in order finally to attain a combined view of the whole. The effort to eliminate false alternatives is the driving force of the employment of the dialectic from Plato to Hegel. The task of developing the details of the dialectical method, and of showing

it applicability to the solution of the present problem, belongs
to a later chapter;[1] here we are concerned merely to indicate,
in the most general way, why the problem is dialectical and
what a dialectical solution would involve.

C

The formulation of this type of solution is one thing; its
application to this specific debate is quite another. The struggle
of these two tendencies in philosophy has been actually fought
out in what is at least believed to be factual and logical debate.
It will therefore be necessary to examine this debate critically
and in detail.

Modern philosophy has been preoccupied with this debate
and, as a result, an immense literature has grown up about the
problem and the argumentative details which the debate has
engendered have gradually crystallized into certain well-known
arguments. There is what we may call an idealistic train of
thought and a realistic train of thought. When these two have
met, the meeting has given rise to argument and counter argument—to refutation and refutation of the refutations—among
which is to be found some of the most intensive thinking of our
time. The field has been fought over and over again, positions
have been taken and retaken. Idealism is protean in its forms
and is able to raise its head again after every blow—to find a
form for every cultural and scientific climate. Realism is the
Antaeus of philosophy; and, like that hero, renews its strength
every time it touches the ground of natural instinct or prejudice.
Each of these tendencies has crystallized into a 'logic' of its own
—has in fact made its own logic based upon its own assumptions.

Our first task then will be to seek to understand this debate
and to disengage the logic of the two positions. The two immediately following chapters will be concerned with this. They will
inevitably involve a rehearsal of the arguments *pro* and *con*
which the conflict has engendered. There will be the study of
typical arguments, old and new, and thus inevitably the thresh-
ing over of much old straw—but these arguments will be
approached from a new angle and viewed in a new perspective
—in the perspective namely which our present conception of
the problem entails. More especially we shall go behind the

[1] Chapter v.

specific arguments to the epistemological intentions of the two positions which, as we have seen, are continuous throughout all the transformations of idealism and realism—in short, to the driving force of idealism and the resistance of realism.

The necessity of this new perspective is increasingly realized. Of this very problem Moritz Geiger keenly remarked that 'the game of discussing the arguments alone without discussing the attitudes back of the arguments is lost before it is begun.'[1] It is just this hopeless game that we have been playing and it is its very hopelessness that demands a complete change of perspective and the change of venue described above. In this sphere theory is inseparable from attitude and to discuss the arguments for the theories without understanding the judgments of value which give the driving force to idealism and the resistance to realism, in all their varied forms, is indeed to thresh over and over again the old straw, which makes of this debate the very symbol of futility in philosophy. Such understanding must, however, be mutual, and mutual interpretation must be the first stage or condition of such a solution of the problem. This involves that we shall, as Plato said in the *Theataetus*, 'distinguish between mere disputation and dialectic' and cultivate that 'friendly and congenial spirit,' that magnanimity of mind, which he ascribes to the true philospher.

Just 'this charity of mutual interpretation is,' however, as Royce justly complained, 'ill developed among philosophers.' Why is it that philosophic polemic—and no more constantly than in this very debate—bandies about so freely the charge of absurdity when, in reality, nothing is so foolish as to bring the charge of absurdity against positions which history has shown to be well-nigh ineradicable?. The first condition of such mutual interpretation is the recognition of the fact that the great philosophers are not only men of good will but also men of good mind, and that in a sense they all think better than they speak. This means that we should discourage the cheap tricks of ordinary controversy, the retort, courteous or discourteous, the search for merely verbal inconsistencies, for the spirit of their

---

[1] Moritz Geiger, *The Philosophical Attitudes and The Problem of Subsistence and Essence*, Proceedings of the Sixth International Congress of Philosophy, 1926, pp. 272 ff. The paper is in part an argument for the phenomenological position as a means of transcending these dogmatic oppositions.

utterance is likely to be better than their words. Philosophical criticism is all too likely, as Bergson pointed out, to concern itself with the formulations of the less intelligent scribes, taken in their bare and unqualified literalness, whereas what we should above all seek is the meaning the statements bore to the great philosophers who first gave these historic positions currency. Unless we take the trouble to find out what they were really driving at and face the task of learning their own particular idiom, we shall not only paralyze our own powers of under-standing, but also make it impossible to overcome the strife of systems which has arrested the spiritual initiatives of present-day philosophy.

In all that has been said, it might reasonably be maintained, we have little more than the general ethics of controversy, applicable perhaps especially to philosophical debate. In reality the matter goes much deeper. It concerns what I should call the strategy rather than the tactics of philosophical debate—namely, the mutual seeking of understanding and truth rather than the confounding of an opponent. In making this distinction I have in mind particularly one aspect of the debate which, not only makes impossible such understanding, but in the end con-fuses the fundamental issues involved.

Both parties to the dispute constantly charge their opponents with introducing considerations extrinsic to the logical issue involved. Thus it is repeatedly said in varying words that idealism 'has profited genetically by an intimate ego-centric appeal over and above the argumentative cogency it may possess.' On the other hand, it has just as frequently been claimed that realism has profited by the same kind of appeal, in this case 'to the anxiety of ordinary thought to interpret the reference to a beyond (in knowledge) in terms of an independent real world which shall transcend all consciousness whatsoever, an anxiety which is due to manifold motives and in part to relatively unphilosophical motives whose strength is largely social.'

In a sense, of course, both of these charges are true. In both cases there is always an appeal to extrinsic motives in the sense of motives other than purely logical; the real question at issue is whether they are extrinsic in any ultimate and therefore dyslogistic sense. From one point of view this appeal to logically unsupported judgments of value is of the very essence of the dispute. From the blatant philistinism that kicks the stone and cries, 'I disprove it thus,' to the argument of the most sophisticated modern realist—to the effect, for instance, that 'not only science but all progress depends upon the belief in independence,' the appeal is ultimately if not to 'prejudices' at least to the acknowledged beliefs and values of one's fellow men. From the most naïve 'that art thou' of Indian idealism to the most modern and most subtle turn of the idealistic argument, there is always an 'intimate ego-centric appeal' to that which is important and significant to man. The final appeal of both realism and idealism alike is then an *argumentum ad hominem*, but in the case of ultimate issues it is only such arguments that really have any force and in which any one very much believes.

This appeal to so-called extrinsic motives has been called the fallacy of illicit importance. It is my contention that, despite what some self-deceived logicians may say, there is, in ultimate philosophical argument, no such fallacy. In all argument concerning first and last things, nothing significant to man is alien to the philosopher—nothing that is 'important' can be irrelevant, and therefore no appeal to it illicit. To call such appeals illicit is to assume two things both of which are highly questionable if not demonstrably false. It is to assume, first of all, that any appeal to 'importance' or value is merely emotional and subjective, an assumption which itself can be shown to be fallacious. But it is also to assume—and this is even more questionable—that logic itself has significance and importance apart from the ends and values which it subserves. Logic—at least in the context of philosophical debate—is but the *Moral des Denkens*, and this 'morality,' important as it is, is meaningless apart from the cognitive values and the ensuing obligations which logic itself must acknowledge and fulfill.

D

We have discussed critically the tactics employed in this endless debate between idealism and realism. It is, however, a commonplace that tactics have no meaning except with reference to the larger strategy to which the tactics are related and to the larger objectives which they subserve. If we may carry this analogy over into philosophy we may ask, what are the objectives of this debate and the larger context in which the debate takes place? What, so to speak, is the grand strategy of philosophical discourse without which the tactics of disputation are futile and meaningless?

I think it must be clear by now that this particular debate has no significance except as seen in the larger context of metaphysical philosophy, as the story of realism and idealism in the history of philosophy has shown. There are those, it is true, who think that it may be separated from this larger context and, as a single problem, solved by the methods of empirical and logical analysis; but in this they are, I think, greatly deceived, for as we have seen, there is no empirical criterion by which the question may be answered one way or another. It must be clear also that, except as seen in the context of modern sensationalistic empiricism, the opposition in its present form is without meaning. As, therefore, the problem is hopeless if we attempt to discuss the arguments without discussing the attitudes behind the arguments, so also it is only in the light of the larger objectives of philosophy that the epistemological issue has any meaning. The clear envisaging of these larger objectives of philosophical thought is the *sine qua non* of any fruitful discussion of specific philosophical issues.

It cannot be denied that idealism has been more conscious of this larger strategy than realism. In the long perspective of history idealism, in the metaphysical sense, is seen to have accepted more consciously and definitely these larger objectives of philosophical thought and consequently to have adopted tactics of a more eirenic sort. Modern idealism in many of its later forms is in so far eirenic that it has sought to evaluate both the motives and conclusions of realism, and, indeed, to incorporate the essence of realism in its larger vision. The spirit of realism has unfortunately on the whole been more sectarian. It is no doubt irritating to have idealism blandly propose to incorporate what it calls the partial truth of realism in its more comprehensive system, but irritation is not the best preparation for impartial philosophizing. In any case, when one has once grasped the larger strategy of philosophical dialectic, this issue which has divided philosophy and engendered a form of strife which has arrested all spiritual initiative, may well be seen to fall into a wholly secondary role.

This larger strategy of philosophy is, I think, increasingly realized among philosphers. This is conspicuously true of what have been called the 'life philosophies,' those philosophies, namely, which insist that philosophy is not a device for dealing with the problems of philosophers but rather a method cultivated by philosophers for dealing with the problems of men. Of the many who might be called to witness I shall choose a statement of this position by a French philosopher which brings out clearly the recognition of this larger strategy of which I have spoken.

In an address before a philosophical conference in France, M. Paulhan offered the following suggestive interpretation of philosophy. The actual *'lutte philosophique'* and the *'division des croyances'* is, he holds, an inevitable characteristic of philosophy. The struggle for existence and division of labour among our philosophical creeds is a necessary consequence of the practical and social character of philosophy. Each one of the main parties, chief faiths, has its own particular work to do; it represents a tendency useful and even necessary to society. Opposition in society, of diverse needs and different tendencies, when translated into the world of ideas, takes for instance, among other forms, the appearance of the struggles of materialism and spiritualism, realism and idealism. In a well constituted social organism these different tendencies would not, perhaps, be more irreconcilable than eating and breathing in a physiological organism. But man is apparently condemned, perhaps irremediably, to this struggle.

The role which M. Paulhan assigns to the more enlightened thinker is then an eirenic one and, in a sense, above the battle. But is it indeed necessary that mankind, as a whole, should be condemned irremediably to this struggle? Is it not more likely that an opposition such as this is due, not so much to the stupidity and intolerance of the opponents as to the peculiar character of the opposition itself? May it not be possible that a real understanding of the significance of these beliefs is the beginning of the transcendence of the opposition itself? Because they are necessary to life, life reconciles them in a certain way and to a certain degree. When we recognize that they are life forms of the human reason, may not reason itself find means of reconciliation? To all these questions this book hopes to give affirmative answers. Life of itself, even when spelled with a capital letter, solves no philosophical problems, least of all this perennial opposition of realism and idealism, with all that it implies. Nevertheless, precisely this vital reconciliation of which Paulhan speaks gives us a right, I believe, to expect a reconciliation in theory as well as in life. This expectation I believe to be justified and it is this reconciliation in theory which constitutes the main object of the book.

Chapter II

The Driving Force of Idealism. The Idealistic Train of Thought.

I — A

WHEN one reflects on idealism in the different stages of one's life something like the following usually happens. At first, as a youth, we smile over its silliness; somewhat further on the way we find the idea interesting, clever and forgivable—we discuss it readily and gladly with people who are still, according to their age and development, in an earlier stage. With maturity we are likely to find it meaningful, to annoy ourselves and others with it, but on the whole scarcely worth disproving, and contrary to nature. It is hardly worth the trouble of further thinking because we feel that we have thought often enough about it already. But later, and with more earnest reflection and more extensive knowledge of human life and its interests, idealism acquires a strength which it is difficult to overcome.

This statement, in substance a quotation from Lichtenberg's papers, written in 1853, is still for countless minds as true as when it was first written. It expresses admirably that driving force of idealism which we are now to attempt to understand, and it is for this reason that I have begun my discussion with the quotation. The inherent strength of this belief—the driving force of the idealistic train of thought—is, then, the theme of this chapter. We shall be concerned first of all with idealism as a life form of the human reason, as a way of thinking which, while clothing itself in logical argument, gets its real driving force, as Lichtenberg says, from earnest reflection and fuller knowledge of human life.

But what is this idealism, which many, like Lichtenberg, have found it so difficult to overcome? To this question, as we have already indicated, no single answer can be found. Nevertheless, an identity of intention runs throughout the entire series of changes which constitute the history of the notion. It is this continuity of intention, suggested briefly in the preceding chapter, which we have now to develop more fully. In presenting the idealistic train of thought the driving force of idealism, we shall allow, in so far as possible, idealism to speak for itself—to express, as it were, its inmost soul, its deepest initiative and its ultimate intentions. We shall, accordingly, avoid all problems of criticism except such self-criticism as idealism has developed from within, or such criticism from without as it has accepted as part or basis of its own constructive belief. On the other hand, criticisms of realism will of necessity enter in, but only in so far as they are part of the idealistic argument.

It is reasonable to suppose that it is the idealists themselves who best know what they really mean and are therefore best able to interpret to us the continuity of intention which underlies all its forms. Despite differences of language, there is little difference among them in essential meaning. Idealism, in this most general sense, has frequently been defined as 'any theory which maintains that the universe is throughout the work or embodiment of mind.' Since mind is inseparable from value, Dean Inge is, I think, in principle right when he says that 'idealism is most satisfactorily defined as interpretation of the world according to a scale of value or, in Plato's phrase, the Idea of the Good.' We may agree then with Brightman that 'any philosophy may be called idealistic if it embodies the reasoned conviction that ideals and the values they presuppose belong to the very objective structure of the universe.' I think he is also right when he insists that this alone is necessary to modern idealism.

These are the attempts of idealists to express the inmost intentions of the position they represent. But apparently non-idealists and realists recognize the truth of this characterization. Thus C. D. Broad writes 'By idealism I understand the doctrine that the nature of the universe is such that those characteristics which are "highest" and most valuable must either be manifested eternally or must be manifested in greater and greater intensity and in wider and wider extent as time goes on.' G. E. Moore writes in much the same way. 'Idealism in the larger sense,' he tells us, 'is the metaphysical assertion that the universe is spiritual,' and it is because he believes that there is one argument necessary to this belief that he seeks a refutation of idealism by attempting to refute this particular argument.[1]

[1] See chapter iv, pp. 104 f.

These statements, we may then assume, represent more or less adequately the deepest spiritual initiatives as well as the ultimate intentions of the entire idealistic train of thought. They embody that *metaphysical* idealism which, as has been already indicated, has been the dominant strain of European philosophy from the beginning. With this metaphysical idealism has, however, always been connected some theory of knowledge with which, it is supposed by its supporters, to be inseparably bound up. It is supposed by some, as for instance Mr Moore, that there is one argument which is considered necessary to their position by all idealists, 'namely, the trivial proposition that *esse est percipi.*' Whether this be true or not—I think it is not—certainly some epistemological position seems involved in idealism 'in the larger sense.'

B

This, then, is the idealism which we are to attempt to understand. In order to understand it we must, at the very beginning, dispose of a widespread misconception, which is not only false in itself but makes impossible *ab initio*, any genuine understanding of the persistence or driving force of idealism. It is rather generally assumed—by idealists no less than realists—that realism is the 'natural' attitude of man, that idealism appears only as the result of sophistication or a 'malicious criticism' of human knowledge, and it is to the 'natural man' that appeal is often made. Quite the contrary is really the case. There is a natural idealism and it is only by first examining this natural form that we shall understand either the continuing epistemological intention of idealism or the development of its later more reflective forms.

The 'natural man' is both realist and idealist. The world man lives in—and that is the only world that, in the first instance at least, interests the philosopher—is 'full of a number of things.' It contains the 'furniture of earth,' but also the 'choir of heaven.' It contains many physical things but it also contains innumerable objects which are acknowledged by the plain man to exist only on the 'mental' plane. Yet there are things which every man feels to be real. Love, empire, fame, justice, God— all belong to a transcendental ideal world. By these he lives, for these he is found willing, not only to live, but in his great

moments to suffer and to die. In his great moments of experience these are, in fact, the things which man feels to be most
really real. All these have their reality not only, nor indeed
principally, in their necessity, but still more in their worthiness
to be. Hence they partake more of reality than any mere 'fact'
could do and men, recognizing this, bow to them as the truly
real.

This simultaneous acknowledgment of things at once ideal
and real is primary, and it is out of this primary acknowledgment that all idealism gets its original driving force. But this is
only one side of natural idealism. With it is connected another
element which is equally native and original—namely, the
feeling that the world of the senses is not the real world—and,
as a result of this feeling, the tendency to reduce things in the
mind to ideas. Here various motives are at work in human
experience and later in philosophical reflection. There is the
relativity of all sense perception and perceptual predicates; the
contradictions in our world of common sense objects; and the
humanly conditioned character of our world of empirical
objects. The point to emphasize here is that these motives arise
very early in the experience of the individual and of the race,
and once the consciousness of these facts is awakened, the mind
is started on a path which inevitably leads to the idealistic train
of thought. It is surely a significant moment in the mental
history of any individual when he makes the discovery that
there are deceptions of the senses and perhaps even more
significant when he discovers the deceptions and contradictions
of thought. In such a moment there is not only a healthy shock
to simple trust, but there enters, long before it can be put into
philosophical words, the sense of the phenomenal character and
subjective conditions of all the given. From the fact that I see,
hear and feel, and with my mind so think the thing, it by no
means follows that it is really independent of me and so made.
The world of sense is the world of 'opinion'; the real world is
the world of thought or idea.

In this insight there lies the germ of natural idealism in the
second sense. But only the germ. Unless the ground were
favourable for its growth the seed would not develop. Idealism
would have no chance against the equally primitive and natural
'prejudice in favour of the actual' were it not for a third motive

without which idealism could never come to flower. This third motive I shall call the ideal of genuine knowledge or the natural notion of intelligibility. The first two motives of natural idealism are both deep-seated and powerful but it is the third, as I believe, which constitutes the driving force of epistemological idealism in its most primitive and most developed forms.

This natural notion of intelligibility is that only that which is akin to mind can really be known, and finds its primitive expression in what we call animism. It is the fashion to carry idealism back to this animism and to speak of the historic idealisms of Plato and Aristotle as 'amiable animisms.' I shall not dispute the genesis; in fact I shall welcome it as the deepest spring of natural idealism. That man is primarily an animist no one would, I suppose, deny. The real question is the significance of the fact. The naïve mind supposes, to be sure, that animism is a projection into an independent physical world of 'mental states' and that it thus constitutes the pathetic fallacy on a huge scale. Quite the contrary is, of course, the case. The direct acceptance of things as having meaning and value is the primary form of consciousness; the bifurcation of 'thing' and 'meaning'; the separation of the real and the ideal constitutes the secondary, the artificial and the derived. Natural idealism has then its birth in the 'mythical' consciousness for which knowledge is always oneness of the knower with the thing known. The idealism of Indian philosophy is at once a supreme expression of natural idealism and a fatal stumbling block in the way of all those who find in 'realism' the only natural attitude. Of this idealism, almost racial in character, we must ask how was it ever possible? It is both possible and meaningful if we recognize that Indian thought is permeated by a wholly different ideal of knowledge from that which has characterized Western thought in its later stages—this ideal of knowledge as oneness of the knower with the thing known, native to the human mind as such.

This then is the natural notion of intelligibility—the deepest source of all idealisms. 'The direct acceptance of things as having significance and value is,' as Creighton has said, 'the characteristic mark of idealism as found in the great systems.'

II

The Place of Idealism in the European Tradition.
Natural Idealism and Philosophia Perennis.

A

Greek philosophy is at once a proof of the natural character of idealism and of the sources of the idealistic train of thought in the three motives of natural idealism. Quite apart from the question of the historical relation of Greek to Oriental thought, Platonism carries within its bosom all the motives of natural idealism. In Plato we find at once the feeling that the world of the senses is not the real world; that what we call ideas are the real—especially the idea of the Good; and that genuine knowledge involves oneness of mind with the thing known. An *intelligible* world must be an *ideal* world.

In Plato's system reality does not belong to the ever-changing world of sense; true being is found in the incorporeal essences or ideas which communicate to phenomena whatever permanent existence and knowability they have. These pure forms 'exist' in a supersensuous world and their relation to the world of phenomena is indicated by Plato with the help of metaphors. The 'ideal' world of Plato is thus the true world and the true object of 'knowledge,' as opposed to 'opinion,' is always ideal. Thus arises the idealism, both metaphysical and epistemological, which persisted in the European tradition. The Good is the highest and in some ways all embracing idea, and he formulates in his own way the idea of a self-realizing end which is the heart of metaphysical idealism. That he failed to demonstrate his thesis that the ideas are the all-sufficient explanation of the facts of existence, is undoubtedly true and relapse into dualism resulted. But *in so far* as the world is intelligible it *is* an ideal world. 'The objects of knowledge not only derive from the Good the gift of being known, but are further endowed by it with real and essential existence, though the Good far from being identical with real existence transcends it in dignity and power.'

Aristotle continues the tradition of Plato and embodies in his philosophy all the original motives of natural idealism. In his own way he expresses the primary intention and the original driving force of all idealism. With Aristotle, however, there

43

comes into play another force which is equally present in the European tradition, namely, the resistance of realism. Even in Plato this resistance was present in an irrational factor in knowledge which his idealism was unable to overcome. This dualism constituted the stimulus for Aristotle's own form of idealism. By his profound conception of development he goes far towards overcoming this opposition in Plato's system and doing justice to the irrefutable realistic element in knowledge. But—and this is the important point—in so far as knowledge, intelligibility, is at all possible, it is found in the ideas and again chiefly in the idea of the Good. For in all real understanding it is the teleological rather than the mechancial explanation which is final.

Leibniz was then wholly right in describing both Plato and Aristotle as idealists. So also would he have been compelled to describe the scholastic philosophy had the issue been raised. Christian philosophy, and the scholasticism which grew out of it, continue all the motives of Greek idealism, transformed by the Christian ethos. The metaphors which Plato and Aristotle used to connect the ideal world with the phenomenal world made it possible to transform this idealism into the theism of Christian theology. Whether the cosmic processes are regarded under the Platonic analogy of the 'Demiurge' or under the Aristotelian analogy of the plastic artist, in either case it became possible to incorporate Greek idealism as a permanent element in Christian philosophy. It is true, of course, that scholasticism is often identified exclusively with its Aristotelian form, and the realistic element in this form, as developed by St. Thomas, is taken as the determining element. But it is to be remembered that scholasticism was never a closed system. It includes the ontologism of a St. Anselm as well as opposition to it in St. Thomas. Even in St. Thomas the idealistic element is as prominent as the realistic. Being—antecedent being—is, to be sure, a first principle of this philosophy, as of all scholasticism, but equally primary is another first principle, namely, *ratio est capabilis:* reason can know being because being itself is an embodiment of reason, of the Divine Logos. The one determining reason, however, why scholasticism is, in its entirety, idealistic, is the doctrine of the transcendentals. To say that 'whatever is, in so far as it is, or has being, is at the same time and for that very reason also true, good and beautiful,' is to assert the essence of idealism as we have defined it, namely, the notion of intelligibility which underlies the entire idealistic movement.[1]

Continental rationalism continued this idealistic tradition in modern philosophy; it may, indeed, in this respect be viewed as a series of footnotes to Plato and Aristotle. I am not, of course, unmindful of the difficulties which such a classification involves. Descartes and Leibniz have both been described as idealists, but also as realists. Both believe in the reality of an independent world and that genuine knowledge presupposes this independence. In this sense they are realists and it is from this angle that we shall study them in the succeeding chapter. But in both the idealistic motive is dominant. It is not an accident that for both of them the ontological argument, with its essential Platonism, is the key to their metaphysics. Still less is it an accident that for both *ratio est capabilis* and reason is thus able to know because it reflects in its own 'innate' ideas the Divine Logos. The natural light of reason is, indeed, darkened o'er by the gathering clouds of sensationalism and subjectivism, but the light is still there and it is the same light that lightened the entire Greco-Christian tradition.[2]

B

Otto Willmann in his *Geschichte des Idealismus* gives the name Idealism to the entire European tradition in philosophy as we have described it above and, in the sense that we have thus far used the term, such a characterization as just. All the original motives of idealism are present throughout this entire tradition and all the philosophies examined conform to the definition with which we started. On the other hand, we have also insisted that this same traditional philosophy is above the battle of realism and idealism in the modern sense and this fact was one of the motives for our proposal to find a way to transcend the opposition. How then shall we resolve this paradox?

One way, of course, is to say with Willmann that the idealism of the European tradition is the true idealism, that which has developed since Descartes and Locke the false. But this is an entirely too simple answer to the question. The truth of the

[1] For a fuller development of these points, see chapter x, pp. 246 f.

[2] For a further development of these points, see the concluding chapter, pp. 247 f.

matter is that something happened of a decisive character which made it necessary that *if* the driving force of idealism should continue, it must take on new forms. Idealism, in the sense defined by Leibniz and to which he confesses his allegiance—the idealism of Plato and Aristotle—in a sense comes to an end with Leibniz. The change in the meaning which took place at this time represents a change in the very conditions and presuppositions of thinking which necessitated a change in standpoint and in the idealistic train of thought.

This change, as has already been indicated, was the 'physiology of knowledge' introduced by Locke. With this naturalization of the intelligence went the last possibility of idealism in the historic sense. Until the essentials of the notion of 'innate ideas' were restored in the more critical *a priorism* of Kant and his successors, no idealism in the older sense was possible. But the change, as every one knows, went much deeper than this: it involved—to put it epigrammatically—a change in the meaning of 'idea' itself. Ideas now become largely our name for sensations and their combinations in complexes, and inevitably idealism itself suffered likewise a total change in meaning—a change which the idealism of Berkeley necessarily reflects.

This, then, is the purely local historical situation out of which idealism in the modern epistemological sense arose. The belief in the spiritual character of reality, the natural notion of intelligibility which characterizes all idealism, remains, but it can express itself now only in terms of the new type of epistemological argument. The driving force of all idealism is still powerful but it finds itself unable to function in the new situation except by embodying itself in new forms. Thus arose the dialectical movement in modern philosophy which necessitated certain stages in the development of modern idealism. The forms through which this idealism has passed are generally recognized to be the following: (*a*) subjective idealism or mentalism; (*b*) critical or transcendental idealism; (*c*) logical or absolute idealism; (*d*) axiological idealism or the idealism of values. In following these phases in their dialectical development we shall be able to disengage the continuity of epistemological intention which gives the driving force to all forms of idealism.

III

Subjective Idealism or Mentalism: The Berkeleyan Train of Thought.

A

It is, accordingly, the idealism of Berkeley that first really set the problem of idealism in the modern world and called out the challenge of realism. It was, as we have seen, apparently with reference to Berkeley and his followers that the term idealism in a derogatory sense was first used and against idealism in this sense that Wolff protects the name of Plato with all energy. It was an unfortunate day for philosophy when Sidgwick applied the epithet mentalism to this form of idealism for it fails utterly to grasp its real driving force, but it was this subjective aspect of the position which is most in evidence and it is with this that we must begin.

The real driving force of this idealism is the same as that of the idealism of the entire European tradition. All the motives of this natural idealism are present but there is nothing natural or naïve left in its expression. The way in which it expresses itself is conditioned by the highly sophisticated intellectual world created by the modern physics of Galileo and Newton and the modern psychological analysis of Locke. The sophisticated character of this form of idealism is evident on almost every page that Berkeley writes. One oft quoted passage must suffice. 'It is indeed,' he writes, 'an opinion strangely prevailing among men, that houses, mountains, rivers, and in a word, all sensible objects, have an existence, natural or real, distinct from their being perceived by the understanding.' To Berkeley this opinion has become strange. The mere fact that it has become strange indicates the enormous change in the intellectual context which it reflects, but even more significant are the reasons for the strangeness.

The strangeness of this opinion, and the curiosity of its prevalence among men, lay for Berkeley ostensibly in two things: (*a*) that it is 'plainly repugnant to our reason' that any one of our 'ideas' or sense data, or any complex of them, should exist unperceived; and (*b*) that a double world of sense and of objects is both unnecessary and contradictory. These are the ostensible reasons, and we shall consider them presently, but the real reason in Berkeley's mind—and that which constitutes, as I believe, the real driving force of his argument—is something much deeper. Strange indeed, that men, who might have a familiar world—one immediately intelligible—one which should be directly accepted as having meaning and value—should be perverse enough to prefer one wholly unfamiliar and remote, and in the last analysis impenetrable and unintelligible—a world as he says of 'unthinking things.' Here, through all his sophistication the original and primitive driving force of all idealism breaks through. If this be the primitive animism out of which all natural idealism arises it is animism in a very sophisticated form and one which, in contrast to the *naïveté* of the ordinary man, is describable only as superlative insight.

B

There can be no question, I think, that the real driving force of the Berkeleyan argument lies in this implicit assumption as to the nature of genuine knowledge. In Berkeley's idiom the world 'is a visual language—a most coherent entertaining and instructive discourse,' and only so conceived can it be genuinely known. But the secondary motives of natural idealism are also present and these give rise to his explicit arguments which, although also part of natural idealism, are conditioned in their form of expression by the intellectual context in which they were formulated.

These arguments are so well known that they need not be repeated in detail. Moreover, they will inevitably be brought forward for examination when we come to the study of the refutations of these arguments by realism.[1] It is however desirable to view them in the large. They were, as we have seen, expressed in the ostensible reasons given for the denial of the plain man's strange view of the world, namely, that it is plainly repugnant to our reason. This repugnance, while in a sense deeper than all argument, is nevertheless explained and justified by argument. The arguments advanced by Berkeley are of both an empirical and dialectical or logical character, and since his time all arguments for or against idealism have been of these two types.

The empirical argument starts with acknowledged facts of

[1] Chapter iv, pp. 104 ff.

the physical analysis of his time. His opponents 'acknowledge that colours, sounds, heat and cold, and such-like secondary qualities, do not exist without the mind'. Now if it be certain that these original qualities are inseparably united with the other sensible qualities (primary), and not even in thought capable of being abstracted from them, it plainly follows that these also exist only in the mind. Again, great and small, swift and slow, are allowed to exist nowhere without the mind, being entirely relative and changing as the frame and position of the organs of sense varies. The extension therefore which exists without the mind is neither great nor small, the motion neither swift nor slow, that is, they are nothing at all.[1]

Now to be sure, Berkeley's opponents may refuse to acknowledge the premises from which the argument starts, and indeed it is, as we shall see, upon the denial of the starting point that all modern 'refutations' of his idealism rest, but this is not the whole of his argument, nor indeed the weightiest part. There is still the logical or dialectical argument. It is repugnant to our reason—both unnecessary and contradictory—that a double world of sense and of objects should exist. Berkeley, to be sure, criticizes the copy theory of knowledge or representative realism —and it is upon these criticisms that the argument partly depends—but the true inwardness of his thinking is expressed in the following passage: 'As to what is said of the absolute existence of unthinking things, without any relation to their being perceived, that seems *perfectly unintelligible* (italics mine). Their *esse is percipi*, nor is it possible that they should have any existence out of the minds of thinking things that perceive them.'[2] It is therefore the unintelligibility of natural or physical realism, the impossibility of giving any intelligible expression to such a belief, that constitutes the nerve of his argument.

It is, then, the argument from intelligibility that, on the epistemological side at least, constitutes the driving force of the entire Berkeleyan argument when viewed as a whole. This argument is seen to rest for its driving force on a certain ideal of genuine knowledge. Berkeley felt that the natural world view —the more ancestral one of direct converse with reality—was

[1] *Of the Principles of Human Knowledge*, Bohn's Philosophical Library, Vol. I, pp. 183 f.

[2] *Op. cit.*, p. 180.

the only intelligible one; the secondary view—of a world of independent entities and of knowledge as an external orientation to these meaningless entities—was the strange one. For him 'the phenomena of nature which strike on the senses and are understood by the mind, do form, not only a *magnificent spectacle* (italics mine) but a most coherent entertaining and instructive *discourse.* . .' 'This language or discourse is studied with different attention and interpreted with different degrees of skill. But so far as men have studied and remarked its rules, and can interpret right, so far they may be said to be knowing in nature.'

C

It is this form of idealism which, doubtless, Lichtenberg had chiefly in mind when he said of it that in youth we smile over its silliness, but in maturity find it meaningful and, although contrary to nature, ultimately difficult to resist. There are, of course, those who will always remain youthful and always find it silly; there are others who in maturity will want to think about it no longer and to drop it, as well as the entire epistemological problem, from their minds. There are others, however, who will wish to understand it and to evaluate it properly.

I have already said that in presenting idealism I shall refrain from criticism except in so far as criticism of some specific form of idealism has entered into the development of idealism itself. Criticism of the cardinal principle of mentalism has, however, become part of the later developments of idealism and it is solely from this standpoint that we shall consider it here.

It is almost the unanimous opinion of modern idealists that the driving force of idealism has not got itself adequately stated in Berkeley. For the most part, they agree with the realistic critics of mentalism that the subjectivism of his statement cannot be maintained. So far as its cardinal principle is concerned, that *esse est percipi*, they would quite generally hold that it rests upon certain ambiguities of language and certain paralogisms of reason which, when cleared up and detected, deprive it of most of its argumentative force. They would agree with Kemp Smith that his main argument for the mind-dependent character of sense data is not necessary for idealism. But, on the other hand, they would be equally in agreement that refutation of this form of idealism—even if such refutation is possible, does not constitute a refutation of idealism as such. Above all they would be unanimous in the opinion that while idealism does not get itself adequately stated in Berkeley, even his form contains an element that is irrefutable and an undying element in any adequate vision of the world.

As to the possible refutation of idealism, even in this form, it behoves both realism and idealism to be careful. It has been frequently said that no one has ever refuted it and nobody has ever believed it. This is undoubtedly extreme, for certainly many have at least believed themselves to have refuted it and certainly there have been many—even some scientists to-day, who have believed. A more careful statement is that of Broad to the effect that while this idealism 'represents a position which it is difficult to disprove it is still one in which few would care to believe.' Whether a refutation of this form of idealism is indeed possible, and, if so, whether it constitutes a refutation of idealism in general are questions to be considered in a later context.[1] Here the sole issue concerns the repudiation on the part of later idealism of mentalism as its necessary form.

It is the fashion now rather to condemn the good Bishop and his 'vision glorious' as Fullerton called it. Even modern idealists, in their haste to cut themselves loose from so naïve an idealism, with its paradoxes and paralogisms, have been over-ready to join in this general depreciation. For after all the real driving force of this idealism does not lie in the cogency of its logical arguments so much as in something very much deeper. After all, it *was* a vision glorious, and the glory of it lay—and indeed still lies—in the fact that Berkeley saw with unexampled clarity that only idea, mind, can be ultimately intelligible. In his perhaps limited eighteenth-century way, he saw what all thinkers of the first rank have always seen, namely, that knowledge must not only be possible, but that it must be made intelligible and that no science or metaphysics that makes it impossible can stand. This Kant was to see much more clearly and fully. It is the belief of many later idealists that Berkeley's thought, rough hewn though it many respects it may be, is nevertheless in its essentials a significant expression of the perennial driving force of idealism. That, to change the figure, Berkeley's reach far exceeded his grasp is undoubtedly true, but

[1] See chapter iv.

51

his reach was very great. However inadequate its expression, Berkeley's philosophy is an important version of perennial idealism—a version which, while it shocked every right-minded man when Berkeley propounded it, and still has the power to outrage even the most hardened philosopher—nevertheless was the only version possible in terms of the language which he found himself compelled to speak.

IV

Critical or Transcendental Idealism.
Kant 'the Reluctant Witness for Idealism.'

A

It is clear from the preceding that, as in the case of natural or naïve idealism, so in the form we call mentalism there is an imperishable element which survives all criticism. Nevertheless, it is the belief of many idealists that the true inwardness, the real driving force of idealism, thus inadequately expressed in mentalism, first finds a valid embodiment in what is called transcendental or critical idealism.

When we turn to this form of idealism, when still better we have lived in that world of objective mind or spirit which, since Kant and Hegel, has been the familiar homeland of most of those who call themselves idealists, we realize that we are at once in the same and yet a vastly different world. The sameness of this world with that of a Plato or Berkeley will appear as we proceed; here we wish to emphasize the difference. This difference is of cardinal importance. It is true that realistic critics have constantly attempted to reduce these later forms to mentalism, but the attempt has wholly miscarried. It is true also that most idealists, as many are ready to admit, 'tend to express their meaning in language that lends itself readily to subjective interpretation and to a superficial identification with that of mentalism,' but only the literalist or the mentally blind could really be deceived. The driving force in both is the same, but the forms of expression belong to wholly different orders of ideas.

It was Kant who introduced European thought to this world,

but curiously enough, he did so by 'refuting' idealism, or that form of it called mentalism. Kant has been described as a reluctant witness for idealism. If he was a witness at all, it was because the force that drove him so to witness was quite independent of the particular arguments for idealism in the form of mentalism. If he was reluctant it was because he was fully aware of the immitigable element in the resistance of realism and of the impossibility of its being refuted. Indeed, from this latter point of view, he may equally well be described as a critical realist and will be so referred to in the following chapter. This is the famous ambiguity of Kant of which more will be said later and which is so significant for our entire argument. But so far as his own critical idealism is concerned, it may be said that it was possible only after subjectivism and mentalism were refuted. Only then could idealism in its objective form be established, and in consequence Kant's famous refutation of idealism is an essential part of his entire argument.

B

Kant's refutation of idealism is directed against the assumption of Berkeley and Hume that the only indubitable certainty is the certainty of our own internal states—'ideas' in the modern sense—and that this certainty constitutes the starting point of knowledge. It is also directed, of course, against the same assumption in Descartes whose doctrine he called problematical idealism in contrast to the dogmatic idealism of Berkeley. This idealism starts with the 'self'—the empirical self in Kant's terminology—but the very notion of the self, in this sense rests, according to Kant, upon the opposition of inner and outer. This opposition or contrast is itself, however, only possible when an empirical object independent of the self is also postulated, for the self finds it possible to become conscious of its own changing states only in that it refers them to an enduring object in space. Stated in another way, the very form of the spatial intuition carries in itself the necessary reference to an objective existent, to a reality in space.[1]

This is the kernel of Kant's refutation of idealism in the sense of mentalism. Two things about it are especially significant for

[1] For an excellent analysis and evaluation of this 'refutation', see Ernst Cassirer, *Die Philosophie der Symbolischen Formen*, Vol. I, p. 152.

our present study (*a*) first the refutation itself, its nature and significance; and (*b*) its place as a necessary step in the development of Kant's own form of idealism.

As regards the first point, the argument is obviously dialectical in the sense of our definition. It has been said that this refutation consists primarily in turning the logical trick played by Berkeley against himself—and with even greater justice. Berkeley's refutation of realism consisted in attempting to show the self-contradiction or unintelligibility of the postulate of the absolute existence of unthinking things. Kant seeks to show the unintelligibility of not postulating them. Now this refutation does not, of course, refute in the sense that Kant supposed it to refute 'idealism'—we shall find that no such refutation is possible—but it does bring to light the real character of all such attempts at refutation, namely, the dialectical argument from unintelligibility.

The second point is even more significant in our present context. In the very moment that Kant finds it necessary to refute 'mentalism' he is forced to become, although reluctantly perhaps, the witness for another version of idealism. He was forced to see that while no intelligible theory of knowledge is possible which does not postulate an object independent of the empirical self, it is equally true that no intelligible theory can be constructed which does not postulate mind-dependence in some sense—that there could be no genuine knowledge unless the thing known were, in some degree and in some fashion, formed or fashioned by the mind. In the last analysis only that which is ideal is intelligible. Thus was born critical or transcendental idealism. No idealism can be called critical which does not include in it the postulate of mind-independent objects in some form, but it is equally true for Kant that no realism can be called critical which does not recognize also the dependence of the object on mind for its meaning and intelligibility.

C

We have now seen what made Kant a reluctant witness for idealism. It was the irrefutable element in realism, the resistance to mentalism and subjectivism which any intelligible theory of knowledge must embody. Let us now see why he witnessed to idealism at all, however reluctantly, and what form of idealism he felt compelled to hold. It is called transcendental or critical idealism.

All three motives of natural idealism were present in Kant as they were in Berkeley. The feeling that the phenomenal world of the senses is not the ultimately real world, that what we call ideal or spiritual is real—especially the idea of the Good, and that genuine knowledge involves in some sense oneness of mind with the thing known—an intelligible world must be an ideal world. Of the first two we shall speak presently: it is with the epistemological side of Kant's idealism that we are first concerned.

It is well known how Kant conceived his problem at this point. In the Preface to the second edition of the *Critique of Pure Reason* he proposes what he calls a Copernican revolution in epistemology or the theory of knowledge. The assumption that the object of knowledge is wholly independent of the knower leads to insoluble contradictions. Let us then change the point of view. Let us assume that the object of knowledge is dependent upon the mind for being known in any genuine sense and see what results.

The story of what followed is too well known to be repeated here. The empirical reality but transcendental ideality of space, time and the categories; the distinction between the empirical and transcendental selves; both emerged as necessary consequences of this revolution in standpoint. So also the well-known solution of what appeared to Kant to be hitherto insoluble problems in the theory of knowledge. This is not the place to enter into detailed study of this really significant revolution— that has been done over and over again. Two aspects stand out, however, and are especially significant in our attempt to tell the story of modern idealism. The first is the element of transcendentalism; the second the form in which the natural notion of intelligibility finds its expression in Kant.

The element of transcendentalism in Kant is the outstanding feature of his version of idealism. Some element of transcendentalism has always been present in traditional philosophy and is an essential element in historic idealism. It is Kant's version of transcendentalism, the special turn he gave to the notion, which is significant. Locke's physiology of knowledge of which he speaks—not without a certain element of disdain—

had consequences which although apparently not fully realized by Berkeley (even in the later Platonic phases of his thought) were fully realized by Kant. It generated a purely naturalistic conception of knowledge—(a 'naturalization of the intelligence') which culminated in the scepticism of Hume and thus made some other conception of knowledge, and of the knower, imperative—if genuine knowledge were to be possible. Otherwise stated, the essence of Kantian transcendentalism is the denial that knowledge, in its true character of truth and revelation of reality, is empirically describable as an observable relation between empirically observable and describable existents. It is a unique relation, understandable only in terms of a knower which transcends nature. This version of transcendentalism has become an essential part of all idealism since Kant, for the real opposition in modern philosophy is not between idealism and realism but between idealism and naturalism.

No less important for the understanding of this 'critical' idealism is the notion of genuine knowledge, and therefore of intelligibility, which underlies the entire Kantian way of thinking, and which constitutes its inmost driving force. It is the same natural notion of intelligibility which was present in Berkeley as in all idealists, but transformed in a significant way. The essential thesis of Kant, when his philosophy is taken as a whole, is that pure reason, reason when abstracted from its reference to ends and values is *non capabilis*. When taken in its fullness and completeness, *ratio est capabilis*. It is for this reason that, from introduction to conclusion of the *Critique of the Pure Reason*, the primacy of the 'practical reason' is asserted, and in the canon of the pure reason the idea of the good is made the determining principle of *all* forms of the employment of the reason, including the pure reason itself. In this version of idealism the Platonic conception of the primacy of the Good and the scholastic doctrine of the transcendentals both find a modern restatement.[1]

D

The driving force of idealism, if it were to maintain itself historically, had, I believe, in so far as the nineteenth century is

[1] See for a development of this entire position my article 'Kant and Modern Axiology' in *The Heritage of Kant*.

concerned, to embody itself in this 'transcendental' form. As Taine has said, all the germinal ideas of the nineteenth century were made on the other side of the Rhine. How shall we evaluate this form? What shall we say of this stage in the development of modern idealism? We are, in so far as possible, allowing idealism to speak for itself, and criticism is therefore no part of our study of idealism at this point. Nevertheless, there are two aspects of the Kantian position the criticism of which by succeeding idealists themselves that are of especial significance for what is to come.

The first of these we may describe as the ambiguity of Kant. Kant is held by many to be thoroughly ambiguous on this fundamental issue of realism and idealism and for this he is often held up to scorn by forthright thinkers. As a matter of fact it is precisely for this reason that he is so significant in the history of modern philosophy. Kant is a grudging thinker and concedes only what he has to. Reflection on knowledge, and still more on the fundamental issues of life, compels him to witness for idealism in its fundamental intentions. But he cannot and will not concede what is an equally irrefutable element in realism. For this reason Kant can be treated just as well as a critical realist as critical idealist. Both the driving force of idealism and the resistance of realism are equally present in his thinking. Kant's ambiguity is to his eternal honour, and one of the strongest proofs of my main contention, that neither an exclusive idealism nor an exclusive realism is possible, that a position must be found which is beyond realism and idealism.

The second point of criticism—made indeed by idealists themselves—is to question whether Kant's version of idealism is really a continuation of the idealistic tradition or rather a break with it—whether the critical philosophy does not mark the end of the movement and the beginning of modern agnosticism and naturalism. Now it must be admitted, I think, that the negative side of Kant's thinking has, on the whole, been the more influential—not because it represents the true Kant, but because it expressed that which for other reasons, was becoming the dominant mood of the modern world. As for the true Kant, the charges of *physicalism* and *moralism* made against him, as for instance by Gilson,[1] misrepresent him completely. So far as his

[1] Étienne Gilson. *The Unity of Philosophical Experience*, chapter ix.

fundamental metaphysics is concerned he represents a continuation of metaphysical idealism. It is, however, with the criticism of succeeding idealists that we are here concerned. These appeared at two chief points: (*a*) the dialectical argument, as for instance in Hegel, against the agnostic element in Kant, with its unknowable thing in itself; and (*b*) the extension of Kant's primacy of the practical reason, with the primacy of the value categories, to the entire field of cognition—an extension which, as I have already suggested, was implicit in Kant. Thus arose two forms of modern idealism: absolute idealism with its emphasis upon logic, and axiological idealism or the idealism of values. It is in these two forms that the driving force of idealism, its inmost epistemological intention, finally receives full expression.

V

Absolute Idealism: Logical Forms of Idealism.

A

After Kant it was evidently impossible for the driving force of idealism to be adequately expressed in terms of mentalism. Indeed, part of almost every statement of idealism is a denial of mentalism as the cardinal principle of idealism. It has been said that the way to philosophy is not through Kant, but around him. However that may be for philosophy as a whole, certainly no idealist can go round him without paying dearly for his adventure. In any case, all succeeding forms of idealism have gone through Kant. Among these is one which believes itself to have gone beyond him, namely, what is called Absolute Idealism.

The motives of this movement are of course those which have constituted the driving force of idealism from the beginning, but to these has been added one which may be called the logical motive, *par excellence*. In principle it seeks to express the driving force of idealism in strictly logical form.

This logical motive found its classical expression in Hegel. It was he who sought to show logically or dialectically that the 'half-idealism' of Kant was only a half-way house: that the thing in itself to which Kant so stubbornly held involved a self-contradiction and could not remain an element in any intelligible theory of knowledge; that all genuine knowledge must be knowledge of the whole, and that this whole must be of the nature of mind. I shall, however, present it in the form given it by Bosanquet who has, I think, caught the true inwardness of the entire movement, at least on its epistemological side. He has, moreover, expressed it in a form especially suited to our present context.

'The driving force of idealism, as I understand it,' writes Bosanquet, 'is not furnished by the question how mind and reality can meet in consciousness, but by the theory of *logical stability* (italics mine) which makes it plain that nothing can fulfill the conditions of self-existence except by possessing the unity that belongs only to mind.'[1] In other words, the driving force of idealism—that force which has always driven idealism to postulate mind as the ground of the universe—is primarily logical and arises out of the insight that only an ideal world is a knowable and intelligible world.

Before examining more closely this attempt of idealism to get itself adequately stated, let us note first of all that the argument embodied in this statement is 'the exclusive property of later idealism and is largely overlooked by its realistic opponents. It has nothing corresponding to it in the earlier forms of mentalism.' Let us see how this changes the form of the problem.

As Berkeley saw the problem, there could be no genuine knowledge unless the thing known were like the knower, were an idea in the mind. As Kant saw it, there could be no genuine knowledge unless the thing known were, in some fashion and to some degree, formed or fashioned by the mind. The form of idealism we are here considering sees the problem differently. It is not a question of how mind and object can meet in knowledge, but rather the much more fundamental question: what must be the nature of the object of knowledge if knowledge in any genuine sense is to be possible. Genuine knowledge can be only of the whole and the wholeness or unity necessary for such knowledge is found only in the region of mind. Matter, for instance, cannot display genuine unity in difference: two particles are not capable of being the same particle. Even life, with its category of organism, falls short of such unity unless mere

[1] Bosanquet, *Logic*, 2nd ed., II, p. 322.

life, in the biological sense, be reinterpreted in terms of spirit—
the 'life' of mind.

All these are, of course, the commonplaces of this form of
idealism and need only to be stated to be understood. The point
I wish to make here is that the driving force of idealism thus
expressed is the same driving force which, beginning with
natural idealism and expressing itself in Plato, Berkeley and
Kant, finds a final statement in 'logical terms.' It is a far call,
indeed, from the primitive animism of natural idealism, but the
distance is not so great that they cannot understand each other
when they speak. The ideal of genuine knowledge which underlies this very sophisticated form of idealism is again that only
that which is akin to mind is really intelligible.

B

There is one aspect of this argument which demands special
attention, both for itself, and by reason of the fact that it is the
supposed refutation of this argument—from the internality of
realitions—which constitutes the ground for the resistance of
certain modern forms of realism to be examined in the following
chapter.

The universe, it is maintained, must be logically a many in
one if it is to be really known. In other words, genuine knowledge, which is always knowledge of relations, is possible only if
the relations are internal or intrinsic to the things related. This,
as we have seen, is the inmost ground for the metaphysical
aspect of this idealism, which holds that since mind alone has
this character, reality must ultimately be of the nature of mind.
But there is a further aspect of this argument which is even
more important for the epistemological idealism which we
are specifically studying. Knowing is a relation between the
knower and the thing known. Genuine knowledge requires,
not only that the object of knowledge shall be a many in one—
a system of internal relations—but that the relation between
the knower and that which is known shall be 'internal' also—in
other words that there shall be mutual involvement of mind
and object.

The first aspect of this argument has already been considered,
but may be restated in order to bring out more fully the significance of this logical doctrine. It involves a certain conception of

'facts,' or of the relation of the data of knowledge to the notion of knowledge itself. The realist emphasizes the knowing of facts, but despite the importance of the factual, no brute fact has of itself any significance. A mere collection of facts has no meaning, and therefore does not constitute real knowledge unless the mind sees in the facts a law or an idea which the facts somehow embody or express. Facts do not constitute genuine knowledge unless related internally in an ideal. In the words of Hegel, 'Truth is the whole.'

The second aspect of the argument with which we are more particularly concerned applies this same principle to the knowledge relation itself. Genuine knowledge is impossible, it is held, unless the relation between the knower and the object known, between the subject and object, is an internal relation in this sense. In any intelligible theory of knowledge, mind and object mutually imply each other, or there must be mutual involvement of mind and nature.

C

The driving force of this argument, in its double aspect, is still felt by many minds and still remains for them unimpaired despite repeated 'refutations'. Of these refutations we shall have more to say presently. Here our task is merely to disengage this driving force of 'logical' idealism and present it as adequately as possible.

First of all, it must be made clear that those who hold this form of idealism believe it is possible to dissociate themselves completely from the form called mentalism. Creighton and others insist that 'it can accept the world in very much the sense that it is presented to us by common sense and science.' 'A thorough going idealism,' writes Caird, 'will not fear to admit the reality of that which is other than mind, and even in a sense diametrically opposed to it: for it rests upon the perception that these opposites are yet necessarily related, and that both are different and correlated aspects of the whole.' This would, of course, be denied by many realists, but the mere fact that idealists so believe, indicates that, while this idealism has the same ultimate driving force as the Berkeleyan type, that force has, as Bosanquet says, 'been transferred to another point.' It is this that we must now seek to make clear.

The generic kinship with this earlier form is evident. Both forms argue negatively against the ultimacy of matter; both argue positively for the ultimacy of spirit. The ultimate argument in both cases is, if we may use a phrase of Berkeley, that it is ultimately 'repugnant to reason' that the opposite of the idealistic position should be maintained. But at this point an important difference enters in. For Berkeley it is plainly repugnant to our reason that ideas should exist independent of the mind, and that there should be a world of unthinking things. For this later idealism, it is repugnant to reason that there should be any genuine knowledge unless the world has the type of organization of the many in one which is characteristic of mind.

It is, then, this *dialectical* argument from the logical or speculative impossibility of knowledge except on these conditions—which constitutes the driving force of this logical idealism. Thus the theme of all idealism—only the ideal is ultimately intelligible—started by Plato, developed by Berkeley and Kant, finds renewed expression in this logical idealism. The driving force of the argument is held to be logical and on the truth or falsity of this supposition much hinges. It is well known that from the standpoint of logic itself the doctrine of internal relations has been increasingly impugned and criticism of this doctrine constitutes the chief basis for the refutation of this idealism as developed by later forms of realism. Of this we shall take due note in the proper place.[1] Here, where we are concerned merely with the most general evaluation of various forms of idealism, I shall make but one comment. There is one criticism—made by idealists no less than realists—which, to my mind, has special significance in this context. It is that this 'logical' idealism is essentially circular in character, involving a *petitio principii* of the more glaring sort. It begs the question of the nature of genuine knowledge, or, in other words, itself rests upon a logically unsupported judgment of value. It is the recognition of this circle which has led to the development of a further form of idealism.

---

[1] Chapter iv, pp. 114 f.

VI

The New Idealism: The 'Idealism of Values' and the Axiological Argument.

A

There can be no question that we are getting ever deeper into the heart of idealism. We have no longer merely natural idealism with its extrinsic appeals; no longer merely mentalism with its idealism of consciousness in the form of either the 'small' or great consciousness; we have rather a form of idealism which gets its driving force from an ideal of genuine knowledge, from the affirmation of a conception of the world which, it holds, must be acknowledged if genuine knowledge or any intelligible logic is to be possible. But even this is not the last word of idealism. Nor indeed, can it be if we once recognize the real character of the argument we have been considering. For many, therefore, the real driving force of idealism has not yet got itself fully and adequately expressed.

There are those for whom this driving force arises not from the logical or speculative impossibility of the existence of unthinking things—of a world either unperceived or unthought, but from an impossibility of an entirely different kind which we shall call *axiological*. There is a form of idealism which, it is held, can still maintain itself even if the fallacies of mentalism and the *petitio principii* of logical idealism are fully admitted. Indeed, the formulation of this form of idealism rests upon an explicit recognition of this *petitio principii:* in fact it glories in it. This form of idealism has been called the idealism of values.

The line of thought I have here in mind has been expressed in many forms and by many schools of thought—alike in certain later idealisms of the Neo-Kantian schools and in those that derive from Fichte and Hegel. It would be possible to find formulas for it in Rickert or Münsterberg, or in the later writings of Bosanquet and Royce. I have chosen to allow Pringle-Pattison to speak for the idealist at this point because the phraseology he employs is peculiarly fitted to bring out the difference between this and the forms of idealism that have preceded it.

'Ultimately,' he writes, 'I believe it is true, as I have argued

63

all along, that we cannot take nature as existing *per se*; it has to be taken as an element in a whole which cannot be expressed except in terms of conscious values. All values depend on feeling, on some form of conscious or living experience. Familiar with values in our own experience, we feel it impossible to conceive anything devoid of value (such as an unconscious material system would be) as ultimately real and self-subsistent, in other words as a whole, as *res completa*. It is this *moral impossibility* (italics mine), I think, rather than any speculative contradiction, of a world existing absolutely unknown, that is the driving power of the idealistic argument.'[1]

What then is meant by 'moral' in contrast to logical and speculative impossibility? It evidently has reference to a certain kind of evidence. In the field of legal discourse, for instance, the term 'moral certainty' is used to denote a form of conviction which, although it does not reach the level of logical demonstration, nevertheless constitutes a certainty on which any responsible and rational being is supposed to be willing to act. This element is undoubtedly present in the notion of moral as here used, but there is something more, and this *more* is of greater significance. It is the recognition of the fact that meaning is not merely an empirical or logical category but that it cannot ultimately be separated from value. The distinguishing note of axiological idealism is the conscious recognition, not only of this fact, but of the equally important fact that the two notions intelligibility and value are inseparable. It is only natural, then, that it should be equally understood that the driving force of idealism has always been the consciousness of this fact—the feeling that the idea of a *res completa* wholly devoid of value is ultimately unintelligible. Since, however, this consciousness of unintelligibility is possible only to minds which acknowledge values it may properly be called 'moral' rather than logical and speculative.

The argument here, then, like the other idealistic arguments, is an argument from intelligibility. It does not, however, argue, like Berkeley, that the absolute existence of unthinking things is 'perfectly unintelligible,' it can undoubtedly be conceived, nor, like logical idealism, that a reality which does not possess the unity of mind is ultimately unknowable and unintelligible,

[1] A. Seth Pringle-Pattison. *The Idea of God in the Light of Recent Philosophy*, p. 200.

for that involves the prior assumption as to what constitutes genuine knowledge. It argues rather that intelligibility is bound up with value and that if these are disjoined, unintelligibility necessarily follows. Since, however, in the last analysis, value cannot be separated from mind, metaphysical idealism is implied in it.

The great significance of axiological idealism is that it recognizes explicitly that which, from the very beginning, has unconsciously been the driving force of all forms of idealism. It recognizes that, as we pointed out in the introductory chapter, the problem of knowledge is part of the problem of values at large and cannot be separated from it. With the recognition of this fact we are in a position to understand also a further statement of Pringle-Pattison in this connection. 'Every idealistic theory of the world,' he writes, 'has as its ultimate premise a logically unsupported judgment of value—a judgment which affirms an end of intrinsic worth and accepts thereby a standard of unconditional obligation.' Whether this is true or not of every idealistic theory—I hold that it is—it is certainly true of any idealist who has become self-conscious and recognizes the real driving force of all his thinking. This logically unsupported judgment of value is precisely the ideal of genuine knowledge which drives him on. But because it is logically unsupported, both inductively and deductively, it does not follow that it is without support at all. There is the 'moral' necessity of which Pringle-Pattison speaks, and this may give to the judgment of value, implied in all idealism, a support which no argument, either inductive or deductive, can give. Nor does it mean that because idealism rests upon a logically unsupported judgment of value it is in this respect at a disadvantage compared with realism. This we shall find true of realism also. That the realistic conviction is a 'moral assurance,' and that it also, in the last analysis, rests upon a logically unsupported judgment as to what genuine knowledge is and must be, is also recognized by all critical and self-conscious realists. The really significant thing is that both these perennial tendencies, in philosophy and in the theory of knowledge, rest finally on the same kind of grounds— a fact which is of determining significance for our entire study.

C

The preceding interpretation of the ultimate driving force of idealism is significant from a number of points of view. It represents, for instance, a certain necessary correction of the exclusively intellectual or logical forms of idealism which, in the hands of certain thinkers such as Bradley, eventuated in a criticism of experience and knowledge which was, in its own way, as 'malicious' as that of Hume, and led necessarily to powerful reactions in idealism itself and to certain modern forms of realisms. But the really important point is the recognition that the driving force of idealism is really 'moral' or axiological in the sense that it springs out of a realization as old as Plato, that 'it is from the idea of the Good that objects of knowledge derive the gift of being known.' In the words of Kant, for whom this is as true as it is for Plato, 'the ideal of the highest good is the determining ground of the ultimate end of the pure reason itself.'[1] Knowledge itself is oriented towards value.

Our discussion of axiological idealism involves no critical evaluation of the position at this point—criticism in this sense is excluded in principle from this chapter. It is rather an interpretation of this form of idealism as an expression or embodiment of the ultimate intentions of idealism as such. Thus viewed, it may be looked upon as the last stand of idealism. It connects modern idealism explicitly with the entire idealistic tradition in European philosophy and makes plain what has always been its inmost driving force. It makes plain also what has always been the inmost logic of modern epistemological idealism. It is the true inwardness of Berkeley, of Kant, and, as I believe, of the entire post-Kantian movement. It is only in this last form that idealism speaks with a clear and certain voice. It has come to full consciousness of itself, and in that consciousness it now knows the meaning of its irrepressible and irrefutable force.

[1] Kant, *The Critique of Pure Reason*. [tr by Norman Kemp Smith], p. 635 [A804–B832].

VII

The Irrefutable Element in Idealism: The Idealistic Minimum.

A

In the preceding pages we have tried to let idealism speak for itself and by so doing to make clear the driving force of idealism as it has come down through the ages, and especially as it has expressed itself in the protean forms characteristic of modern thought. The underlying thesis has been that while the forms have changed—changed as dialectically determined by the formulations of realism as they have appeared, and by the logic of its own development—the driving force, the primary episte-mological intention, remains the same. This we may describe as the idealistic train of thought, and it is only in the latest and most sophisticated forms of idealism that its true inwardness has become fully self-conscious and the unity and continuity of the entire movement becomes fully understandable.

Part of the driving force of idealism has always been the deep-seated feeling that the postulate of the absolute existence of unthinking things, without any relation to mind, is 'repugnant to reason' and, in Berkeley's terms, 'perfectly unintelligible.' Out of this feeling has arisen the negative aspect of idealistic argument in all stages of the development of idealism, namely, its refutations of realism. A brief consideration of the character of these refutations will make even clearer the nature of the idealistic argument itself.

Strictly speaking, refutations of realism as such did not begin until the modern era. For the idealist naïve forms of realism have always been repugnant to reason, but specific arguments in refutation did not arise until realism itself found self-conscious formulation, as opposed to self-conscious idealism. In this sense Berkeley's criticism of the view 'so strangely prevailing among men' constitutes the first specific refutation. It followed two lines, an empirical and a logical, and since his time all refuta-tions have followed more or less this general scheme.

The empirical line of thought takes the form of attempting to show that the proposition that there are objects wholly independent of the knower cannot be empirically verified, and that therefore, 'it should not be believed.' The second or logical line of argument takes the form of attempting to show that the proposition that there are wholly independent 'unthinking things' is in some way logically contradictory, and is therefore repugnant to reason. It is true, of course, that while all refutations follow this general scheme, they vary in important ways according to the form of realism which it is sought to refute. As there is no single form of realism to which all types can be reduced so there is no single refutation which applies to every formulation of realism, but all refutations contain this double appeal to fact and to logic.

Now, as we have already indicated in the introduction and will show more fully in the following chapter, neither of these types of argument really refute. There is no empirical proof or disproof of realism for there are no possible experiences which the disputants might have which are relevant to this solution, one way or another. There is no logical proof or disproof of realism, for there is nothing self-contradictory in the notion of objects wholly independent of the mind. The argument, as we shall see, is neither empirical nor merely logical, but dialectical in the sense already defined.

This is, indeed, what all these so-called refutations have always been. The common element in all—from Berkeley to the latest form of logical or axiological idealism—is the supposed demonstration of the impossibility of genuine knowledge if the object of knowledge be conceived of as wholly mind-independent. But it is equally clear that they do not have the slightest force unless some evaluation of knowledge, some 'logically unsupported judgment of value,' is presupposed. This is undoubtedly true and will be shown in a later context.[1] But in so far as the driving force of idealism is concerned, refutations of realism, in this dialectical sense, are of great significance. Such a refutation is never an *argumentum ad rem*, but an *argumentum ad hominem;* but it is precisely this *argumentum ad hominem* which is so meaningful. Realism itself cannot be refuted, but in the very attempts to refute it is displayed an element in idealism which itself is irrefutable.

C

It is just this element in idealism which, as Lichtenberg says, makes it so difficult to overcome. The newer forms of idealism

[1] Chapter iv.

68

serve only to emphasize the force of Lichtenberg's remarks. We may at the beginning find idealism silly, hardly worth disproving because, as we say, it makes no difference to the facts. We may find it difficult to disprove and yet a form of belief which we should scarcely like to accept. Or we may disprove it over and over again (it is the best refuted of all theories) and still find that there remains something that is irrefutable. The fact remains that, 'with earnest reflection and more extensive knowledge of human life and its interests, it acquires a force which it is difficult to overcome.'

Idealism is, as Ludwig Stein has said, the phoenix of philosophy, and any philosophy reckons ill that leaves it out. The imperishable element in idealism is the curious fact that, in so far as its essence is concerned, whenever we deny it we somehow affirm it. It was for this reason that Royce liked to hear condemnations and refutations of idealism for they served only to bring out more clearly the irrefutable element in idealism.[1] Such criticism is merely a refining fire, and out of the ashes the phoenix of philosophy arises only the stronger.

This is why, as Royce says, 'the idealistic movement, although frequently repressed, although often deliberately ignored, has been as constant as the movement of a great river beneath masses of winter ice. Every now and then the ice breaks or melts and the idealistic tendency comes to the light of consciousness. It is irrepressible because it is human. It is true because truth itself is inevitably an ideal which cannot possibly be expressed except in ideal terms. One who has become aware of this universal significance of the idealistic tendency becomes indifferent to the general hostility towards either philosophy or idealism which is so often expressed by the unreflective.'[2]

Idealism is irrepressible because it is human, and for that reason it not only continues to express itself in varying forms, but shows itself to contain an element which is irrefutable. It is true because truth itself is inevitably an ideal which cannot possibly be expressed except in ideal terms. It is entirely clear from the immediate context what Royce here means. It is precisely what we have described as the driving force of idealism throughout this entire chapter. As Royce puts it, 'the question,

[1] *Lectures on Modern Idealism,* p. 240.

[2] *Op. cit.,* pp. 237 f.

how ought I to conceive the real is logically prior to the question what is the real itself?' He quotes Rickert to the effect that the ought is prior to the nature of the real 'The proposition I "ought to think thus" is prior to the proposition "This is so".' In other words, truth being an ideal, always has reference to value. Only an ideal world in this sense is an intelligible world, and in so far as knowledge involves intelligibility, any adequate theory of knowledge must contain an idealistic element.

This, it seems to me, is the *minimum* of idealism which any meaningful or intelligible theory of knowledge must contain. It is true, as we shall see in the next chapter, that any intelligible theory of knowledge must also contain a realistic *minimum*. It is the very purpose and nature of knowledge to be true to something beyond itself, and unless the content of knowledge is recognized as having a condition in some respect independent of the mind the very significance of knowledge is lost. But this fact by no means excludes the fact that other conditions are necessary to the significance of knowledge, and these conditions we have sought to formulate in the preceding paragraph.

It is these conditions that the various forms of idealism have sought more or less successfully to express—the mentalism of Berkeley, the critical or transcendental idealism of Kant, the logical and axiological forms of later idealism. All these forms are seen to be subordinated to one fundamental epistemological intention of idealism—the intention, namely, which arises out of the recognition of the fact that an ultimate separation of mind and values from reality makes impossible an intelligible theory of knowledge no less than an intelligible theory of life. The excessive claims of certain forms of idealism may be found untenable, and even unnecessary, to the realization of the primary intention of idealism—these will have to be considered in later contexts[1]—but this minimum remains.

[1] Chapter ix, pp. 221 ff.

Chapter III

The Resistance of Realism. The Realistic Train of Thought.

I — A

THE World We Live in is the way the modern realist likes to describe that view of the world which he has elected to defend against the malicious criticism of the idealist. His is the actual world as contrasted with the world of romantics and idealists. He professes to be outraged by what these conscienceless thinkers have done to the 'plain man's' world and proceeds to take it under his defence.

It is this note of outrage that primarily and fundamentally is heard in all the protests and resistances of realism. Let us listen to that note as sounded by a modern realist. 'If common sense realism is outraged by the reduction of the visible and existent universe in all its vast extent to mere mental content, with a constant belittlement in power and magnitude, the new or Platonic realism of the present day is *still more outraged* by the idealists' relegation to the status of subjective dependence upon consciousness of the even vaster realm of abstract subsistence. For the invisible region of the subsistent comprehends the infinite totality of essences and values—of truth, beauty and goodness—and the laws of its structure possess a degree of validity which, to the realist, far transcends the validity of inductive inference as to the laws of nature.'[1]

It is, I repeat, to this sense of outrage, this natural morals of the unspoiled human understanding, that all realists first and last appeal. As Royce complains, 'they hold it to be more or less immoral not to believe in transcendent realities.' This appeal to morals is one of which the simple chronicler of realism should not complain but one rather which he should note, mark and inwardly digest. If it is an extrinsic appeal, as in a sense it undoubtedly is, that is as we have seen, not a matter to complain of. If idealism is, in the last analysis, a gigantic *argumentum ad hominem,* so also is realism. There is then no ground for quarrel with the realist because of his moral pathos. His indignation becomes him, both as philosopher and as man. One can justly

[1] W. P. Montague.

71

complain only when he is disingenuous in his appeal, when he would have us believe that this plain man's world is necessarily the world of science and philosophy also.

B

But what is this 'realism' which is so outraged by idealism in its various forms? Here, no more than in the case of idealism is there a simple answer. As there is no 'cardinal principle' of idealism to which all forms of idealism can be reduced, so also there is no cardinal principle of realism. In the passage quoted, at least one fundamental distinction among realisms is made, namely, between common sense realism and the new Platonic realism, and many other distinctions will have to be made in the course of the discussion. In addition to this common sense realism there will be representative realism, various forms of critical realism, to say nothing of the new Platonic realism. Is it possible to find any persistent element, any continuity of intention underlying all the changing forms?

Here also, as in the case of idealism, we should like to allow realism to speak for itself. A difficulty arises, however, which does not appear in the case of idealism. The former, being the original and creative element in philosophy—the driving force of idealism being the driving force of philosophy itself—is more fully conscious of its motives and of its inseparable relation with a spiritualistic metaphysic. Realism, on the other hand, being largely the party of opposition, although often of a highly organized opposition, can express itself mainly in negations, and the form of these negations is determined by the type of idealism which it opposes.

The extrinsic appeals which create the hidden resistances of realism are of the most varied nature. They may be a stubborn materialism which says 'all is matter and motion: the rest is moonshine.' They may, on the other hand, be moral enthusiasm which expresses itself in a stubborn resistance to an idealistic monism which would absorb the individual in the whole and, therefore, affirms a spiritualistic pluralism or personalism. The chief source of resistance, in the modern world at least, is a form of naturalism which sets itself stubbornly against the transcendental elements in idealism. Realism is, then a party of organized opposition and the members of the party are non-descript in the sense that the members of all oppositions are likely to be. This adjective non-descript—need I point out?—is meant in no derogatory way but merely in a descriptive sense. Despite these facts—and the difficulties which they entail, there is a primal element—a continuity of epistemological intention which I shall seek to bring to light.

'What,' asks J. Loewenberg, 'is the common thread that runs through the manifold forms of realism? To this question,' he continues, 'there is unfortunately no unambiguous answer. But when technical disguises are laid aside all realism appears to consist in the conviction that reality is prior to the knowledge of it, and *that consequently mind has a status which is derivative* and not pivotal (italics mine). It is misleading, I think too, to state the case for realism by saying that reality is independent of being known. . . Every philosophy, to be philosophy at all, must rest upon the supposition that between being and knowing there is some linkage. What distinguishes realism from other views is not insulation but emancipation of being from knowing. . . Not in extruding from reality all relations consists the work of realism, but rather in investing it in respect of knowledge with a particular kind of relation, the relation of priority.'[1] Now I should agree with the writer that the 'common thread' of all realisms is this belief in priority. Common to all forms of realism, from the most naïve to the most sophisticated, is the postulate of antecedent reality. But this does not at all imply the second part of the thesis, namely, that mind is derivative and not pivotal. That is not the essential of historical realism, but solely of modern naturalism with which epistemological realism has become increasingly associated. This distinction is of the utmost importance for all that follows.

The essential realist—the one who remains when all technical disguises have been laid aside—is expressed in the cry of outrage with which we began. It is this essential realist, present in every man, whether naïve or sophisticated, who in this chapter is to be allowed to speak all that is in his mind and heart—to express to the full all his outrage, his hard headed, sometimes almost sullen, resistances. Or, expressed in other terms, it is this perennial tendency—this basal epistemological intention, which is to

[1] J. Loewenberg, 'Problematic Realism,' *Contemporary American Philosophy* Vol. II, pp. 55, 56.

be allowed to express itself in all its varying forms. Here, as in the case of the idealist, we shall perhaps find that, whatever his prejudices and errors, he is in possession of an incontrovertible truth, that, as is almost always the case, he thinks better than he speaks. Here also we shall perhaps find, when all is said and done, that, as in the case of idealism, there is if not a convincing train of argument, at least a fundamental faith that it is impossible to overcome.

II

The Place of Realism in the European Tradition.

A

Realism, in the epistemological sense, is a wholly modern phenomenon and arose in dialectical opposition to the subjective idealism or mentalism which constituted the first form of modern idealism. In the sense that genuine knowledge requires that its object shall be antecedent being, independent of the individual mind, the idealism of Plato and Aristotle, of mediaeval philosophy and of continental rationalism, is realistic also. Traditional philosophy is beyond realism and idealism in the modern sense.

Platonic realism is a case in point. It is idealistic in the sense that the real is ultimately idea and genuine knowledge is possible only of that which is ideal, but this does not in the least affect the belief that ideas are independent of the individual mind. Nor does this form of idealism exclude the presence of an irrational factor in reality—one that cannot be made wholly intelligible—a factor which makes it necessary to express oneself in metaphor and symbol. It is a mistake, however, to contrast with this idealism of Plato, the so-called realism of Aristotle. In so far as the real driving force of Aristotle's philosophy is concerned, it is as much 'idealistic' as Plato's. In the sense that a privileged position is given to mind and 'idea' in the interpretation of reality it is in every way a continuation of the tradition of European idealism, as Bergson and many others have come to see.

Nevertheless, in as much as the realism in scholasticism, and in later European developments, is often associated chiefly with

Aristotle, the realistic element in Aristotle and in the forms of scholasticism derived from him requires special comment.

The significant element in Aristotle from this standpoint—and one which became increasingly influential in European thought—is his emphasis upon the primacy of the physical object in his theory of knowledge. It is the thesis that the physical object is first in the order of knowledge and that all other knowledge is mediate and inferential, that distinguishes Aristotelian scholasticism and which, from this time on, becomes, so to speak, the criterion of realism. It is my contention, however, that the 'principle of being,' or more specifically of the priority of being, characteristic of all scholastic philosophy, involves in no sense the principle of the primacy of the physical object in knowledge. That is the presupposition or 'prejudice' of but one form of scholastic realism, as I shall attempt to show more fully in a later context.[1] The essence of Greek and Mediaeval realism is to be found rather in the realism of universals, whether extreme or 'moderate.' In the European tradition as a whole, realism means this and only this, and as such, is wholly consistent with what we have described in the preceding chapter as the idealism of that tradition. It is a fundamental blunder to identify realism, in this general sense, with the Aristotelian version, and still more to identify it with modern epistemological realism.

We have for reasons which seemed good and sufficient placed European rationalism in the idealistic tradition. It would, however, be a mistake to fail to recognize a realistic ingredient also in this movement. The 'realism' of Descartes and Leibniz is, in fact, one of the forms which will especially interest us in the development of modern realism.

It goes without saying that realism, in the sense of the realism of universals, is an essential part of this entire movement. The mere fact that for Descartes, Spinoza and Leibniz the ontological or Platonic argument for the existence of God is basal, suffices to show that the element of Platonic idealism had been restored after its decadence in later mediaevalism. But realism in a second sense was also beginning to assert itself as an essential part of this tradition. This was, of course, due to the analysis of knowledge by Descartes. The movement to subjectivity in

[1] Chapter x, pp. 249 f.

75

Descartes, the finding of primary certainty only in the thinker or knower, led to the problematical or possible idealism of which Kant later wrote. Idealism in the modern epistemological sense became at least a possibility in the sense that it was never quite possible in the earlier European tradition.

But this problematical idealism which Kant sought to refute was really never probable to Descartes himself. Descartes had a genuinely realistic conviction in the sense of an antecedent reality independent of mind—even a genuine conviction as to the reality of the 'external world' although he was intelligent enough to see that it was not an intuition, but a conviction or faith, justifiable only on dialectical and value grounds. So also in the case of Leibniz, as we shall see. For Leibniz also there was never any question of antecedent being as the necessary presupposition of genuine knowledge. But he too was critical enough to see that realism in this genuine and irrefutable sense is not in contradiction with an equally critical idealism, and that the principle of antecedent being does not necessarily imply the primacy of the physical object in knowledge.

In concluding this sketch of realism in the European tradition we may then say, without any hesitation that this tradition was realistic throughout, but only in the sense that for it the postulate of antecedent being, or that 'the first principle of all knowledge is being' is primary. But realism in the sense of the primacy or privileged position of the physical object in knowledge is but a secondary motive of this tradition and not necessary to it. Nevertheless, precisely this secondary element becomes the determining presupposition of all discussions of knowledge of the modern world. It is the uncriticized assumption of the entire empirical movement beginning with Locke and, when joined with the derivative conception of mind later developed through evolutionary naturalism, gives rise to an identification of realism with naturalism which has become increasingly characteristic of present-day thought.

C

From this point on, the story of modern epistemological realism is understandable only in terms of the universe of discourse of Locke and Berkeley, and of the underlying assumption of the primacy of the physical object which determines that universe. The analysis of the physical object in terms of sensations and sense data is the starting point, and the issue of idealism and realism is understandable only in the light of that analysis.

In this sense the opposition, as we now understand it, is a wholly local and modern problem. Realism, as a self-conscious position, is possible only after the subjectivism and mentalism of Berkeley which followed upon this analysis. Not only its reason for being, but also the very nature of its arguments are determined by this resistance. There is, to be sure, a natural common sense realism, 'a natural world picture' which until the problems are raised is taken for granted and exists side by side with the equally primitive and 'natural' idealism of which we have spoken. But once this natural world picture is challenged, as for instance by Berkeley, the natural resistance of realism which is indigenous to the human, takes on the various technical disguises of which Loewenberg speaks, and we have the manifold forms in which it has embodied itself—representative realism, critical realism and the new or Platonic realism of modern epistemology. We shall now follow this primal resistance through its manifold forms and disguises.

III

Common Sense Realism and The Transition to Representative Realism.
The Natural World Picture.

A

Man is, as we saw, naturally no more a realist than he is an idealist. But while realism is not exclusively the natural attitude of man, there is nevertheless a natural realism—the realism of common sense to which philosophical realism may make powerful appeals. This is a wholly different matter. This natural realism, as has already been suggested, is part at least of the basis of human social intercourse and communication and, as such, is never doubted.

The world of natural realism has been repeatedly described, but nowhere better perhaps than in the words of Lotze. 'Naïve consciousness always takes sensation to be perception of a *complete externally existing thing* (italics mine). No doubt disturbs the assurance of this belief, and even the illusions of the senses,

insignificant in comparison with the preponderance of con-
sentient experience, do not shake the assurance that we here
everywhere look into an actual world that does not cease to be
as it appears to us, even when our attention is turned from it.
The brightness of the stars, seen by the night watcher, will, he
hopes, continue to shine over him in slumber, tones and per-
fumes, unheard and unsmelt, will be fragrant and harmonious
afterward as before; nothing of the sensible world will perish
save the accidental perception of it which consciousness formerly
possessed.'[1]

This natural world picture is the opinion which Berkeley
found 'so strangely prevailing among men.' Now while this
opinion, when examined, may itself seem strange enough, it is
not strange that it prevails among men. The opinion is due to a
very natural prejudice which has been described as animal faith.
The genetic sources and 'practical' justification of this prejudice
are obvious enough and should not be minimized. We have
good reason to think that it is the result of biological necessities
which could have led to no other result. But while this is true,
there is no more reason for taking natural realism and its
prejudices as final than for taking natural idealism with its
tendency to hypostatize ideas as final. What has happened here
is that mankind has made a very natural inference from the
psychological priority of sense data to their ontological priority,
and there is no necessary reason for this.

That the opinion called natural realism is in essence a prejudice, is recognized by many modern realists themselves. The
'prejudice in favour of the actual' as Meinong calls it, in favour
of the primary reality of the actual world as it first appears to
us, is one which, however natural it may be, is little more than
'animal faith' and could be corrected without in the least
affecting the cardinal principle of realism. Be this as it may, this
natural realism, however natural it may be in the first instance,
immediately discloses difficulties and speedily gives place to
more critical forms of realism.

B

While then it is not strange that natural realism should prevail
among men, this world picture itself is strange enough when

[1] *Microcosm*, Bk. III, chap. v.

once it is examined. But in order to see its strangeness and its difficulties it must be more definitely stated.

As technically formulated by C. D. Broad, natural or 'naïve' realism is the theory that the sensa which are the appearances of a physical object are literally spatio-temporal parts of that object and that the spatio-temporal parts that are not manifested in sensation are of precisely the same nature as those which are not thus manifested.[1] It is natural that men should think thus, that they should think that the colour or odour of an apple are literally in the apple as a spatio-temporal object. It is natural also that they should think that the parts of the apple which they do not see or smell are of the same character as those which they can see and smell. It is natural enough, but this fact does not in the least prevent it from being very strange when once we come to know the real character of these qualities —their relativity to human perception—and still more the real character of the entities in terms of which science explains or interprets the inside of the apple. When this strangeness is realized it leads inevitably to the idealism of a Berkeley or to a realism greatly different from natural realism.

The specific difficulties which led to the final breakdown of natural realism are the common-places of philosophy. After the analyses of modern physical science, and their exploitation by Descartes and others, it could not possibly survive. If the secondary qualities are not literally spatio-temporal parts of the physical object, how do I know the real nature of the physical object? If I am deceived in a part of my natural faith in the actual, how do I know that I am not deceived in all? If I do not know the physical object as it is immediately given, if psychological priority is not necessarily ontological priority, then my sensations or 'ideas' cannot be literally parts of the spatio-temporal object. These difficulties might not necessarily lead to the mentalism of Berkeley and Hume, but if realism were to survive it must obviously take on other and more sophisticated forms.

The innocence of natural realism was forever destroyed by the distinction between primary and secondary qualities. If realism is to survive, then these sense data must in some sense be 'copies,' not parts of the object. But if this is so, how then can

---

[1] C. D. Broad, *The Mind and Its Place in Nature*, 1927, pp. 422 ff.

I get out of the circle of my own sense data or ideas, to know that they correspond to reality? Thus is born representative realism, or representative perception with all its problems. From the standpoint of our present study, it means the sweeping away of the first defences or resistances of realism, namely, the natural prejudice in favour of literal truth of the natural world picture. By one of thought's little ironies it was by the very natural science to which realism has constantly so disingenuously appealed that its defences were first undermined—and indeed continue to be undermined. It had to find new defences and out of this need arose new statements of realism, the first of which we shall describe as representative realism.

IV

Representative Realism. The Copy Theory of Knowledge.

A

Realism, as a self-conscious philosophy—with its characteristic appeals *ad rem* and *ad hominem*, begins, then, only as a resistance to 'mentalism' in some form, or to the view that reality is mind-dependent. As such, it is possible only in the 'psychological' period in which 'things' have been analyzed into 'ideas' in people's minds. Such a self-conscious realism can, however, be, in the first instance at least, only a representative realism. For once the dualism between ideas and things has been created, knowledge can be thought of only as a copying or representative function.

This account of the rise of representative realism may seem scarcely to do justice to the historical facts, for the representative realism of Descartes and Locke actually preceded the mentalism of Berkeley, and it was rather the realism of the Scottish school and the indignant protest of Kant which constituted the direct reaction against Berkeley and Hume. But to insist upon this would be to overlook one very important fact—namely, that the seed of disillusionment with the natural realism of common sense, which was later to flower in Berkeley and Hume, was already germinating in Descartes, Malebranche, and others. With the distinction between primary and secondary qualities, the worm of subjectivism had already begun to gnaw at natural realism and the hardest problems of knowledge had already forced themselves into the open. In the very nature of the case the reduction of any part of the 'thing' to ideas was the beginning of a path that had to be trod to the bitter end. Realism had already entered upon the path of sophistication which it has never since been able to leave.

Realism was, then, forced to a doctrine of representative perception and to a copy theory of knowledge. But we know the kind of questions which a Descartes, a Locke and a Leibniz were immediately compelled to face. How do we know that there is a world independent of us, and how do we know that our 'ideas' give us true knowledge of this world—true copies of the independent things? The answers which they gave to these questions have been found by many to be among the most artificial and sophisticated in the entire history of philosophic thought. Yet it is precisely in these answers and in the arguments with which they are supported that the real source of the realistic conviction first clearly appears and, to my mind at least, it is precisely where they appear most artificial that the true inwardness of realism stands most completely revealed. They are so important for our entire story of realism that I shall give these answers in some detail.

Descartes had a genuine realistic conviction, but he rested that conviction on the 'goodness of God.' 'But after I have recognized the existence of God and because I have at the same time recognized the fact that all things depend upon him and that he is no deceiver and that in consequence of that I have judged that all that I conceived clearly and distinctly cannot fail to be true, . . . no opposing reason can be brought against me which should make me ever call it in question; and thus I have a true and certain knowledge of it.'[1] Of the independent existence of material things Descartes was sure that he had a clear and distinct conception and for the moral reasons given above was sure that he could not be deceived. But the point is that they are *moral*.

Leibniz also believed in the existence of an external world, but he confesses in many passages that 'there is no exact demonstration that the objects of sense are outside us,' and insists that the existence of the external world has only 'moral certainty.'

[1] End of Meditation v.

To obtain even this requires first the existence of God which has, he holds, absolute certainty. The Cartesian form of the argument, it is true, he rejects. The argument by which Descartes seeks to demonstrate the existence of material things is weak. It would have been better, therefore, not to try. 'God might,' he says, 'have excellent reasons for deceiving us and in any case the deception could be undone by our own reason.' For Liebniz also belief in an external world has only moral certainty. So also is it with Locke. Locke admits, likewise, that our assurance that there are things existing without us cannot reach demonstration. 'Yet it is,' he holds, 'an assurance that deserves the name of knowledge.'[1]

B

The necessary transition from natural to representative realism brings out clearly, not only the reasons that forced that transition, but also the deeper moral reason which leads realism to reassert itself in ever new forms. The reasons given in the characteristic expressions of the philosophers we have been examining are, I think, most enlightening and for our argument of outstanding significance. Some further comment on this situation is accordingly desirable.

In the first place, the primary resistance of natural or naïve realism is still present in representative realism, but it has been significantly transformed. If we may make use of a term already employed, animal faith has been transformed into moral faith. No faith in the reality of the external world is, of course, ever merely animal for it is a faith, not mere animal instinct, and it is exercised by man, but in contrast to the faith of natural realism, with its biological and pragmatic conditions, the faith of these philosophers is obviously of a wholly different order.

In the second place—and this is of equal importance—the philosophers concerned *recognize* that their certainty *is moral* and not logical. That this moral certainty is based on a prior certainty of the existence and goodness of God makes it for our modern feeling a very sophisticated kind of certainty—especially if we do not understand what Descartes and Leibniz really meant. But the essence of their position is clear. It is a theological

[1] *An Essay Concerning Human Understanding*, Bk. iv, chapter xi, sec. 3.

form of statement of the principle, as old as Plato, that it is from the Good that objects derive the gift of being known.

Finally, Locke's way of stating the situation deserves special notice. While admitting that our assurance that there are things existing without us cannot reach demonstration, either empirical or logical, he thinks, although he is perhaps not wholly sure, that it is 'an assurance that deserves the name of knowledge.' Why knowledge and what sort of knowledge? Apparently, although Locke was far too simple-minded to grasp the implications of his position, it deserves the name of knowledge because on this assurance rests the reality or genuine character of all other forms of knowledge. There seems to be no other reason than the belief that genuine knowledge presupposes the independent reality of the object known. If this is Locke's reason, then we have a type of thinking which in our terms is dialectical. In any case—and this is the important point—there is for Locke no demonstration, no proof, empirical or logical, for the belief that things exist without us. It is belief, either animal faith or that moral faith which, like the fundamental faith of the idealist, embodies a logically unsupported judgment of value. If any grounds for such an 'assurance' are possible they must be of the nature of dialectical argument—an argument which should 'show' that unless this postulate or presupposition of mind-independent being is acknowledged, no genuine knowledge is possible.

V

Critical Realism and The World We Live In. The Undermining of Representative Realism.

A

Representative realism, with its inevitable element of moral faith, was not only the natural but the only possible reaction to the disintegration of natural realism. The copy theory of knowledge is the one which first appears when any theory of knowledge becomes necessary, and knowledge is not merely taken for granted. But the insufficiency of this statement of realism was also soon to make itself felt and to give place to various forms of critical realism. To these we shall presently turn. It will, however, be well before we enter these more remote worlds to emphasize the fact that the world of these realisms is no longer 'the world we live in' and that the appeal to this motive of 'common sense' or natural realism is both disingenuous and extrinsic. By no stretch of the imagination can the world of any of these critical realisms be identified with that of the 'plain man'. It is a greatly changed world and one changed in very important respects. For one thing, it is an impoverished world. Even certain modern realists may be heard to wax indignant over the effrontery of other realists who have stripped the world of its colours, sounds and smells which plain man and poet alike both know and love.

Critical realism cannot, then, avoid some impoverishment of the natural world picture. But even more important, perhaps, is the fact that its world is in many respects an artificial world. From this point on all realisms are highly artificial and sophisticated. Having been compelled to yield one by one all the natural prejudices to which such a realism could confidently appeal, it must now be content to conceive the world in such a way that in it the plain man can only with the greatest difficulty find his way about. Often by constantly reassuring him, often quite disingenuously, that this is his old familiar world, can the modern realist keep touch with the plain man. This is especially the case when the appeal is made to the realism of science. There is undoubtedly an element of realistic faith in science, as indeed in all human activity, but the illusion that modern physical science is but glorified common sense, or that whatever realistic element there is in modern physics is the realism of either common sense or of representative perception, is finally dispelled. So far as this particular issue is concerned science is, as we shall see, as much idealistic as realistic.[1]

B

In the broader sense of the word, 'Critical Realism' must include all the realists since Kant, not omitting Kant himself, although he was in one aspect of his thinking a reluctant witness to the driving force of idealism. It must include the New Realists as well as the Critical Realists in the narrower sense of the term, namely, those who object to the epistemological monism of New Realism.

It will be first of all enlightening to recall the various descrip-

[1] Chapter vii.

tive names which the latter realists have given to their theories. In all these terms the break with the plain man's world is implicitly recognized. Thus, in addition to Kant's 'empirical realism,' we have the 'transfigured realism' of Herbert Spencer, which means that 'some objective existence, manifested under some conditions' separate from and independent of subjective existence is the final necessity of thought, and yet that the perceptions and objects in consciousness are not the reality and do not resemble it, but only *symbolize* it.' Lewes had what he called a 'reasoned realism' which he distinguishes, not only from crude and natural realism, but also from transfigured. It asserts that the reality of an external existence, a not-self, is given in feeling and indissolubly woven into consciousness.

The element common to all critical realism is really expressed by the word transfigured. The ancient resistance of realism is present, but it is so transformed that it is only in spirit, and not in letter, that it bears any resemblance, to either natural or representative realism. This transformation is chiefly expressed in the dictum that the contents of consciousness are not the reality and do not resemble it, but rather symbolize it. On certain fundamental points all forms of modern critical realism are agreed, but Critical Realism *eo nomine* differs from the New Realism, later to be examined, on issues so essential from our standpoint that we shall first consider critical realism for itself, leaving the New Realism for later consideration.

Critical Realism *eo nomine* differs from both natural and representative realism in regard to the place which it gives to sense data in its conception or theory of knowledge. Having in mind our preceding formulation of natural realism, we may also turn to Professor Broad for a definition of critical realism. Critical realism, according to him, is 'the theory that *sensa* are not literally spatio-temporal parts of the physical objects of which they are appearances; that there are certain characteristics which belong to *sensa* and not to physical objects and there are other characteristics which belong to both, although not necessarily in the same determinate order. In so far as they do not literally copy or represent the physical object, the relation must be described as symbolic.'[1]

---

[1] *Op. cit.*, p. 422 ff. It is this form of realism which is most characteristic of the new epistemology of physical science. See chapter vi.

It is, of course, this changed notion of the knowledge relation —from that of copy to that of symbol—that is all-important for the development of our general theme. For it means, not only that a large part of the primary defences of realism have been yielded but that the defence which remains has shifted to another point. Nevertheless, the aspect of critical realism upon which this view depends—namely, the characteristic differences between the *sensa* and physical objects—arises out of the critique of representative realism, and to this criticism we must therefore now turn.

C

Critical realism in all its forms is the result of criticism exercised on both naïve and representative realism. To be sure a large part of this criticism was developed by idealism, but these elements have been taken over by realism itself in the course of its development and have, therefore, become part of its own logical structure. It is, therefore, solely as an element taken up by realism in the justification of its own resistances that we shall consider them.

The fundamental difficulty with Representative Realism is its doctrine of representative perception. This doctrine was based upon two assumptions, both of which have proved themselves untenable. The first of these is the assumption of the identity of sensation and *sensa*. The failure to distinguish between these led to mentalism and, as we shall see, certain refutations of idealism rest upon this distinction. The second assumption was that sense perception must be identical with absolute knowledge. The relativity in certain respects, of sense data to the subject made impossible the notion that they could be in any literal sense representative of the physical object and made necessary another notion of the knowledge relation. To these 'logical' difficulties in the notion of representative perception itself have been added also those which have appeared as the result of biological knowledge and reflection. The main assumption underlying all conceptions of representative perception, namely that sense perception was developed mainly for knowledge, has been made more than doubtful by a genetic view of sense perception which seems to make it clear that sense perception was made primarily for adaptation and only secondarily for knowledge. The idea that sense perception gives us

86

a literal copy of the physical object seems everywhere to be a thing of the past.[1]

The net result of this critique has been what is, in every respect, a critical realism—critical in respect to its doctrine of sense data and their relation to the physical object, but critical also in respect to its conception of the status of the physical objects inferred from the sense data. The essential point is the substitution for the notion of literal copy that of symbolic representation. The fact that modern physical science with its 'new epistemology,' reaches the same critical conclusions substantiates the view that any realism to be possible in the world of modern knowledge must be of this general type.[2]

D

Critical Realism marks a complete break with both Natural and Representative Realism—a break which includes a disagreement with the entire conception of the nature of knowledge as previously held. Knowledge had been uniformly thought of in realistic circles as a direct or indirect apprehension of an object. This tendency, which bears witness to the continued influence of natural realism, the critical realist believes must be resisted at all costs. Knowledge is an affair of judgment and of the reference of judgment. This break is in large part due to the deadly critique, on the part of idealism, of the copy theory of knowledge. It is, Sellars admits, to the credit of the objective idealists that they have recognized this fact, i.e. that knowledge is an affair of judgment.[3]

This, then, is the point at which the transformation of realism is conditioned by its reactions to the criticisms of idealism, but it is also the point at which the nature of the essential resistance of realism appears with increased clearness. Critical realism is no longer merely the natural animal faith of naïve realism in the objectivity of the natural world picture as given; no longer the merely 'moral' faith which is an inevitable part of all forms

[1] For a summary statement of this position see Kemp Smith *Prolegomena to an Idealist Theory of Knowledge*, to which reference will be made in a later context [chapter ix, pp. 222 f].

[2] See chapter vii, pp. 168 ff.

[3] R. W. Sellars, *Essays in Critical Realism*. In his essay in this volume, entitled 'Knowledge and its Categories,' as well as in his *Critical Realism* 1916, there is an excellent account of the 'twistings and turnings' of Realism.

of representative realism, but in a special sense a reasoned faith, a reasoned realism as Lewes describes it. Knowledge, being an affair of judgment—not of apprehension either direct or indirect —it is the reasons for that judgment which become increasingly significant. As the realism itself is transfigured, so also is the resistance of that realism. Although it still has its roots in animal faith, that faith has now been transformed into a conscious postulate—into a judgment of cognitive value which, while itself logically unsupported, is itself the support of the entire theory of knowledge.

VI

The New Realism. Platonic or 'Logical' Realism.

A

It has been our contention all along that each reinstatement of realism, each new resistance developed to the driving force of idealism reveals ever more fully its true inwardness. We shall not be surprised, then, to find that in what is called the New Realism, this primitive strength survives in a highly sophisticated form. The appeal is still at bottom an *argumentum ad hominem*, but the man to whom the appeal is made is a vastly different one and the arguments embodied in the appeal are of a significantly different order. The sense of outrage is still there but, as now invoked, it is one which only a highly cultivated intelligence can feel. It is no longer merely the world of common sense, but still more the invisible realm of subsistent essences and values which this new realism takes under its defence.

Powerful movements in both Anglo-American and German philosophy have led to the formulation of this new type of realism. The New Realism of England and America may, indeed, be distinguished at many points from the realism of Meinong and Husserl, but in so far as the main issues are concerned they may be viewed as one. Both movements arise out of a reaction against subjectivism in varied forms. The reaction against psychologism in logic and ethics is, of course, part of it, but no less important is the reaction against idealism in both its mentalistic and logical forms. The Anglo-American form of this New Realism has, indeed, the Berkeleyan form as an opponent; but its dearest enemy is the logical idealism of Hegel, especially in the form made so influential by Bradley against whom so many of the leaders were in conscious revolt.

There are then two aspects of this form of realism which require equal emphasis. The first of these concerns the status of the *sensa* or sense data, which has always been the crux of the various types of realism; the second consists in a logical motive which consciously sets itself in dialectical opposition to the logical motives of objective idealism.

The essential of realism—the source of all its resistances—has always been the postulate of independence. This driving force is still present in the New Realism but in a highly subtle and sophisticated form. The New Realists have taken to heart the difficulties of the earlier forms of realism and the criticisms of it from Berkeley to Hegel; they now assert a doctrine of independence which is wholly compatible with the immanence in consciousness of the sense data. The cardinal principle of this realism has, therefore, been described as 'the independence of the immanent.' The stimulus to this new statement of independence was partly given by developing the distinction between sensation and sense *data* which constituted the basis of G. E. Moore's *Refutation of Idealism* of which more will be said later.[1] This doctrine, it is true, extends the character of independence to various universals, including essences and values, the relegation of which to a subjective status arouses, as we have seen, such a sense of outrage in the modern realist, but it is, after all, the status of the sense *data* which, now as always, constitutes the crux of the resistance of realism.

The second motive we described as the logical. This logical realism, as it is called, includes, in addition to the New Realism of England and America, the type of realism developed by Frege, Meinong and Husserl, and while the latter may differ from the former in certain respects, they are all one in the fact that the appeal is no longer primarily to instinct or faith but to logic. This appeal to logic includes, as we shall see, the setting over against the idealistic logic, with its doctrine of internal relations, of a doctrine of external relations based upon logical analysis. But it also—and indeed even more fundamentally—makes the argument for realism rest upon a supposed logical contradiction at the very heart of idealism, by attempting to

[1] See chapter iv, pp. 103 ff.

show that a doctrine of mind-dependence is self-contradictory and that the 'axiom of independence' is the necessary presupposition of genuine knowledge and *bona fide* logic.

The cardinal principle of the New Realism is then the independence of the immanent. The object of knowledge is mind-independent, but this independence is held to be wholly compatible with the denial of transcendence of consciousness.

The fundamental axiom of this realism is that every act of knowing involves an object to be known other than the knowing of it. In all our meanings, in all our thinking, we refer to an object of thinking. Even if we speak of a unicorn or a square circle, if we use a false proposition or a true one, we always refer in our thinking to the objects or the propositions as something different from our thinking. All constitute a realm of fact which we do not create but discover. This axiom, it is obvious, must turn anything that can be talked about at all into externality. In opposition to the supposed pan-subjectivism of Berkeley we have an equally thorough-going pan-objectivism. It is the sense *data* which, as we have said, are by this axiom primarily given external 'existence'—and it is upon this independence of the sense data that significant attempts at the refutation of idealism have been based—but the universals, including in some versions even round squares and golden mountains, have been sent pell-mell after them. As idealism, in the extreme form of mentalism, assimilates the object to the subject and tends ultimately to a solipsism of the subject, so realism, in this latest form, assimilates the subject to the object and tends to a solipsism of the object. Both are novel worlds—the one as remote from that of the plain man as the other.

The doctrine of the independence of the immanent brings with it a second element which shows clearly the break of this form of realism with all previous types, namely, the doctrine of epistemological monism. The essential of all forms of realism hitherto has always been some form of epistemological dualism. From natural and representative realism, through the various forms of critical realism, independence of the object of knowing has always meant that the sense data have been in part subjective and that between idea and thing, subject and object, there is a break which in a sense can be bridged only by some act of faith, animal or 'moral.' The doctrine we are here considering believes that it can eliminate this issue. The entities which are thus independent are 'neutral' essences, neither mental nor physical, which may enter into relations—that are purely external—with mind or with objects; epistemologically they are one.

It is at this point that the logical aspect of this form of realism may be emphasized. As logical idealism depends upon a doctrine of internal relations, so this logical realism depends upon a doctrine of external relations; to refute this later form of idealism it is necessary only to show that relations are external. Into the arguments for the externality of relations we shall not for the present go; they belong to the logical refutations of idealism which will be considered in a later context.[1] Here the sole point to emphasize is that the argument for realism, as well as the refutation of idealism, is primarily logical in character.

B

The novel atmosphere of the New Realism is obvious—its difference from all preceding forms apparent to the most cursory gaze. This world of neutral entities, this spectacular universe, is wholly unrecognizable as the world we live in. It wipes out distinctions which for the plain man have been immemorial landmarks. It is not strange, then, that to some realists also, this 'epistemological monism,' with all its consequences, should appear only as a 'remarkable *tour de force*,' as a belated attempt to restore natural realism with its doctrine of direct knowledge which criticism should have made impossible. A *tour de force* it certainly is, but because it is such it by no means follows that it is without significance. It is precisely its violent and arbitrary character that is significant. Like all violent turns of thought it witnesses to some inherent necessity which, if it cannot find expression in simple and natural thought, will find a more sophisticated way.

This *tour de force*, as has been already indicated, is the assertion of independence of consciousness of that which, for common sense and for all preceding forms of realism, has simply not been independent. It includes, as we have seen, in its pan-objectivism even the independence of illusion and error. It is, however, not

[1] Chapter iv.

with these aspects of the position that we are now concerned—criticism is no part of the task which we have set ourselves in this chapter—but rather with the inherent necessity which has compelled this *tour de force*. There are doubtless many aspects of this form of realism which simply cannot endure. Being products of purely local and temporal conditions in the present scientific and philosophical world, they will pass also. But the inherent necessity which gave rise to this *tour de force* will not pass. This necessity, created in the dialectical development of realism, is supposed to be logical. Actually, it is neither empirical nor logical; it is axiological or 'moral,' precisely as the driving force of idealism is ultimately axiological and moral. You may call it a prejudice if you will, and a prejudice it is in the sense of a pre-judgment, but it is one that is necessary, not only for life but for knowledge. It is a cognitive value which must be acknowledged if knowledge itself is to have any meaning or be intelligible.

C

In the preceding paragraphs we have examined the ways in which the New Realism seeks to maintain the essentially realistic contention against the main theses of mentalism and logical idealism. There are, to be sure, many appeals to fact in these well-known arguments, but after all the 'nerve of the argument' is to be found in the axiom of independence—the thesis that to deny this axiom involves a logical contradiction—a contradiction, moreover, which G. E. Moore maintains 'no idealist has ever yet succeeded in avoiding.' An examination of this 'axiom' will at the same time bring out the full meaning of the New Realism and reveal the inmost source of the resistance of all forms of realism.

This axiom has been well stated by Meinong and in a way, moreover, which brings out clearly the dialectical character of the argument which I wish here to emphasize. 'No thought,' he writes, 'can have itself as object of the thought . . . The object of the thought is always transcendent to the thinking. Every claim of an identity of the experience of apprehending with the object to be apprehended, or claim that the last is determined by the first is a case of subjectivity-objectivity and therefore *widersinnig*.' It is claimed that the opposite of the realistic axiom is a self-contradiction and therefore makes epistemological non-sense of any theory of knowledge which maintains it. What, then, is the nature of this self-contradiction?

In the first place, it cannot be properly maintained that the opposite of this 'axiom' involves a logical contradiction. There is no logical contradiction in saying that an object exists now and that it does not exist when it is not experienced.[1] Nor can it be said that the denial of this realistic axiom is intrinsically *wider-sinnig* or nonsense. It is contrary to sense *only if I make a prior assumption of a certain ideal as to what constitutes genuine knowledge.* Only if this assumption is acknowledged can the denial be shown to be contrary to sense. This is so important that it must be developed at more length.

Let us take any case of 'knowledge,' any judgment whatsoever that appears to refer to an independent or transcendent being. It may always be so transformed that it merely asserts facts of consciousness, and only in this form is it really beyond doubt. I say, for instance, 'the sun shines'. Instead of saying this I may say 'I see the sun'. Only in this latter statement is there anything like immediate certainty, the denial of which is in any sense self-contradictory. On the other hand, denial of a transcendent object is always possible. Nor is it necessarily *wider-sinnig*. It is contrary to sense only if I assume from the start that genuine knowledge requires and presupposes this distinction between the fact of consciousness and the object. In other words, the subjective version of my judgment is contrary to sense only because of a prior assumption on my part as to what constitutes genuine knowledge, or of what conception of knowledge we must have in order to 'make sense.' If you do not acknowledge this prior assumption, no argument is possible. This assumption, however, like that which underlies the idealistic theory, is a logically unsupported judgment of value.

But, it may be said, to deny this 'value,' and the obligation which follows from it, is to make all our statements meaningless. Precisely so. The acknowledgment of this axiom, or postulate, is the condition of all intelligible discourse, of all communication between man and man. It is doubtless *wider-sinnig* to deny trans-cendent being—and I would be the first to recognize this fact—but *it is so* only because *Sinn* (meaning, sense) implies values

[1] For a fuller development of this point, see chapter iv.

which must be acknowledged. Those realists of whom Royce complains, that they hold it more or less immoral not to believe in transcendent realities have, after all, a great deal to say for themselves. Genuine knowledge and *bona fide* logic depend for their genuineness and their *bona fide* character upon this axiom and its acknowledgment, but the demand for its acknowledgment is axiological, not logical.

This I shall describe as the last stand of realism just as axiological idealism, or the idealism of values, may be called the last stand of idealism. As in the case of the latter, so in the former the ultimate premise is seen to be an unsupported judgment of value. It is this judgment, with the obligation which it entails, which constitutes the true inwardness of all forms of realism. As for idealism the driving force lies in a moral rather than a speculative impossibility, so for realism, when it becomes fully self-conscious, the root of its stubbornness is a moral, not a logical, certainty. This is the meaning of the animal faith of natural realism, of the reasoned faith of critical realism and, finally, of the 'axiom of independence' of the latest and most sophisticated forms of realism.

VII

The Irrefutable Element in Realism: The Realistic Minimum.

A

We have attempted, in so far as possible, to allow realism to speak for itself. In doing so we have followed the transformations of realism and the gradual transference of its resistances from one point to another. First, the appeal was to the natural prejudice in favour of the actual, justified to a certain extent by considerations of a biological nature. Then the appeal is to a certain kind of 'moral certainty'; Descartes, Leibniz and Locke were all keen enough to see the nature of this appeal. Finally, the appeal is to what I have described as axiological necessity—to the axiom of independence which must be acknowledged if knowledge itself is to retain its meaning and value.

This I have described as *the last stand of realism*, and with the transference of its resistance to this point we have finally become aware of its inmost drive and of the 'continuity of epistemological intention' throughout. This I shall also maintain is the irrefutable element in realism—that which remains when all particular formulations are subjected to criticism, whether from within or from without. This continuity we have now seen in its historical and dialectical movement. Part of that dialectic has always been 'refutations of idealism'. In the development of realism they have played precisely the same part that refutations of realism have played in the development of idealism. A consideration of the principles underlying these refutations will serve further to bring out the true inwardness of realism.

The first refutation of idealism was that of Dr Johnson, who, kicking the stone, said, 'I disprove it thus'. I cannot see that any of the many refutations since his time differ in principle from his. They are all arguments *ad hominem*, appeals to the logically unsupported judgment of value which underlies all the resistances of realism in whatever form they appear. This first crude, behaviouristic refutation has, indeed, become refined and subtle as the dialectical argument has proceeded, but when carefully examined, as we shall seek to do later it will be seen that they never lose their original character and force.

It is true, of course, that they have taken the forms of empirical and logical refutations. Mentalism has been 'refuted' by supposed appeal to fact—to ever more adequate study of *sensa*, their relation to sensation and the physical object—in other words by attempting to show the fallacies in Berkeley's and similar forms of argument. Logical idealism has been 'refuted' by appeal to logic—by attempting to show that relations in general—and more specifically the relation between the knower and the object known—are external to the things related. But none of these arguments really refute idealism, as I shall attempt to show in the following chapter. The only argument which can be said in any sense to refute idealism is that which we have described as the last stand of realism—and that argument is dialectical. It is an *argumentum ad hominem* and, to have any force at all, presupposes upon the part of the mind to whom the argument is directed, an acknowledgment of a certain conception of genuine knowledge which begs the very question to be proved.

In this sense, then refutations of idealism, like the refutations of realism, are really arguments in a circle, as indeed they must be, in the very nature of the case. But this fact does not deprive them of significance. For it is precisely the value of circular argument to show us that we cannot get out of it—that we cannot escape the assumption which appears in our premises and conclusions alike. Circular arguments are not necessarily vicious; they are so only when we do not understand what their circular character means. Realism can then never really refute idealism, but its very attempt to refute it serves to make clear an equally irrefutable element in realism. This we shall call the realistic *minimum* and with an attempt to formulate it we shall close this chapter.

B

Idealism we have described as the phoenix of philosophy. Realism may be described as the Antæus of philosophy. Every time it touches the ground it arises with renewed force. The original source of that force is undoubtedly in animal instinct, in that prejudice in favour of the actual which makes the physical object the object of knowledge *par excellence*, and the natural confusion of psychological with logical priority. This primal force is never wholly lost. The sense of outrage which leads the realist to take the plain man's world of common sense under his protection is, to be sure, both moderated and modified in the course of reflection—it may, indeed, be transferred to the world of essences, subsistences and values as we have seen—but it remains in principle the same. Every time this Antæus touches the ground he renews his force, *but the force is moral*.

This ultimately moral source of the resistance of realism has been well expressed by Jacques Maritain in the following impressive words: 'Idealism strikes at the very life of the intelligence: it misunderstands radically the intelligence even when it affects to exalt it. At the same time and for the same reason one discovers it (idealism) at the roots of all the ills from which the mind is suffering today.' Strikes at the roots of the intelligence! A revealing phrase. In the words of our discussion, idealism makes genuine knowledge and *bona fide* logic impossible. We may doubt whether all the manifold ills from which the mind is suffering today can be laid to this single cause. We may deprecate the over simplification which thus includes all forms of idealism in one sweeping charge. But we can well understand that there are theories of knowledge which *do* strike at the roots of intelligence—denature it and take all the meaning out of it. To the realist, idealism is one of these forms. Here then we have the essentials of realism and of its resistances in so many and varied forms.

There is, then, it seems to me, a realistic *minimum* which any intelligible theory of knowledge must retain, just as I attempted to show in the preceding chapter, there is a necessary idealistic *minimum*. Here I shall merely indicate the nature of the *minimum* briefly, leaving its detailed development for a later chapter.[1]

Genuine knowledge, the realist rightly sees, presupposes antecedent reality, the mind-independent character of the object of knowledge *in some sense*; the denial of this primary principle of all knowledge is, as Maritain says, to strike at the very roots of the intelligence. For unless the content of knowledge is acknowledged as having a condition independent of the mind the 'peculiar significance' of knowledge is inevitably lost. The very purpose and meaning of knowledge is to be true to something beyond it; its very intent is to be governed by it and dictated to in certain respects. All this is indisputable, although it cannot be 'demonstrated'. It is a logically unsupported judgment of value.

This, then, is the *minimum*, but with the bare statement of this minimum the problem has only begun. The real issue is to determine just what this independence means. Only a critical realism can determine that fact, and when the results of a truly critical realism are compared with those of an equally critical idealism, it may be found that the two are 'separated only by a word.' Whether this is true, whether a consistency between realism and idealism can be shown, is yet to be seen. But that does not in the least affect the conclusions of this chapter, any more than it affects the conclusions of the preceding chapter. There is a necessary *minimum* of realism in any theory of knowledge worth the name.

[1] Chapter v, pp. 139 f.

97

Chapter IV

The Transcendence of Realism and Idealism. Conditions of Transcendence.

I — A

EARLIER we had occasion to speak of the disconcerting situation created in philosophy by the perennial opposition between idealism and realism. It seemed more than likely that an opposition such as this is due not so much to the stupidity or intolerance of the opponents as to the peculiar character of the opposition itself. The sources of the opposition we have now found to lie in certain 'prejudices' or presuppositions of thought which are, in a very real sense, ineradicable. The ultimate premise of either position is a logically unsupported judgment of value, and, in so far as these judgments are felt and acknowledged, they are immitigable.

We have spoken of these ultimate premises as 'prejudices' and in a sense they may be so called. Both the driving force of idealism and the resistance of realism are in part psychological and it is just as well to recognize this fact. It is for this reason that Jung finds them ineradicable and both necessary to life.[1] It is for this reason also that, as we have seen, Paulhan finds them necessary for the life of society and, therefore, in principle ineradicable. In a deeper sense, however, they are neither merely psychological nor social and cease to be prejudices in any dyslogistic sense. They are 'moral' in the sense already defined, and it is this moral 'assurance', felt by both parties to the opposition, that makes all 'refutations' of either position futile and the opposition in some sense for ever ineradicable.

Both idealism and realism are then ineradicable. But because they are ineradicable it does not follow that they are irreconcilable. Both are equally indigenous to life; idealism is as natural as realism. Life, in fact, creates the opposition, but it also knows how to reconcile it. Both are necessary 'life-forms of thought', and precisely because both are necessary both must be possible. Life does not say merely either or; it says both real and ideal. It gives its ontological predicates with equal readiness

[1] See chapter v, pp. 119 f.

to both the actual and the ideal. Now 'Life' with a capital letter of course solves no philosophical problems; the 'intuitions' of life can take the place neither of conceptual thought nor of philosophical interpretation. Yet 'this vital reconciliation gives us every right to expect that a mode of reconciliation must be recognized in theory as in life, as normal to the entire process of consciousness.' This reconciliation, both vital and theoretical, is the theme of the present chapter. Such a reconciliation involves, however, as its preliminary a fuller understanding of the nature of the opposition and of the conditions which alone make possible its transcendence. Our present concern is, therefore, with the conditions of transcendence.

In the introductory chapter we stated these conditions in general form. The problem was described as one of mutual understanding and interpretation. This may be stated in a psychological or in a more 'logical' way. We may say that in order to understand and evaluate the arguments of idealism or realism respectively, we must go back to the attitudes which lie behind the arguments—that discussion of the arguments without reference to the attitudes is a game lost before it is begun. But we may also say that the ultimate premises of both these arguments are logically unsupported judgments of value. It is these judgments, together with the obligations which they entail, which constitute the true inwardness of the driving force of idealism and of the resistance of realism. It is the understanding and interpretation of these facts that constitute the conditions of the transcendence of the opposition.

These conditions may be summarized as follows. There is, first of all (a) the fact of the ineradicable character of these two beliefs and the reasons therefore. There is secondly (b) the impossibility of either proof or disproof of either of these positions and the reasons for this situation. Thirdly, there is (c) the recognition that the conflict cannot be eliminated by their own means—that is by the unneutral logics to which both appeal—and consequently the necessity of a change of venue, the transference of the case to another court. These facts and conclusions have, indeed, emerged more or less clearly from our historical studies. It is now necessary to state them more explicitly.

II

The Ineradicable Character of the Two Beliefs. The Impossibility of the Elimination of Either.

A

If idealism (epistemological) is true, says Meinong, it occupies an anomalous position. To the usual run of things in science the realistic belief in independence remains a curious exception—that the old knowledge is not supplanted by the new. The Berkeleyan or other arguments may for a time convince, but the old realistic conviction returns with all its pristine vigour. This is undoubtedly true. But the humour of the situation is that the same holds for realism. The critique exercised by realism on idealism has been no less conclusive and damnatory, but the damnable heresy seems to flourish all the more. Many of the wiser realists have come, therefore, to admit that they 'see no argument by which idealism can be disproved,' although still professing to see in it a position 'which they would not like to accept.' History should long ago have indicated the unlikelihood, if not impossibility, of eliminating either one of these alternative positions. An insight into the nature of these beliefs indicates that neither proof nor disproof of either of them is really possible.

The reasons for this have already become apparent in the preceding chapters. There are the extrinsic appeals of both idealism and realism which, while we may call them illicit, can never really be eliminated. In the second place, while the problem is not psychological in meaning, it is, as Jung maintains, partly psychological in origin. But more fundamental than either of these reasons is one which must have become fully clear after these studies. It is that neither idealism nor realism is 'knowledge' in the sense that their champions believe them to be. Locke, with more than his usual subtlety, while admitting that 'the assurance that there are things existing without us cannot reach demonstration,' yet feels that it is somehow an assurance that 'deserves the name of knowledge.' Had he been just a little more subtle he would have phrased his statement differently. If it deserves the name of knowledge, as in a sense it undoubtedly does, it is not because it rests upon demonstration, either empirical or logical, as he himself clearly saw, but because it is a postulate or presupposition of all genuine knowledge, one that alone makes genuine knowledge possible—in short, a logically unsupported judgment of value. Had he stated it thus, the story of modern philosophy might have been significantly different.

It is, however, the negative side of Locke's position which concerns us here, namely, that realism is indemonstrable either empirically or logically. This general truth should be evident by now, but the point is so important that I shall venture to press it just a little further. It is often said 'either objects are independent of the subject or they are not. Is not this a simple matter of fact, the propositions like any other propositions, and therefore either true or false, capable of proof or disproof?' Thus it is said that the truth of the proposition, reality is independent of the knower, rests upon an induction by the method of agreement. Every particular object is independent of myself, and consequently I conclude that reality as a whole, the all-of-reality, is independent. But to whom is the fallacy of such an argument not immediately evident? Even from the standpoint of formal logic the argument is fallacious. I might just as well say that because every physical object is heavy the physical world as a whole is heavy. But the difficulty is more fundamental than this. It is that, as Locke saw, such a proposition (and the same is true of the corresponding thesis of idealism) is not a proposition, like other propositions, capable of demonstration, either empirically or logically. If such propositions deserve the name of knowledge, it must be knowledge in another and quite different sense.

B

The reason for the anomaly in the case of the beliefs in realism and idealism—namely, that the old knowledge is not driven out by the new—is, then, the fact that neither is knowledge in the sense that its champion supposes it to be. Not being knowledge in this sense, it cannot be driven out by such knowledge.

This general situation is, as we have seen, recognized by some logical positivists. As there are no possible experiences relevant to the proof of idealism or realism respectively, and no formal logical procedure which could conceivably demonstrate either position, so equally there are none that can refute them. In this the logical positivist is fundamentally right, although, as we saw, it does not follow that for these reasons the opposition is meaningless. It is then the thesis of the irrefutable character of either position that we have now to maintain. This means that none of the famous refutations, either of idealism or realism, really refute. To prove this very important point it is necessary to examine these supposed refutations in detail. Before doing so, however, it is desirable to recall certain characteristics of all such refutations which we noted in a preliminary way in the preceding chapters.

In the first place, these refutations of the opposing position are always parts of the positive argument for realism or idealism respectively. Refutations of idealism—from Kant to G. E. Moore—are always a part of such argument. So also refutations of realism from Berkeley to Stace. When, however, we examine these so-called refutations we find that they never refute idealism or realism *as such*, but only some special form. Both positions have gone through many transformations and the refutation of one form does not necessarily mean refutation of others. Jaurès is said to have remarked concerning the 'sacredness of property,' first tell me what sort of property you mean. Similarly, if you speak of the refutation of idealism, for instance, you must first tell us what kind of idealism you mean. It follows from this that the first condition of the refutation of idealism, or of realism also, is its reduction to a single proposition to which it can be shown that any form of idealism or realism, as the case may be, must subscribe.

This, then, is the preliminary step in all attempts at refutation and the indispensable condition of there being any refutation at all. Granted that this is possible, there follows a second character of all such refutations. They always take two lines, appeal to fact and appeal to logic; an empirical and a logical refutation. Thus, supposing, for instance, that idealism can be reduced to a single proposition, let us say, *esse est percipi*, it can be refuted, conceivably, in two ways: (*a*) by showing factually that there are data mind-independent and (*b*) by showing that to deny this involves a logical contradiction. Both are, for instance, employed by G. E. Moore in his supposed refutation of idealism.

Both are also employed by Stace in his supposed refutation of realism. It is claimed that there is no empirical evidence for mind-independent entities and that to postulate such involves some sort of contradiction.

These, then, are the general characters of all such refutations. It is now our task to examine these supposed refutations in detail. We must ask whether the reduction to a single cardinal principle, on which all refutation depends, is possible. We must then ask, whether these appeals to fact and appeals to logic constitute valid refutations. To both these questions we shall find it necessary to answer in the negative. As to the second question we shall maintain that there is no empirical disproof of either position because of the nature of the propositions involved. Nor is any appeal to logic possible. I shall attempt to show that no logical contradiction is involved in the holding of either position and that, therefore, neither can be refuted logically.

III

Attempted Refutations of Idealism and Realism. Their Significance.

A

It is now my purpose to apply these general considerations to actual supposed refutations of idealism and realism. I shall begin with the refutation of idealism for two reasons. According to my view, the issue is essentially a modern one and arose in a specific context. It was idealism which first challenged the refuters, and it is only proper that we should begin with this refutation. There have been many such supposed refutations, but since, as we have also seen, there is no refutation of idealism as such unless it can be reduced to a specific proposition, we shall consider the now famous refutation of G. E. Moore which begins with such an attempt at reduction.

Of this well-known paper the author later writes that he is doubtful whether he should have included it in his *Philosophical Studies* (published in 1922). It appears to him now, he writes, 'to be very confused and to embody a good many downright mistakes.' This I would not dispute, and it would have been enlightening if in the later reprinting he had shown us where these confusions and mistakes lie—and still more enlightening if he had told us whether he now believes that it really constitutes a refutation of idealism. This I do not for a moment believe.

Professor Moore recognizes, of course, that idealism in the larger sense, namely, the metaphysical assertion that the universe is spiritual, is not refutable in this way and perhaps not refutable at all. He therefore attacks one argument which he thinks is necessary to the belief. In his own words, 'I shall therefore attack at least one argument which, to the best of my belief, is considered necessary to their position by *all* idealists . . . if my arguments are sound they will have refuted idealism. If I can refute a single proposition which is a necessary and essential step in all idealistic arguments, then no matter how good the rest of these arguments may be, I shall have proved that idealists have no reason whatever for their conclusion.' the trivial proposition which he proposes to dispute is this: that *esse est percepi.* . . .

Now I do not believe that this argument is necessary to idealism, and I should certainly challenge Professor Moore's statement that it is considered necessary to their position by all idealists. But granted that he is right on this point, even this proposition cannot be refuted by his arguments and, in my opinion, cannot be refuted by any arguments. It cannot be shown, either empirically or logically, that unexperienced entities exist and this would be necessary to refute idealism, even as defined by Professor Moore.

The supposed refutation is so well known that it is necessary to state it only very briefly. 'The idealist maintains that subject and object are necessarily connected mainly because he fails to see that they are distinct, that they are two at all. When he thinks of yellow and then he thinks of the sensation of yellow he fails to see that there is anything whatever in the latter which is not in the former.' The entire argument then rests mainly on a supposed experiential distinction between yellow and the sensation of yellow, and secondly, on a supposed logical contradiction in identifying them when they are thus different. But let us hear his own words:

'Accordingly, to identify either blue or any other of what I have called "objects" of sensation with the corresponding sensation, is in every case a self-contradictory error. It is to identify a part either with the whole of which it is a part, or else with the other part of the same whole. If we are told that the assertion "Blue exists" is meaningless unless we mean by it that the "sensation of blue exists", we are told what is certainly false and self-contradictory. If we are told that the existence of blue is inconceivable apart from the existence of the sensation, the speaker probably means to convey to us, by this ambiguous expression, what is self-contradictory error. For we can and must conceive the existence of blue as something quite distinct from the existence of the sensation. We can and must conceive that blue might exist and yet the sensation of blue not exist. For my own part I not only conceive this, but conceive it to be true. Either, therefore, this terrific assertion of inconceivability means what is false and self-contradictory, or else it means only that, *as a matter of fact* blue never can exist unless the sensation of it exists also. (P. 19) "No philosopher," he adds, "has ever yet succeeded in avoiding this self-contradictory error; and the most striking results both of idealism and agnosticism are only obtained by this identification of blue with the sensation of blue".' Clearly the appeal here is in the first instance to matter of fact (empirical) and secondly to logic, namely, self-contradiction.

As to the former, I have already indicated in principle why such disproof is impossible. Let us now see it in detail. It may be said, in the first place, that the acts of sensing to which Moore and modern realists in general appeal, and for the ignoring of which they reproach Berkeley, are completely inaccessible to observation and cannot be appealed to as empirical proof or disproof. But even if they were accessible, and if the difference between sense data and our awareness of them—on which the entire argument depends—were empirically established, the distinction would neither prove realism nor refute idealism. It might prove that blue or yellow are not mental, but such a proposition is perfectly consistent with idealism, as Bosanquet and Stace have both shown. But it certainly does not prove that the unexperienced entities exist—which is the thesis of realism. Nor does it disprove the idealistic thesis that such entities do not exist. Neither proof nor disproof is empirically possible here.

The real nerve of the refutation—if it be such—lies then elsewhere, namely, in the sphere of logic. Now there is, I insist, no self-contradictory error in saying that blue never can exist unless the sensation of it exists also. But, granted that there is, this is no refutation of idealism. The essential of idealism, even as defined by Moore, consists in saying that an object does not exist when no one is experiencing it. There is no self-contradiction in saying that an object exists now and does not exist when it is not experienced. It may be something that we find difficult to believe, but it contains no logical contradiction. More of this later.

This refutation of idealism does not then refute. Nor, according to my view, can any refutation. Obviously, I cannot prove a statement of this sort, as I cannot here examine all supposed refutations. But I may point out that the impossibility of such refutation is conceded by many realists. Mr Broad finds it something that cannot be proved but which he yet believes. Many find realism nothing more than animal faith, and Mr Russell goes so far as to say that 'belief in the existence of things outside my biography must, from the standpoint of theoretical logic, be regarded as a prejudice, not a well grounded theory.' Granted that idealism cannot be refuted—either empirically or logically—it does not, however, follow that the supposed refutation is without significance. Certainly, realism is not mere animal faith nor mere prejudice. What then is its significance? It is, as I have said, dialectical. In the very attempt to refute is brought out the irrefutable element in realism itself, the logically unsupported judgment of value of which the empirical and logical apparatus is merely the technical disguise.

I rather think that Mr Moore has himself indicated this significance, perhaps unwittingly. 'We can and must conceive the existence of blue as something distinct from the existence of the sensation. We can and must conceive that blue might exist and yet the sensation of blue not exist. To hold the opposite is self contradictory error which,' as he says, 'no idealist has ever succeeded in avoiding.' But why this *can* and this *must*? Surely there is no logical self-contradiction here. If I *must* it is only because he assumes that, with him, I acknowledge a certain significance to knowledge. If I do acknowledge it and then 'hold the opposite,' I do indeed refute myself, but self-refutation does not logically refute a proposition. Mr Moore or any other realist can, perhaps, persuade me by this type of argument to acknowledge this logically unsupported judgment of value, but cannot coerce me by any proof either empirical or logical. Perhaps I ought to accept it, but this oughtness is axiological, not logical necessity.

I do not know whether Mr Moore thinks that his supposed disproof of idealism constitutes a proof of realism or not; certainly this is the inference generally drawn. Apparently he does so believe. For, we are told, 'the only reasonable alternative to such realism is absolute scepticism and it is as likely as not nothing exists at all. All other suppositions, the agnostics' that something at all events does exist, as much as the idealists' that spirit does, if we have no reason for believing in matter, are as baseless as the grossest superstitions.' Here the full dialectical character of the argument becomes finally clear. The only reasonable alternative to this evaluation of knowledge is absolute scepticism and, *of course we cannot be such sceptics*. Now I agree that we cannot be sceptics—we have knowledge and the epistemologists' problem is to show how it is possible. If to be possible and significant it must contain the postulate of mind-independent objects—and I am inclined to think it must—then let us make this postulate, but let us also acknowledge that this 'assurance', though it perhaps 'deserves the name of knowledge', is of the nature of neither empirical or logical demonstration. For metaphysical propositions such as this no such demonstration is possible. The argument is wholly dialectical and it is precisely this fact that gives it its great significance.

B

There is, then, no refutation of idealism in the sense ordinarily understood—no disproof either empirical or logical. Idealism is the best refuted thesis in the world and the damnable heresy continues to flourish all the more, invading even the sacred precincts of physics itself—to the scandal of many philosophers. It is tempting for the realist to think that this must be due to stupidity or perversity on the part of the idealist, but it would be well for him to give the question second thought, and to ask whether there is not some more deeply seated reason. The idealist is so certain, that he even proposes to refute realism. Such refutation has always been a part of modern idealism from

Berkeley to Stace. But if idealism is irrefutable, so is realism and to the justification of this thesis we now turn.

It is manifestly impossible to examine all the refutations of realism. For the particular purposes of the present discussion I shall therefore take what is not only probably the latest attempt, but one also that brings out my general points most clearly— namely, that proposed by Professor W. T. Stace in his article, *The Refutation of Realism* (*Mind*. Vol. XLIII, No. 170. April, 1934). I choose it all the more readily for the reason that it is set over explicity against the 'Refutation of Idealism', by G. E. Moore.

'That which is essential to the realist position', Professor Stace holds, 'is that some entities sometimes exist without being experienced by any finite mind.' Realists seem to him to agree in asserting this, and to refute it is therefore to refute realism. The refutation of realism will be accomplished, he holds, if we can show that we do *not* know that any single entity exists unexperienced. The essential point of this refutation is that we cannot prove that any object exists independently of our experience and, therefore, it ought not to be believed. And for him there are only two possible ways of showing this, namely, either deductively or inductively, logically or empirically. Intuition is for him excluded by definition.

The idea of logical proof or of deductive inference may, he holds, be excluded. There is no logical contradiction in my saying that an object exists now and that it does not exist when no one is experiencing it. The view that nothing exists except my personal sense data may be one that no one would care to hold, but there is no logical inconsistency in it. In this he is surely right when one understands what logic really is. There is left then only some sort of appeal to facts, some sort of inductive inference. To refute realism all that is necessary then is to show that there is no such empirical evidence to verify the belief, and therefore, as he holds, it should not be believed.

Now 'inductive reasoning,' so he continues, 'proceeds always on the basis that what has been found in certain observed cases to be true will also be true in unobserved cases. But there is no single case in which it has been observed to be true that an experienced object continues to exist when it is not being experienced, for, by hypothesis, its existence, when it is not being experienced, cannot be observed. Induction is generalization from observed facts, but there is not a single case of an unexperienced existence having been observed on which could be based the generalization that entities continue to exist when no one is experiencing them. And there is likewise not a single known instance of the existence of an unexperienced entity which could lead me to have even the slightest reason for supposing that it ever did exist.' Now I should not want to put the argument in this extreme form. Certainly I should not want to say that there is *not the slightest reason for supposing that unexperienced entities exist*. But in principle I agree with the thesis. It is simply the thesis of the logical positivist, already examined, that for a metaphysical proposition such as this, the empirical criterion cannot be brought into play.

It is true that this thesis of Professor Stace—namely, that there is no empirical or inductive proof for realism—was immediately challenged. His own refutation was immediately followed by a series of refutations of the refutation, as is always so pitifully the case. It was argued that belief in independent entities is a belief like any specific scientific belief when, as we have seen, it is not. Evidence here, it was said, is analogous to the empirical evidence by which we come to believe in the reality of other minds when obviously such evidence is of the nature of the evidence for reality or unreality of an object in Mr Ayer's sense of the terms. Following the same general line of thought, others supposed that an inference to the existence of unperceived entities is like an inference from perceived parts of the moon to a spatially continuous or solid moon, when, as a matter of fact, as the logical positivist rightly sees, they belong to two wholly different universes of discourse.

I hold, then, that these answers do not refute the refutation, and that there is no empirical proof for realism, as indeed most modern realists see and acknowledge. But now we come to the nerve of Stace's supposed refutation. We are told that since this is so, 'the belief in unexperienced entities ought not to be entertained any more than the belief that there is a unicorn on Mars ought to be entertained.' This is one of the most extraordinary pieces of reasoning I have ever seen. There is no analogy between the unicorn on Mars and this belief. I can think of at least one good reason for holding the realist's belief, namely, the postulate of antecedent reality upon which, according to him, genuine knowledge alone is possible. But this is not the point I wish to make here. I wish merely to point out that at no point in the argument is realism actually refuted. We are simply shown that it cannot prove its own thesis. And that, on our view, is precisely what we should find. Neither position can prove its own thesis, nor can it disprove its opponents.

It is, accordingly, no more possible to refute realism than to refute idealism. Nor, according to my view, can any possible supposed refutation, although manifestly I cannot argue that here. But it does not follow that this and other attempts have no significance. Their significance is very real, for they bring to light that which motivates all such attempts, namely, the empirically and logically unsupported judgment of value which underlies all idealism. This is the thesis that genuine knowledge is not possible without mind-dependence of the object of some sort. This has been stated in many ways and with different degrees of convincingness—from Berkeley's 'repugnance to reason', through Kant's reluctant witness to idealism in his Copernican revolution, to the statements of mutual involvement of mind and its object in Hegel and Bosanquet, and to the thesis of axiological idealism.

This significance also comes out, perhaps likewise unwittingly, in Professor Stace's own formulation. He holds that the realist's position ought not to be believed because we cannot prove it either inductively or deductively. Mere absence of such proof constitutes, however, no valid ground for such an *ought*—at least to one who believes that such independence is the necessary condition of genuine knowledge. No, it is really because Professor Stace believes that such independence makes genuine knowledge impossible that he thinks we ought not to believe it. Here, too, he can persuade me to an acknowledgment of this primary unsupported judgment of value, but he cannot coerce me by any argument, empirical or logical.

Does Professor Stace believe that this supposed refutation of realism proves idealism? Apparently he does. He insists that it is no part of the purpose of the paper to arrive at more than a negative result, but he does think that 'the resulting conception is that, in the last analysis, nothing exists except minds and their sense data (which are not "mental") and that human minds have out of these sense data slowly and laboriously constructed the rest of the solid universe of our knowledge.' Now that the 'solid universe of our knowledge' is to an incalculable degree constructed seems to me undoubted—a necessary consequence of the new epistemology of physical science, as we shall see in a later chapter.[1] But that it is wholly constructed out of our sense data, and that nothing but these data and the minds that have them exists, seems to me to be a wholly gratuitous inference. Certainly it does not at all follow necessarily from the negative arguments advanced by Professor Stace. If we are driven to such a view—so contrary to the natural world picture —the driving force of the argument must be quite other, namely, the logical unsupported judgment of cognitive value which underlies every form of idealism.

C

I think, then, that we may say without presuming too much that neither realism nor idealism can refute the other. It is not because men are stupid and perverse that those who are already idealists are not convinced and those already realists remain untouched. It is for very good and definite reasons. They live in different universes and speak different languages. In other words, they start with quite different premises and quite different cognitive values. It is, therefore, a futile game that we have been playing. We have supposed that we have been dealing with empirical and logical arguments when in fact we have to do with 'attitudes' or better with empirically and logically unsupported beliefs or postulates lying back of these arguments—in short, with dialectic.

Josiah Royce seems to have realized the dialectical character of this situation as well as any one. In his *Supplementary Essay* to his Howison Lecture on the *Conception of God* (1897) he examines this endless debate between the idealist and realist and comes to substantially the above conclusions. His thesis is that idealism (what he calls half-idealism) falls a helpless prey to the counter dialectics of the realist, but so also does realism fall a prey to similar dialectics of the idealist. Each theory, he maintains, is helpless to defend its positive theory against its opponents' criticisms and equally powerless to refute the other.

[1] Chapter vii, pp. 169, 185.

The realist asserts: 'Beyond all our experience there is something wholly unlike experience (independent of experience), the thing in itself.' To this thesis the idealist always rejoins: 'What do you mean by your thing in itself—by the reality and by the nature, that you ascribe to it? And in what relation do you mean it to stand to experience? As soon as you tell, you interpret your supposed reality wholly in terms of experience. You never define that transcendent beyond of which you speak. . . . You want to say that beyond our experience there is something transcendent whose nature is never experienced, whose contents always remain outside the world of experience. But you can never tell what you mean by this beyond precisely in so far as it remains beyond. Telling what you mean is transforming your beyond into something within the world of experience. Therefore' (says the idealist), 'I reject your beyond altogether. Experience is all. Yet I admit that much experience remains to us, indeed, only a "possibility".'

Thus the idealist. But now the realist speaks. 'Yes' (retorts the realist), 'but in your last word you have admitted the very essence of my whole contention. For within the range of what individuals do experience you admit that we cannot remain. You admit the possibilities of experience as something genuine. You cannot do without them. Yet as soon as you admit them, you admit an element transcending concrete experience . . . .Your possibilities are either mere illusions or else facts. If facts are not experienced they are beyond experience. And such beyond is all that I maintain. I should, indeed, prefer to say that what you call possibilities exist beyond experience as grounds of experience, unknown natures of things which determine in advance what our experience shall be when it comes. Such a fashion of statement appears to me to be a franker admission of the inevitable transcendence. And our idealist (half idealist) can only retort once more: But what do you mean by the beyond, whether of the possibility or of its ground, known or unknown? Tell what you mean and this beyond becomes no longer unknown, no longer transcendent. It becomes content of experience.'

'And thus,' says Royce, 'the endless conflict may go on,' and I think it does, no matter how the proposition may be formulated. Each theory is powerless to defend its positive position against its opponent's position and, as he adds, equally powerless to refute his opponent. Which is just my contention. Neither position is refutable, because of the very nature of the thesis.

Royce, of course, draws a moral from this situation. Is there, he asks, any way to escape from this dilemma? His answer is that the only way to do so is to formulate a position that transcends this opposition, one that includes both. This he thinks the position called Absolute Idealism does. Now this may conceivably be a way of solving the dialectical problem. I shall not here deny that it is—that such a position, properly formulated and properly understood, does transcend the opposition, although certainly it has not served to finish the dispute between the two opponents. But it is not the moral that I shall draw, but rather a deeper one which is, I think, rather implied in Royce's analysis of the situation itself. If there is any escape from this dilemma—and I think there is—it lies in recognizing the character of this endless conflict, in acknowledging the irrefutable elements in each position, and in seeking to formulate a position which includes the 'values' of both. This is the dialectical solution which we propose and which we shall seek to develop in the following chapter.

IV

The Exclusive Logics of Realism and Idealism. Their Unneutral Character.

A

All of which leads us to the third condition of the transcendence of realism and idealism, namely, the recognition of the fact that the conflict cannot be eliminated by their own means, that is by the unneutral logics to which both appeal. As no refutation of either position is possible by an appeal to experience, so none is possible by an appeal to logic, for the logic to which each appeals is unneutral.

The significance of this appears especially in connection with the later forms, described as logical idealism and realism respectively. The arguments here are, as we have seen, quite different from those of earlier forms, the driving force of idealism and the resistance of realism being, it is held, essentially logical in character. It is accordingly this conflict on the plane of logical theory, between the two doctrines of internal and external relations with which we are now concerned. Here also, I shall maintain, neither can really refute the other, for their controversy is about the first and underivable principles of logic itself. Each can refute the other only if his adversary acknowledges his first and underivable principle and this apparently the adversary will never do.

The unneutral character of both 'logics' is patent. Each presupposes as the first principle of his logic a judgment of value itself logically unsupported. For the idealistic logic relations are internal to the things related because of the initial assumption that only knowledge of the whole is genuine knowledge, and that, therefore, logic, as the instrument of that knowledge, in order to be genuine, must be developed on the basis of that postulate. When Bosanquet tells us that 'for Logic at all events, it is a postulate that the truth is the whole,' he is including as the very axiom of logic the idealist's evaluation of knowledge. But the same is true of realism. When the realist, as for instance Spaulding, tells us that the postulate of a *bona fide* logic is the independence of the object and the principle of externality of relations upon which it rests, he likewise is including, as the very axiom of all logic, his own evaluation of what a *bona fide* logic must be. Being thus unneutral, neither logic can refute the other, for in each case the refutation itself begs the very question at issue.[1]

That neither 'refutation' really refutes is seen on the most cursory examination. If, as the idealist argues, truth is always the whole, then it indeed follows that a theory of knowledge which insists that the object of knowledge is wholly mind-independent, and that thought therefore makes no difference to the thing known, makes any genuine knowledge impossible. But this constitutes no genuine refutation unless the prior assumption or judgment of value is accepted, and this no exclusive realist will do. Similarly, the refutation of logical idealism always consists in arguing that in order that *bona fide* knowledge

[1] The source of the unneutral character of the two logics is shown in detail in chapter iii of *The Intelligible World*. The title of the chapter is 'Genuine Knowledge and *Bona Fide* Logic.' The two quotations are taken respectively from Bosanquet's *Logic*, 2nd ed. p. 2, and from E. G. Spaulding's article, *The Logical Structure of Self-refuting Systems*, The Philos. Review, Vol. XIX, Nos. 3 and 6.

and logic may be possible, the relation between the knower and the object known must be a wholly external relation—in other words, it makes externality itself a postulate of logic as such. But this constitutes no genuine refutation of idealism unless this prior assumption as to what constitutes genuine knowledge is accepted, and this no logical idealist will do. Both logics are unneutral and cannot, therefore, eliminate the conflict by their own means.

Here too, as in the realms of supposed factual argument, the 'endless conflict may go on.' The only way to resolve it, if it is resolvable at all, is to 'go behind the returns' of both 'logics' to the implicit assumptions that underlie them. It is at least possible that when we do, the conflict may turn out to be, not the result of a logical contradiction but merely of a clash of values, an antithesis of cognitive values which are really not mutually exclusive. As a conflict of values it naturally engages the emotions and passions of men—and thus arise the dogmatisms of the two exclusive logics, but it is not inconceivable that when we come to understand the sources of these dogmatisms, we may also learn how to transcend them. This we hope to show in the following chapter; our sole point here is to make it clear why neither logical idealism nor logical realism can really refute one another.[1]

---

[1] The position here maintained is not wholly unrelated to a one developed by Professor W. N. Sheldon in his *The Strife of Systems and Productive Duality* [1918], especially chapter xii.

His plea for the transcendence of realism and idealism occurs in a larger argument against the 'strife of systems' and for a theory of 'productive quality' which shall still this strife and afford a more adequate means for understanding and interpreting the world. With this general objective I am in complete sympathy. This strife *is* a disease of philosophy, as he maintains, and no aspect of the disease is more debilitating than precisely this strife between epistemological idealism and realism which, as we have maintained throughout, is, in its present form, wholly modern. With his conception of the remedy for the disease I am also in partial agreement. The strife between realism and idealism arises from the fact that thought has taken over what he calls the 'practical logic of competition and exclusiveness.' If then, so he argues, we rise to the level of 'pure logic' we shall find the two not inconsistent with one another. Now this strife does indeed arise out of a spirit of competitiveness which means, according to our analysis, that its source lies in logically underivable valuations. I do not see, however, how any conciliation can arise out of an appeal to what he calls 'pure logic.' For, first of all, as we have seen, there is no pure logic, but, even if there were, the conflict is really not between principles of logic as such, but between the cognitive values presupposed by two logics. The problem is therefore meta-logical, as we shall seek to show in the following chapter.

V

The Epistemological Impasse and Its Solution. A Change of Venue.

A

It seems then an inevitable conclusion that the strife between realism and idealism cannot be eliminated by any arguments either empirical or logical. This is true of both idealism and realism in their later as well as in their earlier forms. And thus, as Royce says, the endless conflict may go on. Epistemology finds itself in an *impasse* and can solve its problem at this point only by what I have described as a complete change of venue.

With insight amounting to genius Fichte saw this long ago, and showed, to my mind at least, once and for all why neither realism nor idealism can logically refute each other. He also gave, I think, a suggestion as to the direction along which any solution must be found. If he had seen the full implications of his position and not been too hasty in his conclusions, he might not only have convinced philosophic thought of this impasse in epistemology, but have anticipated the solution to which, as I think, thought must ultimately come.

In his *First Introduction to the Science of Knowledge* (1797) he maintains that two and only two philosophical positions and systems are possible, which he describes as Idealism and Dogmatic Materialism. As the argument develops one sees that for dogmatic materialism, dogmatic realism may be substituted, for it is really naturalistic realism that he is describing and with which he is concerned. Neither of these positions can refute the other, he holds, for their controversy is about 'the first underivable principle.' Each refutes the other only if its first underivable principle is admitted.

First of all, idealism cannot refute dogmatic realism. Every consistent dogmatist is necessarily a fatalist. He does not necessarily deny the fact of consciousness or that we regard ourselves as free. But he proves from his principle the falsity of this view. He denies the independence of the ego on which the idealist builds and makes it merely the product of the thing, an accident of the world, a part of nature. Hence the consistent dogmatist can be refuted only by the postulate of freedom and independence of the ego. And this he necessarily denies. But even as little can the dogmatic realist or naturalist refute the idealist. The principle of the former, the thing in itself, the independent object is nothing, as the defenders of it must admit. It has no reality other than that by it experience can be explained. But the idealist destroys this proof by explaining experience in another way—hence by denying precisely what the dogmatist assumes. The thing in itself is a complete chimæra. There is no further reason why it should be assumed. And with its disappearance the whole structure of dogmatic realism falls to the ground.

The two systems or points of view are then irreconcilable because each starts with assumptions that cannot be proved and which the other will not admit. Both systems seem then to have the same 'speculative value'. But Fichte believes that they cannot stand together—and that thought cannot be left in this impasse. One must be chosen. It becomes then not only an interesting but an exceedingly vital question as to what leads to the choice of one over the other. Reason, logic, Fichte believes, afford no ground for a decision. For the question does not relate to the connecting of one casual or logical link with another where reason alone comes into play. It relates rather to the beginning of the entire thought process which is an absolutely first act wholly dependent upon freedom of thinking. From the standpoint of intellect, Fichte holds, the decision is wholly arbitrary. But while they both have intellectual value one must have precedence over the other from the point of view of practice and of an ultimate view of the world. He closes his discussion with the famous remark that which of these philosophies one chooses depends upon the kind of man one is.

The truth of Fichte's analysis up to a certain point is undeniable. He rightly recognizes that we are not here concerned with a matter of empirical verification, or of logic in the ordinary sense of the word: that the issue concerns underivable first principles and that these principles embody cognitive values. But from this point on, the situation is not so clear and the necessity of Fichte's solution not so obvious. It is not yet wholly clear that when the situation is properly analyzed and interpreted the two standpoints will be found irreconcilable. The mere fact that, as Fichte himself recognizes, both standpoints are indigenous to life creates at least the presumption that both are necessities of thought. In the second place, it is not at all certain that the decision must be, as Fichte suggests, a matter of arbitrary choice. It is not clear, in the first place, that the acceptance of one of these initial principles is itself a matter of personal choice in Fichte's sense. It is true that all acknowledgment of value involves freedom. We cannot be *contrained* as in the case of either sense perception or logic. But there is necessity just the same, the axiological necessity which itself springs from free acknowledgment. Nor is it at all clear that when it is understood that these first underivable principles really involve valuations, we may not also be free to accept both principles as equally necessary to an intelligible theory of knowledge. It is true that we cannot accept two logically contradictory propositions at the same time without disintegration both intellectual and moral; but it is not yet clear that the opposition of these two underivable principles is such a contradiction. Indeed, we have already held that it is not. In sum, then, while accepting the truth of Fichte's analysis up to a point, it seems possible that he has not drawn the proper conclusions from his anlaysis. It seems to me then that, starting from the undoubted truth of Fichte's main insight, it is possible to draw significantly different conclusions—to develop, in fact, an argument for the conciliation of idealism and realism. The change of venue which Fichte proposed involves a much more radical shift than he envisaged —not merely to the practical universe of arbitrary choice, but to a realm of cognitive meanings and values in which the true relation of these underivable first principles to each other are understood and acknowledged. To this higher court of dialectical insight we shall now turn.

Chapter V

Beyond Realism and Idealism: Reconciliation, Vital and Theoretical.
The Concilience of Idealism and Realism.

I — A

WE have now stated the conditions of any transcendence of the opposition of realism and idealism. In the present chapter I propose to attempt to show how on the basis of the recognition of these conditions it is possible to argue for the positive reconciliation of the two positions. This involves the development more fully of the argument suggested at the conclusion of the preceding chapter.

In the introductory chapter we stated in a general way the programme of this part of our study. The necessity of both positions and of the values which they presuppose—for the individual and social like alike—constituted the starting point of our problem. Life, we there maintained, creates the opposition, but life also knows how to reconcile it. 'This vital reconciliation gives us a right,' we further maintained, 'to expect that a mode of reconciliation can be found in theory as in life, as indeed normal to the entire process of consciousness.' 'Life,' it is true, solves only 'existential' problems, never theoretical questions, but it is equally true that no theoretical questions can be permanently solved if the solution does not, in the last analysis, relate itself to the vital problems of existence.

But how shall we state this vital reconciliation in terms of theory? There are, in general, three ways in which this solution may conceivably be attempted. We may describe them respectively as (*a*) the psychological; (*b*) the pragmatic; (*c*) the dialectical or metalogical.

The idea of a vital reconciliation, and of one normal to the entire processes of consciousness leads naturally to the notion that the problem is in essence psychological and can be solved only by transferring it to the psychological universe of discourse. This solution has actually been proposed by C. G. Jung.

The argument developed by Jung is extraordinarily suggestive. He points out 'how, as a rule, the partisans of the opposing positions attack each other fiercely externally, always seeking out the joints in the opponents' individual armour. We see how these disputes as a rule bear little fruit. We see also how when there are waves of realism or idealism, it is not because opponents are convinced, but because the psychological atmosphere has changed and thus makes it possible for the new tendency to be heard.' We see all this and ask, with Jung, 'whether it would not be of considerably greater value if the dispute were transferred to the psychological realm where it actually originates.'[1] Jung denies that it can ever be solved or reconciled 'by any logic-intellectual formula.'[2] Our only recourse is to seek to penetrate beyond the external argument to the 'psychological law which determines the attitude.'

The perennial opposition of these two ways of thinking goes back, he holds, to two fundamental types of mind (the extravert and the introvert) the former tending to assimilate the subject to the object, the latter to object to the subject. He develops his theme with fascinating psychological detail, but this is not the point that is of significance for us. It is rather the thesis that the opposition arises in the depths of the unconscious and consequently cannot be resolved by any logical-intellectual formula of conscious thought. It is only in the vital processes of what he calls 'fantasy' that man actually reconciles the two attitudes, and it is, therefore, only by understanding the psychological laws of the creative imagination that any theoretical understanding of the reconciliation is possible.

All this sounds plausible enough—and I am not disposed to deny a certain real value to the psychological standpoint as a preliminary stage in the solution of the problem. There are, however, certain considerations which make it clear that psychology can represent only a preliminary stage in the understanding of the opposition and is in no position to solve the problem itself.

In the first place, while it is an immediately understandable fact that every philosophy is the philosophy of some person and depends upon personal and psychological conditions, no philosophy is ever the wholly individual or personal thing it first seems. It always has a certain imposing following, a certain objectivity of a social character at least. Such a fundamental

[1] C. G. Jung, *Psychological Types*, 1923, especially chapter vii.
[2] *Op. cit.*, p. 68.

opposition as that between realism and idealism represents something very much deeper than any mere external similarity of the psychological realm. In the second place, any merely psychological solution is in the nature of the case impossible. For if psychology be conceived as a natural science, assuming the naïve realism which is held to characterize its standpoint, it has already begged the question and cannot be employed to explain or to reconcile the opposition between realism and idealism.

Psychology is, then, in itself incapable of offering any real solution of our problem. It can do little more than show us how these 'hardened oppositions' arise and perhaps somewhat soften the opposition by its genetic understanding. Another possibility may be offered, namely, the pragmatic. Pragmatic solutions have, indeed, been suggested. It was, in fact, William James himself who held that the opposition of realism and idealism is unimportant, for the position we hold makes no difference to the facts. And John Dewey in his *The Quest for Certainty* suggests that this opposition arises out of a common prejudice, namely, that knowledge is always knowledge of an antecedent reality and that if this prejudice is abandoned the opposition tends to disappear of itself. In other words, the problem is only a *Scheinproblem.* The position is really very close to that of the logical positivists for whom the question of the real or unreal is a purely empirical one, for whom the epistemological or metaphysical question is meaningless.

Here, as in the case of the psychological solution, we may say that, while the pragmatic standpoint offers preliminary suggestions towards a solution, it itself effects no real reconciliation. The difficulty with the pragmatic solution is that pragmatism itself is in unstable equilibrium. As has been repeatedly pointed out, there are two versions of pragmatism, the one tending towards realism, the other towards idealism. If one accepts the naturalistic version, one has already assumed the exclusively realistic standpoint associated with it, and the pragmatic position cannot be used to solve the problem. If, on the other hand, one accepts the idealistic version, by that very fact also the question is begged and pragmatism is disqualified *ab initio* as a higher court to which appeal can be carried. One can sympathize whole-heartedly with the desire of many pragmatists to throw out this epistemological problem as meaningless, but pragmatism itself is too ambiguous to be of ultimate significance. It is interesting that Jung, while recognizing that the opposition between these two 'truths' demands in the first place a pragmatic attitude—if one desires to do any sort of justice to the other standpoint—insists that it is only a provisional stage, a transitional attitude that shall prepare the way for a creative synthesis of the two positions.[1] It is curious that he should suppose that the psychological standpoint represents the possibility of such creative synthesis.

The conditions of a satisfactory solution of the problem must, then, include insight into the psychological or vital sources of the dichotomy; also into the cultural and sociological significance of the opposition; and finally, into the pragmatic values of the attitudes in question. But the insight which leads to real transcendence and to a real reconciliation—in theory as well as in life—must be more than this. It must be dialectical—dialectical in the sense, namely, that it includes at once insight into the necessity of both positions, and into their ultimate consistency with each other. This requires an 'intellectual' formula.

The possibility of the reconciliation of the two opposites by any logico-intellectual formula is, to be sure, precisely what Jung and many others deny. And if the formula which we shall seek to develop is intellectual and logical in the abstract sense understood by them, we must, I think, agree. But dialectic, as I apprehend it, is not intellectual and logical in this restricted sense. When properly understood, it is a vital reconciliation—a 'creative synthesis' such as Jung desiderates. It involves all the understanding of the opposition which Jung has called psychological and all the considerations which the pragmatist has called practical. In short, it involves a solution which grows directly out of an interpretation of the implications of both experience and logic as such. This, I shall describe as dialectical insight. The philosopher must always transcend the controversies of his fellows, even to understand them, and with this transcendence comes, not only insight into the relativity of the opposition which gives rise to the controversy, but insight into the possibility of their reconciliation. This is the solution proposed in the introductory chapter. The problem, we said, is

---

[1] *Op. cit.*, p. 399.

dialectical; the solution must be dialectical also. The first part of this statement has been argued in the preceding chapter; we must now proceed to the development of the second.

II

The General Character of Dialectic. Its Relation to Experience and Logic.

A

Dialectic is a term used in various senses by philosophers. In the most general sense, it is often nothing more than another name for argument; and, thus understood, it is scarcely distinguishable from ordinary logic, the procedures of logic being always a part of dialectical argument. But in the more technical sense, it is commonly recognized as a distinctive feature of philosophical thinking and as a type of thought different in important respects from 'ordinary logic,' as Kant called it, in the sense of deductive and inductive method. It is frequently held to be identical with philosophical method as such.

Dialectic, when thus understood, is generally recognized as having the three stages already described in a preliminary fashion in the introductory chapter. It consists in the first instance in developing the 'underivable first principles' upon which an opinion or belief rests and forcing the one who holds them to acknowledge them explicitly. In this procedure the method of self refutation is the outstanding feature, as we have seen throughout the preceding studies. It consists, secondly, in comparing antithetical, i.e. apparently mutually contradictory doctrines, for the sake of determining whether they are really contradictory, and thus leading through initial, and perhaps inevitable exclusive theories, to some truth which includes them both. Finally, it consists in exhibiting a complex truth, by looking at one side and then at the other, in order to obtain a combined view of the whole. This insight which follows upon the transcendence of antithetical positions is called the dialectical synthesis.

There is, to be sure, more to the notion of dialectic than this, and this more must be fully taken into account in any interpretation and evaluation of dialectic as a whole. There is dialectic in the historical sense—in the sense, namely, that the contradiction of ideas, the opposition of *motifs* of thought, and of the values which they presuppose, constitute actual driving forces of history. There is dialectic in the metaphysical sense—in the sense, namely, that our thought processes are held to be also an expression of the nature of reality, our subjective meanings also objective meaning, and that the completed meaning of a system of ideas is identical with all that the mind seeks in looking for truth. Both of these aspects of dialectic must be taken into account before its full significance as philosophical method can be determined, but in the present context we are concerned with the aspects described above and which distinguish it from the methods of ordinary logic both inductive and deductive, and from proof and disproof, whether empirical or logical.

B

There is one feature of the dialectic as thus understood, which distinguishes it significantly from ordinary logic. Connected in the beginning with dialogue, it has never completely lost its relation to discourse. It involves, as we have seen, a radical shift from the world of things to the world of meanings and values, and this is the world of discourse. 'Dialectic is essentially an affair of discourse.'[1]

Dialectic has been defined as 'the explication of meanings in discourse.' It is this making explicit our meanings which constitutes the first stage of the dialectic. Such explication involves, of course, logical definition of terms, but it is never merely such definition. It includes also the explication of the 'postulates', or underivable first principles presupposed by the definition. The meaning of a term in this sense is, to use a mediaeval term, determined by its *suppositio*, and therefore by the universe of discourse which the *suppositio* constitutes or of which it is the presupposition. The mutual acknowledgment of this presupposition is the condition of meaningful discourse. It is true that the meaning of a term is often supposed to be merely its reference to the 'thing', and this is said to be the 'meaning of meaning'. There is, of course, in most cases this reference, but an essential part of the meaning is always another reference—to

[1] Mortimer J. Adler, *Dialetic*, 1927, chapter ii, especially p. 28.

the supposition of the universe of discourse in which the term subsists. Explication of meaning, as indeed our explication of the meaning of realism and idealism has already shown, always consists in making explicit the 'epistemological intentions' presupposed by each respectively. This, however, is the general character of all dialectic, which is always concerned, not with the development of logical implication within a system, but with the relations of the assumptions or presuppositions implicit in such systems.

This explication of meanings in discourse brings with it, finally, insight into the nature of the oppositions or antitheses of meanings which give rise to the more fundamental controversies of philosophy. With the comparison of apparently mutually contradictory doctrines, many of them at least are seen to be not really contradictions, but rather antitheses of meanings and values. As such they are seen not to be mutually exclusive but rather to imply one another. The opposition is thus transcended; instead of 'either-or' it is possible to say 'both-and'. This insight into the nature of the negations and oppositions which enables us to transcend them is called dialectical synthesis.

C

The key to the understanding of all forms of the dialectic is, then, a more profound analysis of negation as it functions in discourse. It involves the notion of self-contradiction as employed in the method of self-refutation and, secondly, the notion of negation as involved in those 'contradictions' which give rise to disputation and dialectic in the second sense. Both involve a fundamental distinction between contradiction and opposition or, better expressed, between logical contradiction and metalogical opposition.

Of the first we may speak briefly. The very general use of the principle of self-refutation is itself significant. The sceptic, the agnostic and the relativist have all at different times been silenced by its crushing and damnatory logic. With it, as we have seen, the idealist has 'refuted' the realist, and the realist the idealist; in one way or another it is the last argument that both employ. And in this the instinct of both is profoundly right, for whether consciously or not, they are aware of the dialectical nature of the problem and that, in certain ultimate issues, self-refutation is the only argument possible.

The sceptic is said to contradict himself when he asserts with conviction that there is no knowledge. And he certainly does, as we say 'out of his own mouth.' For this denial, in casting doubt upon all knowledge, impugns his own thesis. For obviously he intends to assert a meaningful proposition and the assertion that there is no valid knowledge has itself no meaning except on the assumption that this at least is a case of knowledge. The method of self-refutation, then, is employed in order to bring to light the tacit assumptions or presuppositions which cannot be denied without in some sense being assumed. The very denial itself, of some important aspect of it, or some assumption involved in presenting and defending it, constitutes an exception to the denial. A presupposition may be defined then as an assumption whose denial is self-referentially inconsistent, and therefore *wider-sinnig*.

It cannot be denied that however constantly we may employ this form of argument, often without being conscious of it, it has in many quarters fallen into disrepute, perhaps not wholly undeserved. It has not always been treated understandingly either by those who use it or those who criticize it. For him who employs it it is frequently merely a trick of disputation such as Plato deplored. For him who criticizes it is an *argumentum ad hominem* and not *ad rem*, and therefore a material fallacy of logic. The chief source of misunderstanding, however, is a misconception as to the nature of the denial or negation involved. When one claims to know that he knows nothing, he contradicts himself, of course, but that does not prove that he knows anything, but only that that which he claims to know he does not know. From the principle of contradiction only analytical propositions can be inferred; the existence of objectively valid knowledge could be determined only by empirical criteria. In self-refutation the inconsistency involved is self-referential, an inconsistency between a proposition and the tacit presupposition of the universe of discourse in which the proposition is made, and not a contradiction between two propositions in the same logical system. Self-refutation is concerned with those presuppositions that one cannot deny without making himself unintelligible. In this sense it always involves an *argumentum ad hominem*, but in the context in which it is applicable it is also an *argumentum ad rem.*[1]

With this understanding of the function of negation in self-refutation we may pass to its role in disputation. The source of all disputation is disagreement, and disagreement involves, of course, negation. But not all negation is denial in the sense of logical contradiction. Contradiction in this latter sense arises from the assertion of two propositions so related by formal implication that the assertion of either is equivalent to the denial or exclusion of the other. It is evident that if all negation were of this type, all opposition and conflict would be final, and no resolution of the conflict, no mutual understanding on the part of the disputants, would be possible. There are, however, forms of denial or negation which, although apparent contradictions, are, upon closer analysis, seen to be only apparent, and to be actually oppositions or antitheses of values, which are no longer logical but meta-logical. The significant thing here is the distinction between logical contradiction and metalogical opposition. It may be stated in the following way. The ruling principle within logical systems is contradiction; but the relation between the presuppositions or postulates of such systems is one not of contradiction but of opposition.

It is often assumed that propositions are entities, that, merely as entities, abstracted from the logical system in which they subsist, may contradict one another, and that by examining them as propositions we may determine whether they do or not. This conception is, I believe, wholly false and based upon a serious misunderstanding. A proposition is always a proposal and has no 'existence' except in the universe of discourse or logical system in which it subsists. It is impossible that two propositions should contradict one another unless they are in the same logical system. In other words, in order that a contradiction may arise between two propositions they must be in the same coherent system, and this very coherence is determined by the supposition which makes the system or universe of discourse what it is. As self-referential inconsistency represents an opposition between a proposition and the tacit presupposition of the universe of discourse in which it is made, so between the tacit

[1] For a further development of this point and for the application of self-refutation in philosophy generally, see *The Intelligible World*, pp. 42–46.

presuppositions of two logical systems there is not logical contradiction but metalogical opposition.[1]

This analysis of negation enables us to understand the nature of the radical shift always involved in dialectic, for metalogical opposition is a relation neither of 'things' nor of entities called propositions, but of meanings and values.

First of all we must realize that, strictly speaking, negation does not occur in the realm of existence at all but only in the realm of discourse. We speak, it is true, of negative numbers, negative quantities, and negative and positive electricity. But negative here has a special meaning: it refers really to a positive distinction among existences. Negative quantities and negative electricity are as much positive entities as are positive numbers and positive electricity. In other words, existence or being does not allow itself to be divided into positive and negative. The negative of existence is non-existence and of being non-being. Non-existence and non-being are obviously not in the realm of existence and being, but only in the realm of discourse and the meanings with which discourse is concerned.[2]

Within the realm of discourse negation has two possible meanings which it is important to distinguish, namely, one which is purely logical and one which involves an antithesis of values. Thus the term in-human may designate a purely logical concept, in which case it is equivalent to non-human, and the terms human and inhuman are contradictories. In the second case, the use of the negative is significantly different. It includes

---

[1] For a fuller development of this point, see my *Language and Reality*, chapter vii, pp. 269 ff.

Another way of saying this same thing is that of R. G. Collingwood. 'Two propositions cannot contradict one another unless they are answers to the same question,' in our terms unless they are in the same universe of discourse and thus relevant to the same *suppositio* which determines it. This is a valuable way of stating it in some contexts, but is, I think, but a special case under our more general formulation. See his *An Autobiography*, Oxford University Press, 1939, chapter v, especially p. 33.

[2] There are, to be sure, logicians who speak of 'negative facts,' in other words hold that negative propositions mean negative facts. But it should be observed that when this is said it does not mean that there are positive and negative elements in existence. To observe that the sun is not shining is very different from observing that the sun is shining. If there is such a thing as a negative fact it is plainly not of the same order as a positive fact. If negative facts are given they are not given through perception as are positive facts. They are inferred or constructed from perceptions—which places them in the realm of discourse, not in the realm of existence.

in its meaning negative values and in the negation is included the normative conception of the invalid, as a part of the meaning. This is true of many other terms, such as the opposition of natural and unnatural. In such cases the antithesis has meaning only on the assumption of some positive evaluation of the human or the natural as the case may be; it is therefore an antithesis of meaning and value, and as such metalogical in its origin and significance. Metalogical opposition always involves this antithesis of values, and since meaning is inseparable from intention, with its reference to value, dialectical opposition can be understood only by making explicit this reference.

First of all, it should be understood, values as such, do not contradict but oppose one another. In his discussion of 'antitheses of value' Nicolai Hartmann makes the statement that 'oppositions between values have not necessarily the character of contradictions.'[1] This is undoubtedly true as his analysis has shown, but I should go further and insist that they *cannot* contradict one another. Values clash, both in the practical and theoretical spheres, but this does not mean that they contradict one another and are mutually exclusive. This is immediately apparent in the sphere of practical, as distinguished from theoretical values. The two natures of love of which Plato spoke in the *Phaedrus* may, indeed, tragically oppose one another—the flesh lusteth against the spirit and the spirit against the flesh—but they are not in contradiction. If they were, the conflict would be final and no resolution would be possible. Practically, the conflict is often of such a nature that in a given situation arbitrary choice alone is possible; but theoretically, there is always the possibility of that dialectical insight which leads to their reconciliation in a higher synthesis. One sees that the lower or physical values are the necessary condition of the existence of the higher, but it is the higher or spiritual values which give meaning to the lower. It is insight into this relation, and into the scale of values presupposed, which makes possible the holding of both together in a higher synthesis.

A similar situation holds, I believe, in the sphere of cognitive or theoretical value, and the principle of synthesis is *mutatis mutandis*, the same. The notion of cognitive values is already familiar from our earlier studies but further comment may serve

[1] Nicolai Hartmann. *Ethics*, Vol. II, p. 77.

to bring out more clearly the nature of negation and opposition in this sphere.

All epistemological argument, we have seen, concerns the conditions of genuine knowledge and therefore involves assumptions or postulates regarding ideals of knowledge—in other words judgments of value which themselves are empirically and logically unsupported. These cognitive values indeed clash, as we have already seen in our study of driving force of idealism and the resistance of realism, but it does not at all follow that they are in ultimate contradiction. It is quite possible that when these values are made explicit, they do not exclude but really mutually presuppose one another. It may be that the realistic valves are the necessary condition of the 'higher' idealistic values, but that it is the latter which alone give meaning to the former. This we shall later attempt to show; the main point here, however, is that many conflicts are not of the nature of logical contradiction but of metalogical opposition and it is a fatal error to turn an antithesis of values, whether practical or cognitive, into logical contradiction. It is insight into this difference which makes possible the holding together of the opposing positions in a higher synthesis.

The third stage of the dialectic, or dialectical synthesis as it is technically called, is essentially a matter of understanding or 'dialectical insight'—insight into the nature of the opposing positions which enables us to transcend them. This insight is the characteristic thing in the dialectic from Plato to Hegel. It is, however, this third stage which is, above all, misunderstood, and is therefore the chief object of attack. Such synthesis is supposed to do violence to both experience and logic. A true conception of the nature of this transcendence of opposing positions and their inclusion in a 'higher truth' is, accordingly, the *crux* of the entire problem of the dialectic.

An element of transcendence is, it is important to recognize, already implied in any genuine understanding of our own or our opponent's position. It is already implied in the explication of meanings and of the logically underivable presuppositions of our beliefs. It is carried further when we come to understand the nature of the antithesis or opposition of our beliefs and reaches its culmination in the recognition of the false alternative which the analysis discloses and the practical truth of both thesis and antithesis. This synthesis of opposites, then, far from being an artificial combination of incompatibles, is merely the extension and technical expression of this initial understanding.

It is the failure to recognize this character of dialectical insight which has, I believe, in large part given rise to the main charges against the dialectical method, namely, that it does violence to both logic and experience.

It is supposed that the dialectic violates the fundamental law of non-contradiction and that, by some logical hocus-pocus genuine contradictions are somehow annuled in a higher identity. It is not to be denied, of course, that the language of the philosophers has often afforded ground for this misunderstanding. In Hegel's hands, the *coincidentia oppositorum* does often seem to suggest that contradictions are absorbed in a higher identity, but this is, I think, largely a matter of language. In challenging his *dictum*, the truth is the whole, we are likely to forget his equally important *dictum* that the truth of the lower category is not annulled, but is taken up into the higher—that life is the truth of matter and spirit the truth of life. Whenever Hegel says 'both-and' instead of 'either-or', he always means, not only that both can be held together, but in this relation of mutual implication one is always higher than the other. The notion of degrees of truth and reality is essentially a value notion and the axiom of the inseparibility of value and reality is so completely assumed throughout his entire system that he does not even find it necessary to state it explicitly.[1]

The charge that the dialectic does violence to experience arises, I believe, out of a similar misunderstanding. It is supposed that by a similar hocus-pocus the concrete objects of experience are somehow deduced from logical propositions and that the dialectical synthesis is some sort of chemical fusion of things. If this were so the dialectic would also merit all the scorn that has been poured upon it. It is true that in Hegel's hands, the dialectic often seems to suggest that 'in some way concrete things are generated in time either by ghostly conflicts or by sublimated matings of abstract categories,' but that again is, I think, a matter of language and results from taking his metaphors too literally. Rather, as Ernst Troeltsch points out, in his

---

[1] See on this point my paper entitled, 'The Philosophy of Spirit: Idealism and the Philosophy of Value,' in *Contemporary Idealism in America*, 1932.

treatment of history Hegel never for a moment considered throwing out the empirical way of handling his subject matter, but presupposes it and only secondarily orders the material according to the principle of the dialectic. His dialectical picture is a reconstruction of intuitive concrete materials into a totality—not an apriori deduction of the happenings of history out of the idea.[1] I think that this is true and I am inclined to think also that the same holds true in his attempts to interpret the results of the natural sciences. Actually, he presupposes the facts of the natural sciences, as then understood, and uses the dialectic merely as a method of reconstruction and interpretation in the totality of human knowledge.

Dialectic then, far from doing violence to either experience or logic, is rather necessary for the understanding and interpretation of both. Dialectical insight transcends, it is true, experience in the sense of the immediately given, but it presupposes it. It merely makes explicit the complicates of such experience, and these are as much a part of experience as the immediately given itself. It also goes beyond logic in the sense that it is not concerned with the formal relations of implication within logical systems but rather with the logically underivable, and therefore metalogical, principles presupposed by such logical systems. It is thus in a very real sense an extension of both experience and logic, for dialectic is necessary to the understanding and interpretation of both. Unless we make explicit that which is implied in experience and the metalogical presuppositions of logic, we shall fail to have attained that kind of knowledge which, as Plato said, constitutes the coping stone of the sciences.

III

The Nature of Dialectical Problems. The Metempirical and The Metalogical.

A

Dialectical problems are accordingly both metempirical and metalogical in the sense defined. They are genuine problems which arise out of both experience and logic, but which cannot be solved by merely empirical or logical method.

[1] *Der Historismus*, pp. 233-4.

The Platonic dialogues are all concerned with such problems. In the *Phædrus* two opposing views of love are set in antithesis in order to depict the truth which justifies both. In the *Theatætus*, on the other hand, the problem is that of the nature of knowledge and it is here, perhaps, that the application of dialectic to theoretical issues is most in evidence. In this 'high argument' the Sophistic assertion of the relativity of all knowledge is shown to be self-refuting, and while no positive conclusions are dogmatically stated in the dialogue itself, nevertheless, through the negation of partial and untenable conceptions of knowledge, certain truths about knowledge emerge which are mutually acknowledged and the way to reconciliation of apparent opposites is pointed out.

The Hegellian dialectic is concerned with the same kind of situations and involves the same general procedures. In the *Phenomenology* it is the tragic oppositions of the spiritual life that are made explicit and the way to their transcendence pointed out. In the *Logik*, on the other hand, it is the perhaps equally tragic oppositions in the life of reason with which Hegel is concerned. When, for instance, common sense realism asserts that the thing or object is immediately known in experience, Hegel asks, but what is this object and what does 'this' here mean? The explication of meaning which follows serves to show that the object of knowledge is never a mere this—a brute existence as common sense supposes—but involves relations, including relations to the knower himself. In the course of this explication all the chief issues of epistemology are canvassed, including the oppositions of subjectivity and objectivity, independence and dependence, and finally, that of idealistic and realistic philosophy itself, which being, as we have seen, for him 'simply bare abstractions,' is 'of no importance for philosophy.'

Herein lies the greatness of Hegel, as also of Plato, and indeed of all those who have known what philosophy is 'all about', that they have recognized the necessity of going 'behind the returns' of ordinary thought and the hardened oppositions which such thought, both practical and theoretical, generates. All have realized that philosophical problems, being problems of interpretation, their solution involves this shift from the world of things to the world of meanings and values in which the dialectical method alone is applicable.

B

Of the problems essentially dialectical in character it is the epistemological which are most significant in the present context and in which the shift to the metempirical and metalogical is most clearly seen. It brings out the significance of knowing, as distinguished from the things known, and therefore the uniqueness of the knowledge problem.

We may put it in this way. What is true of the knowledge of things cannot be true of the knowledge of knowledge: otherwise knowledge would itself become a thing, and, being such, would lose all universal significance, and the whole problem of knowledge be begged. By the same token, the ways of knowing by which we come to the knowledge of things cannot be the same by which we come to an understanding of knowledge. In this respect the positivist is, from his standpoint, right when he insists that problems of epistemology, including that of realism and idealism, have no meaning. The ways of science by which we know whether a particular thing exists or not are incapable of dealing with the metempirical and metalogical problems of the meanings of existence or reality themselves.

This we shall call the 'peculiar significance' of knowledge, namely, that knowledge itself, not being a thing or a relation between things, to deal with it at all involves a shift from the realm of things to that of meanings. Another way of stating this is to say that any theory of knowledge is included in, and is part of, its own subject matter. It is not a theory of things as in the case of the particular sciences whose theories are in this sense external to the material. The significant thing about theories of knowledge and of truth is that they themselves can never be verified by *criteria* devised for the knowledge of things. Thus empiricism as a theory of knowledge cannot be verified by the empirical criterion itself, and from this point of view is nonsense. Bertrand Russell even goes so far, with justice I think, as to say, 'Empiricism as a theory of knowledge is self-refuting since it must involve some general proposition about the independence of knowledge or experience and any such proposition, if true, must have as a consequence that it itself cannot be known.'[1] This is of special interest in this connection for it not only recognizes this peculiar character of epistemological

[1] *An Inquiry into the Nature of Meaning and Truth*, p. 207.

theories, but also, I should suppose, recognizes, tacity at least, that any treatment of them must be dialectical in the manner in which he himself employs it.

Those who deny this peculiar significance of the knowledge problem, and therefore the dialectical character of its solution, do so because they ignore a most important aspect of knowledge. They confine it to what we may call the dyadic conception, according to which knowledge is either perception or conception, either inductive or deductive, and these two aspects exhaust its entire nature. Actually, there is a third aspect which we may call knowledge by interpretation. Knowledge is not completed until the presuppositions of experience are explicated and the logically unsupported judgments of value, the postulates which underlie all logical systems, are developed. Only when such presuppositions and postulates are related in a larger universe of discourse or interpretation is the goal of all knowledge attained. Whether when this goal is attained, when this explication of meanings is completed, it is identical with objective meaning and whether this objective meaning, when thus attained, is also identical with what the mind seeks in looking for truth, is a further problem and concerns dialectic in the metaphysical sense. Of this we shall have more to say later; our sole point here is that dialectic is the coping stone of all knowledge or science and that without it the knowing process, merely as knowing, would not be completed.[1]

IV

Dialectical Insight into the Opposition of Realism and Idealism. The Conciliation of Realism and Idealism.

A

The general character of dialectic and of dialectical insight has, it is hoped, now been made clear. Our further task is to apply these conceptions in detail to the specific epistemological problem of realism and idealism—to show that the opposition is of this general type and that insight into the nature of this opposition makes possible its transcendence and the conciliation of the opposing positions.

[1] *Language and Reality*, chapter v, pp. 219 ff. Also chapter xiii, pp. 676 ff.

That the opposition is really of this character has already been made clear in preceding arguments; it is necessary now merely to summarize the conclusions. Chapters II and III showed that the driving force of idealism and of the resistance of realism arise from the logically unsupported judgments of value which they presuppose. Chapter IV showed that the opposition in question is one neither of fact nor of logic, but of fundamental beliefs or cognitive values. Our examination of the refutations of idealism and realism respectively showed that the reason why neither could demonstrate its own position or refute the other is that the issues involved can be settled neither by an appeal to matter of fact nor to ordinary logic. Let us briefly recall two points.

First of all, we saw that it is simply not a 'matter of fact' that objects are either independent of the subject or they are not. So far as the merely factual aspect of the situation is concerned, they are both. Thus a colour when seen is given as independent, while at the same time it is dependent for being seen on our physiological organism. The two facts belong to different universes of discourse. Actually, both realists and idealists have recognized this situation in their respective arguments. The idealist never denies the *experience* of independence; he bases his entire argument on the fact that an object may be given as independent and not be really independent. The realist in meeting the idealist recognizes the same distinction, for he also maintains that the colour is both dependent and independent; as sensation it is dependent, as *quale* it is independent. It is possible to go even further in this direction. The realist may maintain, as he often does, that independence for knowledge does not exclude dependence even on the creation of man. There are many objects of the creative activity, both of the individual and the race—the artificats of both art and history—which, while thus dependent upon mind for their existence, are yet, as objects of knowledge, mind-independent.

It is accordingly, meaningless to say that independence and dependence are mutually exclusive *facts*. It is equally untrue to say that the two propositions, that the object of knowledge is independent and that this object is dependent are in logical contradiction. It is simply not true that 'like other propositions they are in a necessary relation of mutual exclusion.' The opposition here is not a logical contradiction but rather a more ultimate and significant opposition between two ideals and evaluations of knowing, evaluations which, it is held, must be acknowledged if the arguments of realism and idealism respectively are to have any force. This appears clearly when the refutations of idealism and realism are examined. As refutations in the ordinary sense, either factual or logical, they fail utterly to refute, but as *argumenta ad hominem*, disclosing the underlying cognitive values assumed, they are not only immensely revelatory but have the dialectical force which all such arguments always have. It was recognition of this situation which constituted the insight of Fichte, although he was wrong in thinking that the resolution of the opposition could be one solely of moral choice.

B

The problem then is metempirical and metalogical in the sense defined, and therefore dialectical. Our further task is to develop the dialectic of realism and idealism. We may divide this part of our study into three parts: (*a*) the dialectic of realism; (*b*) the dialectic of idealism; and (*c*) the dialectic of realism and idealism.

The major part of this task has also been done in preceding chapters. The explication of the meanings of realism and idealism in discourse and the study of the transformations of idealism and realism respectively, as determined by the interplay of the two positions, led to the formulation of what we described the irreducible *minima* of these two positions. We now take the problem up at this point with a view of showing that these *minima* are both necessary for an intelligible concept of knowledge, and that, properly understood, they are not incompatible. Let us then to this end state as impartially as possible what each position in epistemology believes to be the irreducible *minimum*.

The first point to emphasize is that the argument in each case concerns what is considered necessary for the significance of knowledge and without which, as it is said, 'the peculiar significance of knowledge is lost'. Significance in this context is, as we have seen, a value notion, for it refers in each case to an ideal of knowledge—to what constitutes genuine knowledge and to what must be presupposed if knowledge is to be genuine.

For realism, the necessary condition of genuine knowledge is the mind-independent character of the object of knowledge and the opposite is considered *wider-sinnig*. The idealistic position, on the other hand, believes that mind-dependence in some sense is necessary for the significance of knowledge—that only an ideal world is knowable in any genuine sense, and that the idea of the knowledge of an object wholly other than the knower is *wider-sinnig*. A realist will thus say, with Maritain, that idealism strikes at the very root of intelligence and all genuine concepts of knowledge. An idealist will say, with Royce, that idealism is irrepressible and not ultimately refutable, because truth itself is an ideal and cannot possibly be expressed except in ideal terms. Each charges his opponent with maintaining a position which refutes itself, and both of them are right. Our task is now to see the sense in which both may be right. This insight is possible only after we have made a further analysis of the meanings of mind-independence and mind-dependence respectively; by showing first what meanings, and what meanings alone, must be retained if knowledge is to retain its significance, and by showing, secondly, that when these *minimal* meanings are understood, they are seen to be compatible with each other.

C

Let us start then with the dialectic of realism. The realist confidently affirms that unless the content of our knowledge is recognized as having a condition independent of the mind, 'the peculiar significance of knowledge is likely to be lost.' For the purpose of knowledge, the value assumed in all knowledge activity, is to be true to something beyond it. Its very intent is to be governed by and dictated to in certain respects. This we may perhaps take for granted, but the real problem is to discover precisely what, in terms of knowledge, can be meant by the 'independence' of the object.

The primary meaning of independence is the postulate that our thought and our desires shall make no difference to the facts. We believe only in that which is independent of our belief. This much of the meaning of independence seems necessary if the peculiar significance of knowledge is not to be lost—namely, independence of my interests and purposes. It is true, as the methodology of the different sciences has conclusively shown, that our procedures cannot be wholly separated from our interests and purposes. But it is part of any genuine conception of knowledge that what I shall find must in a very real sense be independent of any interest or purpose of mine. In other words reality in some way transcends my present knowledge of it and my inferences from the given eventuate in consequences which I also do not create and which cannot be altered by the interests and purposes of my thinking.

This primary meaning of independence is, I think, unquestionable. On no other supposition is error possible and no theory of knowledge can be made intelligible which does not allow for error. But here again there is an aspect of the situation which is often overlooked by many forms of realism. It is part of any intelligible theory of knowledge that inference must eventuate in consequences which the activity of thinking cannot alter. But it is no less true that should something eventuate which in no way conformed to my ways of thinking, in no way fulfilled the ultimate interest and purposes of that thinking, such an eventuality might be said to exist, but certainly not be said to be known or understood; it would have no meaning. It is, of course, necessary to distinguish between my individual and temporal interests and purposes, and the more ultimate purpose of all knowledge. 'Ultimate reasons' always include, as Whitehead has said, 'aim at value'.

The notion of independence includes, however, something more than this primary meaning, namely, the notion of the giveness of the given, whatever the given may turn out to be— our realization that this content, however great or small, *is as it is*, and that our knowing it does not alter it. This is undoubtedly the necessary condition or presupposition of any notion of genuine knowledge, but the *principle* of the giveness of the given does not prejudge the question of *what* is actually given. A realism not sufficiently critical may include as given much that is really not. Earlier forms of realism included in the given much that later had to be abandoned, but the resistance of realism remains immitigable.

The dialectic of realism leads then to an irreducible and irrefutable *minimum* without which the peculiar significance of knowledge is lost. This *minimum* is the necessary presupposition or postulate of all knowledge, but only because to assert the opposite is to enunciate a proposition which is ultimately *widersinnig* or refutes itself. The various transformations and transmutations of realism have shown that while elements in the realistic *credo* have, one after the other shown themselves untenable, the essential postulate of antecedence remains untouched. This, we shall later see, the 'new epistemology of science' what ever concessions it may find itself necessary to make to idealism, has also demonstrated beyond a doubt.

D

The peculiar significance of knowledge is then lost if the postulate of antecedent being—of the independence of the object of knowledge in this minimal sense is denied. But the significance of knowledge is also lost if certain other conditions are denied—if, in other words, the object of knowledge is not mind-dependent in some sense. With this we come to the dialectic of idealism.

The idealist starts out by affirming that unless the content of knowledge is recognized as having meaning for mind, as embodying in some way that which is akin to mind, knowledge in any genuine sense is impossible. The immediate purpose of knowledge is, indeed, to be true to something beyond itself, but its purpose is also to find that something intelligible, and if this equally fundamental purpose is not recognized, knowledge in any significant sense of the word is not possible. Merely to have an object is not to know it. Mind-dependence, in the sense of relevance to mind, is also a *sine qua non* of any intelligible theory of knowledge. What then does this mind-dependence mean and what does it involve?

In the first place, it means that a certain *relativity* of knowledge to mind must be conceded in any intelligible theory of knowledge. The arguments of the idealist have shown that it is meaningless to try to describe anything out of all relation to mind, although from this fact we cannot argue to the quite different thesis that the real object known is completely determined by the mind that knows it. While the giveness of that which is given is beyond doubt—the postulate of antecedent being is as much a necessary part of historic idealism as of historic realism—it is equally beyond doubt that the only way in which being can be known is in terms of those categories in which judgments about it are possible. Whatever immediacy there may be is always a mediated immediacy.

This relativity to mind extends also to a necessary relation to the mind's purposes and values. It is true, as the realist insists, that for knowledge to be genuine or significant, what eventuates in my experience must be independent of any particular attitude or purpose of mine, but it is equally true that no object may be said to be known in the sense of being understood or intelligible unless it satisfies ideals implicit in our reason as such. It is true, of course, that mind-independence in the sense of the independence of the consequences of thought is the condition of judgments being true or false, but it is just as certain that if these consequences are wholly irrelevant to my ideals of meaning and rationality, the very notions of true and false lose all meaning. Truth is an ideal and not a thing, and in this fact is found the irrefutable element in all idealism. Transcendence of the object of knowledge is a necessary presupposition of all genuine knowledge, but the transcendence of the knower, and of his ideal, is equally necessary.

The dialectic of idealism thus leads also to an irreducible and irrefutable *minimum* without which the peculiar significance of knowledge is lost. This *minimum* is also the necessary presupposition and postulate of all genuine knowledge, but it is so because to assert the opposite is to enunciate a proposition which is also ultimately *wider-sinnig* or refutes itself. The various transformations and transmutations of idealism have also shown that, while elements in the idealistic *credo* have, one after the other, shown themselves no longer tenable, the essential postulate of idealism remains untouched. This, too, as we shall later see, the new epistemology of science makes clear. While it, like all knowledge, presupposes the postulate of antecedent being, it also finds itself compelled to 'make concessions to idealism', concessions without which its own scientific conceptions would be unintelligible.

E

The equal necessity of retaining both realistic and idealistic elements in any adequate theory of knowledge has, I think, now been shown. Without either *minimum* the significance of knowledge is lost. But it is equally clear, I think, that both can be held together, and indeed must be, if an adequate theory of knowledge is to be possible. That they can be held together is implied in all that has preceded; it remains merely to make this mutual implication explicit. This we may describe as the dialectic of realism and idealism.

To make this relation clear it is necessary merely to cast our minds back to the analysis already made. There is really nothing incompatible between mind-dependence and mind-independence as thus critically formulated. The postulate of the giveness of the given, necessary for realism, does not in the least prejudice the critical problem of what is given, nor does the postulate that the consequences of thought are independent of my purposes and interests prejudice the critical problem as to whether knowledge is intelligible without an ultimate reference to purpose and value. On the other hand, the postulate of the relativity of knowledge to mind, either in the sense of relevance to our senses and categories or of relevance to purpose and value, does not in the least prejudice the critical problem of how far this relativity extends. The fact that the object is not completely determined by mind does not exclude the fact that it is partly determined. These are further problems for a critical theory of knowledge.

But we may go further than this. We may also say that they *must* be held together in any intelligible theory of knowledge. Denial of either not only refutes itself, but makes the assertion of its opposite meaningless also. This is seen in the essential polarity of these concepts themselves; neither of the notions of mind-independence or mind-dependence has, as notion, any meaning without the other. A pan-subjectivism which puts everything in the mind is meaningless, and for that reason no idealism has ever been a pure subjectivism. But a pan-objectivism is ultimately equally meaningless, and no coherent realism has ever been wholly such. But this may be said to be a merely verbal argument—dialectic in the bad sense, although I do not believe it to be such. The real point is that not only, as concepts, are the two notions mutually dependent, but are, as methodological postulates of knowledge, equally so.

In discussing this same problem—of idealism versus realism—C. I. Lewis comes to a conclusion worth quoting in this context.

'If,' so he writes, 'the idealist should find that there is nothing in such independence' (as described) 'which is incompatible with his thesis, then it may be that between a sufficiently critical idealism and a sufficiently critical realism, there are no issues except false issues which arise from the insidious fallacies of the copy theory of knowledge.'[1] I should go further than this. I should say, not 'it may be,' but that it is really so. Between a sufficiently critical idealism and a sufficiently critical realism there are, I believe, no issues except false issues, and it is precisely this, namely, that we are dealing here with a false alternative, that the present argument seeks to show.

Some of these issues do, indeed, arise from the insidious fallacies of the copy theory of knowledge, but not all. Some, and these the most serious, arise from the misunderstanding of the entire nature of the problem itself—that misunderstanding which I have attempted to point out throughout this discussion—the false assumption, namely, that the issues are 'factual' and 'logical', when actually they are dialectical—the failure to realize the radical shift that takes place in all epistemological discussion, from the realm of things to that of meaning and value. The fallacies of the copy theory itself arise out of the fact that knowledge is treated as a thing and the relation between knowing and the thing known as a relation between things. A sufficiently critical realism no less than a sufficiently critical idealism will recognize the falsity of the issues and, therefore, of the alternative to which they have given rise.[2]

I am, of course, fully aware that this solution of the problem is merely what it claims to be, namely, dialectical and that this conciliation of realism and idealism is, as the critic would say, wholly a matter of theory. To justify fully this claim to the consistency of idealism and realism, something more is doubtless required, namely, a detailed study of the methodology of knowledge within the particular sciences themselves. It is not possible

---

[1] *Mind and the World Order*, chapter vi: 'The Relativity of Knowledge and the Independence of the Real,' p. 194.

[2] I recall also a remark of Fullerton's which is also not without relevancy in this connection. Speaking of Creighton's form of idealism, he said that it was 'divided from realism only by a word.' Creighton denied this, and doubtless with some right, but the fact remains that the dividing line is so thin that it is very often mainly a matter of words. The pity of it is that these words have seemed so significant as to have, for decades, exhausted most of the energies of philosophers.

to supply this 'more' until we have examined the problem of realism and idealism as it appears in physical science and in the humanistic and social sciences. This we shall attempt in Chapters VII and VIII, where we shall seek to show that the methodology of modern science implies both. Our final solution of the problem is found in Chapter IX, entitled *An Idealistic Philosophy Along Realistic Lines.*

V

Realism, Idealism and Communication. The Conditions of Intelligible Discourse.

A

There is a final argument for the conciliation of idealism and realism which, to my mind at least, has compelling force. It is an argument based upon the necessary relation of knowledge to communication and the conditions of intelligible communication.

All knowledge, we shall maintain, presupposes discourse or communication, and any theory of knowledge involves or includes the question of the necessary conditions of meaningful or intelligible discourse. I think it can be shown that communication, and therefore knowledge itself, presupposes both idealism and realism—the minimal postulates of both—and that this fact furnishes a further confirmation of our position regarding this opposition and its resolution. This also is a dialectical argument and in developing it the full significance of the dialectic in the solution of metalogical problems will become evident. Our first task, then, is to justify the major premise, namely, that all knowledge, to be knowledge, involves communication.

Communication is obviously presupposed in all thinking and knowing which involves conversation and controversy. It is not so obvious when knowing is the 'inner' process of individual thought or the 'outer' process of objective investigation which we call science and scientific method. And yet, as Royce has said, 'any conversation with other men, any process of that inner conversation whereof we have seen our inner self-consciousness consists, any scientific investigation, is carried on under the influence of the generally sub-conscious belief that we are all members of a community of interpretation.[1] In other words, communication or discourse is the presupposition, tacit or overt, of knowledge of any sort and any theory of knowledge involves the question of the necessary conditions of intelligible or meaningful discourse.

This 'subconscious belief,' this tacit presupposition has, accordingly, been the postulate of all traditional European philosophy. 'Knowledge,' said Plato in the *Theatætus*, 'is judgment plus discourse,' and from his time on, communicability has been recognized as a necessary presupposition of knowledge. The scholastics continued this tradition. All science as they asserted, assumes it. There is hardly a work of St. Thomas in which this doctrine is not in evidence. Every form, in so far as it is a form, is communicable and communicability pertains to its nobility. Community pertains, however, not only to the nobility but to the intelligibility of forms. It is, moreover, this communicability of forms and patterns that alone makes science possible. *Scientia est de universalibus.*[2]

It is often insisted that communicability is not an essential condition of knowledge but merely a social *addendum*. The essential condition of knowledge is verifiability, and verification, as understood by modern scientific method, consists solely in reference, direct or indirect, to sensuously observable entities; confirmation within the scientific community, while a part of scientific method, is not essential to knowledge itself. This, however, is, I believe, showing itself more and more to be a false reading of the situation. Private sense data, as such verify nothing. They must first be interpreted and interpretation involves, directly or indirectly, a community of interpreters. More and more, in science itself there is a shift of emphasis from verification by sensa data to confirmation in the scientific community, the potentially public character of all genuine knowledge requiring this shift of emphasis. In science, however it may be elsewhere, nothing enters into the sphere of objective knowledge except that which is inter-subjectively public.

---

[1] Josiah Royce, *The Problem of Christianity*, Vol. II, p. 233.

[2] See on this point, *Summa*, Id. 4, q. I, art. I.

B

The fundamental character of this relation of knowledge to communication has been increasingly recognized by all types of philosophic thought, pragmatic and positivistic, realistic and idealistic. It is, however, with the relation, as conceived by realists and idealists that we are here chiefly concerned.

The latest work to make communication central in knowledge is E. G. Spaulding's *A World of Chance*. His essential point—and this is the only aspect of his treatment that we shall here refer to —is that unless we postulate entities or essences independent of the knower, communication from mind to mind cannot be made intelligible, and this he considers a dialectical 'proof' for realism.[1] With this general argument I am in entire agreement. The argument by means of which he shows the impossibility of communication on subjectivistic or merely pragmatic premises I find unanswerable and believe it to be the most fundamental argument for a necessary realistic *minimum* in any philosophy. Spaulding does not find himself justified in extending his argument to include values as having essential being independent of the subject. To my mind, however, intelligible communication is as much dependent upon the mutual acknowledgment of values, upon which ultimately our 'meanings' depend, as upon the mutual acknowledgment of independent 'things'. No theory of communication is possible which does not involve a 'realism of values.'[2]

Realism is then a necessary condition or presupposition of intelligible communication, but an equally necessary condition is an idealistic *minimum*. For after all, *mutual acknowledgment* of independent entities and values is as much a condition of intelligible communication as *the independent entities* mutually acknowledged, and this mutual acknowledgment presupposes transcendent minds or selves. It was Royce who, among English speaking philosophers, saw this truth most clearly, and it was this which led him to formulate his later version of objective idealism in terms of communication and interpretation. It is doubtless true that, under the influence of the psychological and sociological prejudices of his time, he over emphasized these aspects, but after all, the category of communication, as he

[1] *Op. cit.*, chapter viii.

[2] See *Language and Reality*, chapter vi.

understands it, is more than psychological and social. The community of minds he envisages is metaphysical. Knowledge for him involves interpretation and 'an interpretation is real only if the appropriate community is real and is true only if that community reaches its goal.'[1] Mutual acknowledgment on the part of transcendent minds of common meanings and values is as much a condition of communication and genuine knowledge as the independent being of the meanings and values thus acknowledged. Transcendence of both Object and Subject is presupposed.

Knowledge, therefore, and the communication or discourse, with which it is bound up, presuppose this double transcendence, and with it an element of both realism and idealism. No coherent or intelligible theory of communication can be developed on subjectivist premises, and if idealism involves subjectivism idealism must be abandoned. On the other hand, no coherent theory of communication can be developed without the notion of transcendent mind as well as of transcendent objects. Any form of realism that denies this must be abandoned. I should further add, if both realistic and idealistic presuppositions are necessary for a valid or intelligible theory of communication, then no philosophy, since any philosophy presupposes such communication, can ignore either element in its total structure. The *minimum* of any theory of communication— and therefore, ultimately, of any adequate theory of knowledge —must include this doctrine of double transcendence.

It will doubtless be argued that the very thesis that all knowledge, to be genuine, involves confirmation and therefore communication, either tacit or overt, is itself exclusively idealistic in spirit if not in letter. But thus to argue would be to miss the entire point, namely, that communication is a necessary presupposition of *any* theory of knowledge, whether realistic or idealistic. If we hold fast to the introvertible fact that for neither theory is there knowledge in the sense of verified or verifiable knowledge unless it is confirmed, and that confirmation involves communication, then it must be apparent that a theory of knowledge which makes communication a fundamental category cannot be exclusively idealistic. It is true that there are metaphysical theories of communication that are idealistic in

[1] *Op. cit.*, p. 269.

this sense, but they are not the necessary consequence of an epistemological theory of communication such as the present. Such a theory, by reason of the very fact that it presupposes communication, must be beyond realism and idealism in the epistemological sense.

C

This final argument for the conciliation of idealism and realism brings us back to the initial statement of the problem for which the entire argument of this chapter, it is hoped, constitutes the solution. As there stated, the problem was this: Life creates this opposition between idealism and realism, but just as surely life itself reconciles the opposition which it created. This vital reconciliation gives us a right to expect that a mode of reconciliation can be found in theory as in life, as indeed normal to the entire process of consciousness. This expectation has, I think, been shown to have been legitimate, and to have been justified by the developments of this chapter. It has been justified in a pre-eminent degree by the present argument from communication. For communication is itself the *sine qua non* of any life that is more than physical. The fact that communication, both as the condition of a significant life and of the significance of all knowledge, presupposes both realism and idealism and reconciles them both, brings out the full significance of our dialectical solution.

The argument by which this conciliation is shown being dialectical, involves in a sense a 'logico-intellectual formula'. But it is not, I should insist, of the kind which Jung found inapplicable. The oppositions with which the dialectic deals are, as both Plato and Hegel saw, simply abstract expressions of vital conflicts within experience itself. The reconciliation which the dialectic seeks to show forth is but the explication of the sources of the conflict and of the mutual implication already present in life itself when viewed as a whole. The argument by which this conciliation is shown being dialectical, it may be argued that, as such, it is merely explication of meanings and does not give us truth. This objection to our dialectical solution, together with other objections to the dialectic as such, will be examined in the following chapter.

Chapter VI

Beyond Realism and Idealism (continued). Objections to the Preceding Dialectical Solution.

I — A

IN THE preceding chapter we have presented the process of dialectical transcendence by which, as we believe, the enlightened philospher may come to the insight that the cognitive 'values' embodied in the opposition of realism and idealism are not contradictory and that when the irrefutable minimal presuppositions of both positions are critically examined there is no reason why they should not be found complementary.

It goes without saying that a position such as this will scarcely commend itself to the majority of philosophers. For those in whom the opposition is so hardened that defence of their chosen position has become a large part of their intellectual life, the response can be only that of indignant repudiation. For many the method of solution proposed will arouse only amused contempt. With neither of these emotional attitudes am I, of course, concerned. But there are really plausible if not convincing objections, and these it is incumbent upon us to consider. There are at least three points which should, I think, be singled out for special examination. There is (*a*) the objection to the whole idea of the dialectical method in general, and especially to its application to a problem such as this. There is (*b*) the objection that the position described as beyond realism and idealism is in unstable equilibrium and must, in the end, pass over into some form of idealism or realism. (*c*) Finally, there is the objection that, even if such a position were conceivable or plausible, it could not be shown to be true; for dialectic is concerned with explication of meanings, never with knowledge in the sense of verification or demonstration.

B

Any philosopher who introduces the notion of dialectic and dialectical method at all is, of course, bound to be open to the gravest suspicion as to his philosophical competence. He is immediately charged with doing violence to the sacred principle of contradiction, but it is the resolution of contradictions or oppositions in a higher synthesis—a sort of 'heaven of meanings and values' where, so to speak, all philosophical tears are wiped away—which chiefly arouses the critics' mirth. With regard to the former we have perhaps said all that can be said. If a philosopher still holds that the dialectic, when properly understood, involves doing violence either to experience or logic, probably nothing will persuade him to the contrary. Let us then proceed to the second point.

It is, I suppose this idea of a higher synthesis—of a heaven of meanings and values, as it has been called, of which philosophers of the positivistic type are most contemptuous. They admit that most of the problems which exercise the mind of the philosopher—and not the least the present one—are meaningless from the empirical point of view, and therefore 'unreal'. But they would deny that there is any other point of view and hold that any standpoint which pretends to transcend the empirical is sheer nonsense. Now this is scarcely the place to argue for a heaven, either philosophical or other, but if there be none then most of our philosophy has been, as they rightly recognize, in vain. If, on the other hand, there be one, then must it resolve our oppositions and contradictions, 'else what's a Heaven for?' However that may be, it is with the probable objections to the application of the dialectical method to our particular problem that we are here especially concerned. The entire idea of the transcendence of the purely empirical and existential view will seem to many an absurdity, and the dream of the realistic lion lying down with the idealistic lamb a utopian illusion. That it is neither an illusion nor an absurdity we shall attempt to show.

C

Philosophers of various persuasions have, as a matter of fact, argued for this transcendence. Notable among these was no less a thinker than Heinrich Rickert, who found himself faced with precisely the same problem with which we have been concerned and sought to solve it in a manner not unlike that which we have employed. An examination of his argument will perhaps enable us to formulate our own position more clearly and thus meet the objections to the dialectical solution.

Rickert held that this opposition between realism and idealism within the theory of knowledge makes any satisfactory and intelligible theory of knowledge impossible. He held also that a reconciliation or synthesis of these two positions (he uses the term synthesis) is both desirable and possible, and he seeks a way to bring it about. It is entirely clear, he thinks, that no such synthesis is possible by means of terms taken from the sphere of 'existence'—from the sphere of the subject or mind, or from the sphere of object or thing. The problem cannot be solved by assimilating the object to the subject or the subject to the object. Philosophy 'requires here a third thing'—something that is more than existential being—something that is beyond, not only the dichotomy of mind and matter, but the dichotomy of subject and object; it requires concepts which, although themselves not existential, are yet assumed in all cases of existential judgments. What we require for the understanding of knowledge is something which is neither ideal nor non-ideal, but which is implied by both. We have this in the concept of meaning and, that which goes with it, the concepts of value and validity. This then is the *'standpoint of validity'* which, as he maintains, enables us, not only to transcend this opposition, but also to reconcile the two notions. A statement of it in his own words brings out the main point at issue.

'Meaning', he tells us, 'lies rather above and before all being and is grasped by no ontology. That follows from the fact that every case of knowledge, that something exists, presupposes the meaning of it as true, which belongs to the judgment that some thing exists no matter whether it is concerned with physical or mental, real or ideal, sensuous or non-sensuous, immediately given or inferred existences.'[1] The final ground of every existential judgment, he further tells us, is neither in existence itself nor in a transcendent object, but in a transcendent ideal (*Sollen*) which the knowing subject has to realize. In other words, he is maintaining, in terms of his own special idiom, that which we have all along been insisting upon, namely, the shift from the realm of things, whether physical or mental, to that of meanings and values which the epistemological problem involves; that the mind-independence of the object of knowledge is not an intuition but a postulate—a logically unsupported judgment of

---

[1] *Der Gegenstand der Erkentniss*, 6th edition.

value. The opposition of realism and idealism belongs not to the sphere of existence, neither that of the subject or mind, nor that of the object or thing. The object of knowledge is neither ideal nor non-ideal, but something that transcends both.

This, then, is the 'third thing' required, the standpoint of validity, and it is only when we acknowledge this value and the 'ought' beyond all ontological distinctions, that any synthesis of the opposition can be effected. No one will deny, I suppose, that this is a rarefied atmosphere which we are asked to breathe. But I think that, as philosophers, we are required to breathe it. We cannot remain long in it—plain man and philosopher alike must go back to earth—but unless we do breathe it for a while at least, unless we also get some insight into the real character of knowledge and of the origins of our epistemological oppositions, when we do go back to earth we shall fall back again into our old dogmatisms. We shall go over the old errors again—of attempting to assimilate the subject to the object or the object to the subject—of mind to matter or matter to mind—with all the old futile proofs and refutations of the true nature of which we are now surely sufficiently aware.

The issue is presented clearly by Lossky in his book, *The Intuitive Basis of Knowledge*. Criticizing the standpoint of validity, he asks, 'Is there intelligible meaning in saying that anything can be valid and at the same time not be? Contradiction seems to be involved in this line of thought; and for our own part, we turn to the realistic conception of being which instinctively guides us in science and practical activity.'[1] Here speaks the natural man, but does he speak with wisdom? If Lossky thus turns instinctively to the naïvely realistic faith, he must be frankly instinctive in his procedure or else he must define his realism. If he does the former, we have nothing to say to him. Life alone solves no philosophical problems, and certainly instinct no epistemological ones. If, on the other hand, he chooses to define the real, he will find himself treading much the same paths as Rickert found it necessary to explore. Moreover, while it may be true that this realism instinctively guides us in science, it certainly is not true that when we pass from instinct to reason, realism is still the exclusive presupposition of science and the scientific method, as I shall later attempt to

[1] *The Intuitive Basis of Knowledge*, 1919, pp. 248 ff.

show. Not only may one be a thoroughly competent scientist, whether he be a realist or an idealist, but the new epistemology of science actually implies elements of both.[1]

II

Beyond Realism and Idealism in Unstable Equilibrium. Really a Form of Idealism.

A

I think it must be admitted then, that the general position here developed does actually correspond to the facts which an adequate analysis of the knowledge situation discloses—that there is a third realm, neither physical nor mental, in which a formula may be found for the synthesis of realism and idealism. Whatever criticisms we may make of Rickert's way of stating it, the solution itself is sound. But can we remain in this realm of meaning and value? Is not the position in unstable equilibrium, and are we not forced ultimately to fall back into realism or pass on to a form of idealism?

This charge has been made, as it happens, by both realists and idealists against the solution of the opposition in the form offered by Rickert, and by implication, I suppose, against any solution of the problem of this type. It is described by both as a sort of 'half-way house' between realism and idealism.

The philosophy of validity has been frequently called a half-realism. It is admittedly realistic to the extent that for it reality is independent of finite knowledge. Reality is a norm or ideal that cannot be dependent on finite knowledge because it is presupposed by it. Since the final ground of every truth judgment is neither in existence itself, nor in a transcendent object, but in a transcendent ideal (with its 'ought'), which the knowing subject has to realize, it is seemingly partly realistic. The logical priority of the 'ought' (*das Sollen*) to the 'is' (*das Sein*) makes it independent of all approximations of finite knowledge, and it is therefore independent of the subject. But this view, we are told, is really not realistic, for two reasons. In the first place, it accepts no being but that which is immediately given in the 'idea'—it

[1] Chapter vii, pp. 148 f.

moves entirely within the limits of experience. In the second place, it sets over against the judging subject as an object to which it must conform, only an ought, which can have no meaning apart from the activity of thought. In short, things are dependent upon experience and experience on thought, and either form of dependence must be fatal to realism.[1]

Whether this last statement is true or not depends upon the kind of realism. It would be fatal to some types of realism but not to the really irrefutable element in realism, as our analysis of the realistic *minimum* has shown.[2] But this is not the main point here. It is rather that, being a 'half-realism', its fate, if it is to remain realistic, is to be forced back into an *exclusive* realism. This, I think, cannot be maintained. To do so is to fail to grasp what the entire history of the development of realism has shown, namely, that the mind-independence of the object of knowledge is not an intuition, but a postulate—a logically unsupported judgment of value—and this Rickert's view fully realizes. The realistic element in his theory is all that any genuine realism requires.

As for the realist, so for the idealist, the standpoint of validity often appears to be but a half-way house between realism and idealism, and its predestined goal an exclusive and thorough-going idealism. It cannot be driven back into realism—it is too critical a position for that—but it must, by its own momentum, pass over into idealism.[3]

This, again, I think we must deny. The argument has, indeed, a certain force. For precisely this momentum of which the idealist speaks is the very driving force present in all historical idealism. Meaning and validity seem inseparable from mind, at least over-individual objective mind. Nevertheless, I do not believe that the philosophy of validity is forced to take this step. Assimilation of the object to the subject no more solves the epistemological problem than assimilation of the subject to the object. In order really to solve it there must be this third thing,

---

[1] This line of criticism has been developed by various realists, but it is presented in very much this form by R. B. Perry in his *Present Philosophical Tendencies*, pp. 313 f.

[2] Chapter v, pp. 139 f.

[3] This criticism is also developed by many idealists, but it is found in one of its best forms in Royce's *The World and the Individual*, chapter vi.

as Rickert calls it, making possible the double transcendence of both subject and object of which we have spoken.[1] The standpoint of validity can no more be driven forward into an exclusive idealism than it can be driven back into an exclusive realism. It is, as we have seen in our own analysis of the preceding chapter, possible to remain 'above the battle' and to include both elements or postulates in our theory of knowledge.

B

The charge, on the part of both realist and idealist, that the standpoint which we have been maintaining is but a half-way house between realism and idealism does not then disturb us, for it is precisely such a half-way house that we have been seeking, namely, a position which avoids the exclusive logics of either realism or idealism. But there is still a further difficulty to be met. It may be argued that any theory of knowledge which finds its ultimate object or ground, not in a transcendent being, but in a transcendent ideal, must be essentially idealistic in principle, for ideal is a notion inseparable from mind and the very fact that 'truth is an ideal' makes, as Royce believed, idealism irrepressible.

This objection is not without a certain plausibility, although we shall seek to show that it is not ultimately valid. Indeed, the objector might call Rickert himself to witness, for he retains the word idealism, although obviously not wholly satisfied with such a description. 'Idealistic is our position on the one hand,' Rickert writes, 'in so far as in agreement with positivism or subjective idealism, it asumess no other existent than that immediately given in presentation. Yet this would not,' he admits, 'suffice alone to justify the expression idealism.' 'We retain,' he writes, 'the word idealism for two reasons. First, because we find the absolute or the ultimate basis of knowledge not in something existent (*wirklich*), but in something non-existent, that which we are accustomed to call ideal in contrast with the real. Further, the word idealism seems to be suitable because the word ideal, just as the Kantian concept Idea, refers to something unreal or non-existent in the special sense that it is valid or lies in the realm of values. Through the term idealism

[1] Chapter v, pp. 147 f.

is then brought to expression the primacy of the non-existent value as over against the really existent.'[1]

These reasons do not, I believe, suffice to make such a position exclusively idealistic. On the contrary, when closely examined, they constitute excellent grounds for discarding the term. The first is, indeed, a valid reason for not calling it realism. The fact that the transcendent object of knowledge is found in a 'non-existent ideal' marks it off, it is true, from all exclusive realisms, but it does not, I believe, involve an exclusive idealism. The admittedly realistic element forbids that. Nor because the word 'ideal' is used to designate the transcendent object of knowledge, is the term idealism appropriate to the position. Ideal in this context means something non-existent only in the limited sense which confines it to the physical and the mental, but does not, therefore, exclude the notion of antecedent being. The validity of an ideal is its being. I conclude, therefore, that idealism is not an appropriate term for this position, and that any philosopher who has really felt the full force of the arguments that have driven him to this 'third thing,' and to the standpoint of validity which it implies, is neither necessitated nor justified in calling it idealism. Whatever reasons, whether of piety or convenience, may motive the retention of this honoured name, are far outweighed by that deeper necessity of finding an epistemological standpoint which transcends this fatal opposition.

III

The 'Truth' of 'Beyond Realism and Idealism.' Dialectic and Knowledge.

A

Granted the possibility of this third position in epistemology, what of it? Does not the very fact that the solution is dialectical mean that it is not proof? It seeks mutual understanding of oppositions and their meanings, and thus, by understanding these, to transcend them. But is such understanding knowledge? Is the conciliation of the two positions involved itself true? Can we convince or even persuade men of its truth?

The issue here concerns, of course, not merely this specific

[1] *Der Gegenstand der Erkentniss*, 6th edition, p. 360.

problem but the more general question of the nature of dialectic itself and of the truth value of all dialectical solutions. This more general problem has already been suggested in the preceding chapter when we distinguished between dialectic as explication of meanings in discourse and the more metaphysical conception, that in the very explication of meanings truth itself is attained—the basal postulate of the dialectic in this sense being, that 'the completed meaning of a system of ideas is identical with all that the mind seeks in looking for the truth.' This metaphysical version of the dialectic is quite generally denied— dialectic, it is held, giving us meaning not truth. Before considering the specific problem it is desirable to examine this denial in its more general form.

B

This modern conception is widespread at the present time and is found in the most varied quarters. It is stated by Dewey in *Experience and Nature*, by Jaspers in his *Psychologie der Weltanschauungen*, and is one of the main theses of Adler's book entitled *Dialectic*. The fact that it is so generally a part of our present intellectual climate suggests that, whether ultimately tenable or not—I believe that it is not—it yet contains, and indeed must contain, some element of truth which must be taken into account in any final statement of our position.

The idea itself is, to be sure, so paradoxical that it seems almost impossible that it should be seriously maintained. The idea of a process of explication of meanings that 'gets us nowhere,' and of an understanding of these meanings which remains nothing but understanding, is in its essence so futile that it is hard to see how men can take it seriously. One might, indeed, understand psychologically—and such understanding lead us to 'pardoning all'—even the most indefensible of philosophical positions. One might understand sociologically these necessary tendencies in society but such understanding would lead at best to the philosophical tolerance of which Paulhan speaks, at worst to a complete scepticism on all fundamental issues. The idea itself is then ultimately untenable, but, despite that fact, it contains an element of truth as well as of falsity. This we must first try to understand.

It is clear first of all, I think, that dialectic is not proof in the ordinary sense, and that the conclusions reached by dialectical argument cannot convince in quite the same way in which we are at least supposed to be convinced in the case of empirical verification or logical demonstration. It cannot coerce, for it appeals neither to brute sense *data* nor to brute logical necessity, and only these can coerce. But dialectic, we are told, does not wish to coerce: when it knows itself it asks only for free acknowledgment. This, I think, is true. The real issue then is whether this acknowledgment is a form of knowledge, and whether in this mutual acknowledgment and reasonable agreement we attain truth.

Certainly it would seem—at first sight at least—that such understanding and interpretation is a form of knowledge—in fact the flower and fruit of all knowledge. It can be shown, I believe, that all other knowledge presupposes such acknowledgment. Knowledge, as empirical verification and logical demonstration, themselves presuppose, as we have already seen, underivable first principles, neither empirically verifiable nor logically demonstrable, and which, therefore, can only be acknowledged. The empirical criterion itself cannot be verified empirically, and if true, can be shown to be so only dialectically. If empiricism as a theory of knowledge is self-refuting—that is if true, must have as a consequence that itself cannot be verified by its own criterion—how if it is true can its truth be shown?

Behind this entire question of the truth of dialectic lies, as I have indicated, the still more fundamental question of the meaning of knowledge. Knowledge may, as John Dewey says, 'signify tested instances of knowledge, but it also has a sense more liberal and more humane. It signifies things and events understood; it means inclusive reasonable agreement.' If we include this more liberal and humane notion in our conception of knowledge, then among the things included in knowledge is just this inclusive reasonable agreement which dialectic, from the beginning, has sought to bring about. Such agreement is a matter of acknowledgment—not of coercion but of insight—an insight arising from our mutual sharing of common ideals and values. As such it can only be free, and the free acknowledgment involved can be a matter only of persuasion. In such persuasion, however, truth also is found.

C

To the specific question then, is 'Beyond Realism and Idealism' true? is the position verifiable?—we can answer only in the spirit of the preceding reflections. We may say this much at least, I think: it is, in principle, as capable of convincing as either of the opposing positions which it seeks to reconcile.

The truth of realism cannot be 'proved' in any purely empirical or logical manner as the positivists have rightly seen. But just as little can the truth of idealism be thus proved. Both involve general propositions about the dependence or independence of the object of knowledge, and any such propositions, if true or false, must have the consequence that they cannot be known in either of these senses. On the other hand, granted certain conceptions of the significance of knowledge, one can be brought to acknowledge the necessity of both realism and idealism as its necessary conditions. I cannot see how any one who holds that either realism or idealism may be true or false can deny that a view that holds them together may be true or false also. If realism represents an assurance which deserves the name of knowledge and idealism contains a similar assurance, then an assurance which combines them both may be knowledge also.

In the preceding chapter I sought to show that the two positions not only may thus be held together but *must* be in any intelligible theory of knowledge. With regard to the present issue everything turns upon the nature of this 'must'. If it cannot be of the nature of coercion, neither that of brute sense data nor of brutal logical necessity, what sort of a compulsion can it be? I think we shall not be far wrong if we think of it as the same kind of compulsion as attaches to belief in all first and last things. Empirical verification (with its compulsion) applies only to statements regarding particular matter of fact; logical demonstration, with its compulsion, only with respect to propositions in the same limited logical system; when it comes to the ultimate presuppositions of both experience and logic—which are both metempirical and metalogical—the only criterion possible is one to which I have never been able to give any other name than that of philosophical intelligibility. The question concerns what has been described as the peculiar significance of knowledge. If, in order to retain that significance, the minimal postulates of both realism and idealism must be retained and 'held together.' then, since they are the conditions of an intelligible theory of knowledge, the criterion here applied is that of intelligibility, and the 'must' is such as arises only out of this demand. In this case, as in all ultimate philosophical issues, significance and truth tend to become identical.

D

With this we are brought to a final issue which has been present implicity throughout our entire discussion, namely, an evaluation of the metaphysical interpretation of the dialectic. It involves an answer to the question whether 'the completed meaning of a system of ideas is identical with what the mind actually seeks in looking for the truth.' We have been considering dialectic as explication of meanings in discourse; does this explication also constitute truth?

I think that in the end we must give an affirmative answer to this question, but everything depends upon how the answer is formulated. Stated in one way it is true; stated in another it is wholly false.

It seems clear that in most regions of human knowledge this is not true. What the mind seeks in looking for the truth is either adequation of idea and thing, correspondence between our ideas and their objects, or consistency between our propositions. In the limited universe of empirical science there are many propositions which have meaning, but which have not been verified by its own empirical criterion. In the limited universes of given logical systems there are propositions which, since they conform to the laws of logic are meaningful but not necessarily true. All this is clear, but it seems equally clear that this does not exhaust what the mind seeks when it is looking for the truth. There are, as we have repeatedly seen, many propositions, significant for both experience and logic, which themselves are not verifiable either in terms of empirical or logical criteria. What then is the mind looking for when it seeks the truth or falsity of these metempirical and metalogical propositions? One way of answering this question is to say that the mind is looking for a consistent whole of experience or, in Royce's more metalogical terms, 'the fulfilment of our meanings,' and when it has found this it knows that it has the truth, the point being that there comes a point in knowledge, the maximum context which we call metaphysics, where there cannot be any external relation between our ideas and the reality to which they refer. Another way of stating it is that truth is immanent in discourse and the sum total of intelligible discourse is the truth. I prefer the latter way of stating it, for it emphasizes the relation of meaning to truth which has been the issue throughout our study of the dialectic. Dialectic, as the explication of our meanings in discourse, brings us ultimately to the point where meaning and truth coincide. Knowledge, as we have seen in the preceding chapter, is inseparable from communication and the necessary presuppositions of intelligible communication are *ipso facto* part of the truth.[1]

This does not mean that dialectic can at any point constitute a substitute for empirical or logical criteria when they are applicable. The substitution of dialectical method in universes of discourse where these criteria are applicable is precisely the misuse of the method which in many quarters has brought it into disrepute. Nor does it mean that truth reached by the dialectic either annuls or supersedes what we know as empirical and logical truth. Dialectic, far from doing violence either to experience or logic, is merely rather the necessary extension of both. For unless we make explicit that which is presupposed by experience, and develop the metalogical presuppositions of logic, we shall have failed to attain that kind of knowledge which, as Plato said, constitutes the coping stone of all the sciences. As applied to the particular problem of realism and idealism, we shall attempt to show in succeeding chapters that the conclusion thus reached dialectically is confirmed by an examination of the physical and humanistic sciences themselves, namely, that both are beyond idealism and realism in that when their methods are examined, both are seen to contain elements of both.

[1] For a fuller development of these points, see my article, 'The Dialectic of Meaning and Truth.' *Philosophy and Phenomenological Research*, Vol. IV, No. 3, March 1944.

Chapter VII

Realism, Idealism and The Philosophy of Nature: 'The Philosophy of Physical Science.'

I — A

THE preceding chapters attempted to develop an argument for the transcendence of the opposition between realism and idealism and to outline a position which could properly be called Beyond Realism and Idealism. The argument as presented was, however, carried on in the world of discourse or dialectic. The radical shift from the sphere of things to the sphere of discourse involved in all philosophical debate was evident here, but knowledge, 'science', belongs to the world of 'things'—especially the so-called physical sciences —and when we shift back to this world of things, whether of 'common sense' or science, arguments such as the preceding seem to be of a singularly tenuous kind and the position suggested academic and unreal. Here 'dialectic' seems ludicrous. Realism, it will be said, is an essential part of the very structure of physical science, and to be a scientist means by that very fact to be an exclusive realist.

This, as we have already seen, is quite commonly assumed. Indeed, the appeal to science—extrinsic as it may be when properly weighed—is, and has always been, one of the strongest forces in the resistance of realism. It is, I venture to think, this appeal, more than any supposed proof of realism or refutation of idealism, that has determined the predominantly realistic outlook of recent decades. It was partly the supposed failure of idealism, in any form, to do justice to the physical sciences which constituted the chief reason for its decline in popularity.

The situation has, however, notably changed. We find distinguished physicists maintaining idealistic positions in all the varied forms of idealism—mentalism, Neo-Kantian idealism, and even objective idealism. We find them maintaining, moreover, not only that physical science is compatible with idealism, but that there are actual changes in the concepts and methods of modern science which necessitate idealism. The reasons for these changes are known to every one and are part of the cultural climate of the present. Modern physics has undergone such changes, not only in its particular theories but in its general outlook—changes which would have been unintelligible to the science of the nineteenth century—that to many at least they seem to require far-reaching changes in the philosophical outlook also—more particularly in the direction of idealism.

This tendency is, of course, bitterly contested by both scientists and philosophers. Into the debate thus engendered we shall have to go presently—here we wish merely to point out that the appeal to science, as against idealism, is now a wholly extrinsic one—as indeed it has always been. Science as an activity of the human mind is entirely compatible with either standpoint and, as I believe and shall attempt to show, really presupposes both. The simple fact that physicists of the first rank are able to carry on their investigations and to produce significant and verifiable results, whether they are philosophically idealists or realists, suggests that their private philosophical beliefs have nothing to do with their public scientific activity.

The changes which we have noted have taken place primarily in the science known as physics. This in itself is of great significance. In the first place physics is, in a very important sense, the fundamental natural science and its basal concepts cannot fail—in the long run at least—to have a determining effect upon all the other sciences of nature. It is true, as we shall see, that the categories of the other sciences are not wholly reducible to those of physics—that the fundamental categories of biology have a relative independence, but this independence is only relative and fundamental changes in the philosophy of physics must in the end affect the philosophy of science as a whole. In the second place—and this is perhaps even more important in this context—is the fact that the object of knowledge in physics is the physical object *par excellence*. Whether rightly or wrongly, all modern discussions of epistemological realism and idealism have started with the physical object, and knowledge here has, so to speak, been made normative for knowledge in every other sphere. If, therefore, an exclusive realism is no longer tenable in this sphere, inferences as to the exclusive realism of science in general appear to lose their cogency.

B

The theme of this chapter, broadly stated, is, then, the implications of modern science—more especially modern physics—for our problem of realism and idealism. To the question whether physical science is realistic or idealistic we shall answer, neither exclusively—that it is beyond the opposition and includes elements of both. The present chapter may then be looked upon as a specific application, to a specific sphere, of the position and principles of the preceding chapters, and as, therefore, in a sense a confirmation of our general thesis. This general theme and its development will include three specific theses which we shall attempt to prove.

We shall attempt to show, in the first place, that neither epistemological realism nor idealism can ever be proved or disproved by the 'facts' of physics—that the theory of knowledge of physical science, like the theory of knowledge in general is beyond realism and idealism—in fact, implies elements of both. In the second place, we shall attempt to show that both the arguments for idealism in modern physics, and the arguments in refutation of this idealism, while purporting to be in the realm of facts are really in the realm of discourse or dialectic. In other words, they are dialectical and have here the force and meaning which we have already shown to be attributable to these arguments. Thus when the idealistic physicist develops what he calls the idealistic implications of modern physics his arguments are of the same general dialectical character which arguments for idealism have always been, and when the realist, whether scientist or philosopher, seeks to refute him, the refutations are also of this dialectical character. In the third place, we shall attempt to show that modern physics is, both in method and results, actually above the opposition of realism and idealism; that actually elements of both are present and that, while there is an irrefutable element of realism in physics, as in all forms of knowledge, there is also, equally, a necessary element of idealism; in the words of Weyl, 'it must make certain concessions to idealism.' If this general thesis can be maintained the conclusions of this chapter will form a very important part of our general argument. They will not only eliminate the extrinsic appeals to science—whether of realism or idealism and put the problem into the context in which it really belongs, but it will constitute, so to speak, a further confirmation of our main argument.

II

The Changing Backgrounds of the Philosophy of Science. The New Physics.

A

The debate between realism and idealism in the nineteenth century was carried on against a background of ideas and beliefs about nature and the physical world which conditioned not only the terms in which the debate took place, but also the very presuppositions on the basis of which all philosophical discourse was conceived to be meaningful or intelligible. This background may be described briefly as belief in the literal truth of the Newtonian world picture. This belief included (*a*) a conception of matter as an independent entity and (*b*) a copy theory of physical knowledge which looked upon the concepts of the physical object as direct representations of the object in question.

This background has completely changed. The change is reflected in the very titles of the works of many who represent the 'new physics'. Sir James Jeans speaks of *The New Background of Science*, Sir A. S. Eddington writes of *The New Pathways of Science*, Professor Max Planck asks, *Where is Science Going?* stresses the novelties of its direction, and seems to suggest that the implications of its present position are an idealism of a Kantian sort. The change we have in mind—whatever its further implications may be—has, at least, made the debate between realism and idealism in science as it was then carried on, 'largely a thing of the past'.

The reasons for this general change in attitude and perspective are not easy to summarize in a few paragraphs. The chief reason seems to be a general drift, within physics itself, away from a materialistic and mechanical interpretation of the phenomena of nature. This general drift is, apparently, the result of no outstanding discovery or demonstration; in fact the great mass of evidence that has been accumulating rises at no point to the level of demonstrable proof. It is rather, as C. D. Broad has said, that 'the central mechanistic position has been taken by a series of flank movements rather than stormed by a victorious advance'.[1] The general effect of this major drift is to give us a vision of nature which seems no longer expressible in materialistic and mechanical terms and, if expressible at all, only in organic or 'spiritual' terms, however inadequate and misleading these terms may seem to be.

The most spectacular change is what has been described as 'the growing elusiveness of modern matter'. For the nineteenth century physicist matter was a clear, definite and tangible something occupying a position 'out there in space' and subject to certain unalterable laws, such as the law of gravitation and of the conservation of energy. But this traditional conception has become increasingly unsatisfactory. 'The "matter" of modern electrical and relativity theory bears no resemblance to the homely entity in which men had so easily believed. Matter has in a certain sense become more mysterious than mind and distinctly less familiar. It has become more vague, more intangible and its behaviour subject to less definitely known laws.'

The effect then is to change our entire feeling about matter. Modern physics throws doubt upon the entire notion of the solidity and changelessness of matter, revealing in the ultimate constituents that survive analysis entities which, besides being liable to certain cataclysms which completely alter their nature, are composed in the main not of 'matter' at all, but of empty space. A unit of matter is in fact little more than an electromagnetic field which, while theoretically extending over the whole of space, has its greatest activity in a certain region—a very different conception from the solid tangible entity of nineteenth-century physical philosophy. All this is, of course, a commonplace, but it is not sufficiently realized how conceptions such as these insensibly affect our attitude towards that natural realism which was supposed to be implicit in physical science.

Still more drastic changes in our scientific background have resulted from the Relativity Theory. It also has changed greatly our notion of matter, but it has also changed in equal degree our concepts of physical law. The most important consequence of this theory is the introduction of time as one of the conditions or determinants of the physical object. Space is undoubtedly bound up with time, so that it is not possible to make a true statement about space alone or about time alone, but only

---

[1] *Scientific Thought.*

about space-time. The point event is the unity of physical discourse.

Important consequences follow from this new conception. That which is chiefly significant in the present context is that a physical object is no longer a single permanent entity, but a series of fleeting temporal entities. Each member of the series we think of as enduring for a moment only, but is so like the other members that precede and succeed it as to be indistinguishable from it. We have, therefore, come to think of the physical 'thing' as, instead of being persistent in time, rather continually coming into and going out of existence. When we descend into the world of atoms and electrons the permanency and continuity reveal themselves as merely statistical. An inevitable consequence of this has been new and rather startling changes in our conceptions of physical causality and physical laws. This change has gone so far as to permit some physicists to contemplate the possibility of determinism in the physical macrocosm as compatible with indeterminism in the microcosm, and has led some of them to propose that the principle of chance be admitted as constitutive principle in the universe. It is not necessary for our present argument to attribute too much significance to this proposal, but the mere readiness to contemplate such a possibility indicates a significant change in perspective. What it means is that one of the secondary points for which idealism, as a general movement, has always been condemned, has in a sense been acclimated to science. For just as matter is possibly an ideal construction, so also the principle of universal determinism may be not so much a feature of reality as such as of our way of conceiving it.

It is, then, against this changing background that the present idealistic tendencies in science must be viewed. Miss L. S. Stebbing seems to be wholly right when she says that the 'two main factors are responsible for the tendency of modern physicists to adopt some form of idealism'. There is first the change in the conception of matter; secondly, 'the change in the status assigned by many physicists to natural law'.[1] It is not strange that they should be thus responsible for this tendency for, however valid the intrinsic logic of the argument may or may not be, the extrinsic force of the impression these factors make is

[1] L. S. Stebbing, *Philosophy and The Physicists*, p. 266.

undeniable. Nor is it strange that the popularizers of physical science with idealistic tendencies should have little difficulty in carrying large sections of the popular mind with them. Important then as these extrinsic influences have been, the real force of the idealistic train of thought in modern physics is to be found, I believe, in something much deeper—in the recognition, on the part of the physicists themselves, that these very changes reflect still more fundamental changes in the procedure and methodology of physics itself—in short, 'a new scientific epistemology'. Physical science has become self-critical—critical both of its purposes and its assumptions—and in the light of this self-criticism an idealistic element in its theory of knowledge has for many physicists become almost inevitable.

III

The Real Grounds For Idealism in Science: 'The New Scientific Epistemology.'

A

It is generally recognized that there is a strong idealistic tendency among physicists. A number of European physicists, as represented by interviews in the *Observer*, show, as C. E. M. Joad says, 'a tendency to take what might be broadly described as an idealist view of the universe.'[1] The historic forms of idealism which this tendency assumes are varied, but are predominantly of the Kantian type. It is probably true that, as C. B. S. Haldane has said, 'there is a general consensus of opinion among modern scientists that Kant is the philosopher who, more accurately than any other, expresses their instinctive attitude towards the universe.'[2]

Now this instinctive attitude, while having its origin partly in the general outlook which we have been describing, is really a conscious formulation of principles implicit in the methodology of physics itself. The new epistemology contains a number

---

[1] C. E. M. Joad, *Philosophical Aspects of Modern Science*, p. 72.

[2] This is also maintained by Eddington who, in *The Philosophy of Physical Science*, p. 188, writes 'If it were necessary to choose a leader among the older philosophers there can be no doubt that our choice would be Kant. . . . Kant anticipated to a remarkable extent the ideas to which we are now being impelled by the modern developments of Physics.'

of elements which, when closely examined, are really restatements of the older idealism in a new form. Of these we shall select three for special examination. They are (a) a change in that status of the physical object and of the constituents of 'matter'; (b) a change in the status of scientific law; (c) a change in the notion of 'existence' as employed in physics.

B

The first position has been stated in many forms. Thus Jeans holds it to be 'proved' that 'the objective and material universe of the nineteenth-century physicist' consists of 'little more than constructs of our minds' and to this extent 'modern physics has moved in the direction of idealism'.[1] Eddington puts it even more strongly. He maintains that the physicist has found that 'where science has progressed the farthest, the mind has but regained from nature what the mind has put into nature. We have found a strange footprint on the shores of the unknown. We have devised profound theories one after another to account for its origin. At last we have succeeded in reconstructing the creature that has made the footprint, and lo, it is our own.'[2]

I hold no brief either for these extreme forms of idealism or for the particular language in which they have been expressed. I have chosen them purposely to emphasize an aspect of the new epistemology which, whether expressed carefully or carelessly, is an essential element in it. It is that the objects of physics are to an incalculable degree ideal constructions— 'manufactured articles'. What these objects are 'made of' and what they are 'made for' becomes a question not for physics but for the philosophy of physics. The question how far this means movement in the direction of idealism, or, in other terms, a 'concession to idealism,' depends again on another philosophical, not scientific question, namely, the existential status of these objects.

It is for epistemological reasons of this sort that many physicists have moved in the direction of idealism. Another way of stating this is that scientific concepts are symbolic. Eddington speaks of 'the symbolic world of physics'.

We have already described the ways in which physics has

---

[1] Presidential Address to the British Association, 1934.

[2] *Space, Time and Gravitation*, pp. 200–1.

moved from the world picture of the nineteenth century; another significant change is in its conception of the *nature of this world picture*. This picture—and the concepts which make it up—are no longer conceived as copies or models but as symbols. As I have expressed it elsewhere, symbolism has become a scientific principle. The development of this principle—the different types of symbols in physics, the difference between the symbols in macroscopic and microscopic physics, between those applied to particular aspects of the physical world and to physical wholes—above all, the various theories of the scientific symbol—all these are important phases of the topic and the proper development of them would require a chapter in itself.[1] Here we shall confine ourselves to one aspect of the question which has special significance in the present context.

Three main types of symbols are generally recognized which we may describe as the sensible, the pseudo-sensible and the abstract. To the first belong the physical models, the exact correspondence of which to the physical object was, according to nineteenth-century physics, the criterion of truth in physical theory. The second class includes atoms and electrons and other similar entities. The third includes abstract concepts which are wholly insensible. Quantum mechanics actually replaces the electron and other physical systems by an abstract construct of this sort. Now the epistemological problem concerns the question of the correspondence of these constructs with the perceptible world, for upon some form of correspondence any realistic epistemology must rest. Modern physics does not deny all correspondence, but it does deny a one to one correspondence. The world of physics retains its connection with the perceptible world but that connection has now been put on a statistical footing. 'If the physicist were to restrict himself exclusively to the use of the sensible and pseudo-sensible constructs his ideal of an ultimate system of explanation would never come true.'[2]

The abandonment of the copy or model theory for the symbolic theory of physical concepts means at least that the older forms of realism, natural and representative realism, are

[1] This chapter may be found in chapter xi of my *Language and Reality*.

[2] See on this point H. Margenau, 'Methodology of Modern Physics,' *Philosophy of Science*, Vol. II, Nos. 1 and 2.

abandoned. If realism remains a part of modern scientific epistemology it is a very critical realism which makes large concessions to idealism. The element of relativity, which in another connection we saw any realistic minimum must allow for, is inevitable in the epistemology of modern physics. It includes not only the fact that knowledge does make a difference in the facts, but also the relativity which arises from the realization that our symbolic concepts are made for certain purposes and that this relativity to purpose cannot be eliminated from our evaluation of their truth. In any case, such realism as is here involved must be a critical realism.

C

These two elements in the new epistemology—the character of physical objects as ideal constructs and the notion of the relation of these constructs to the external world as symbolic—both raise exceedingly searching questions as to the existential status of these objects and as to the entire notion of existence as employed in physics. There is no question what 'existence' meant for the nineteenth-century physicist. He believed, in the main, that these constructs existed in precisely the same manner as the table of which they seemed so unbelievably to be the constituents. That, however, seems to be largely a thing of the past. The 'matter of modern electrical and relativity theory bears no resemblance to the homely entity in which they so easily believed'.

The question of the existential status of the physical objects arises directly out of the recognition of their symbolic character. The three types of symbols already distinguished, the sensible, the pseudo-sensible and the wholly abstract, although creating somewhat different problems with respect to correspondence, raise the same issue as regards existence. Physicists do not differ on the question of the nature of these objects—that they are constructions and that their relation to reality is symbolic; they disagree merely as to whether they 'exist' or not. This raises the entire question of what is meant by existence in physics, or as Eddington phrases it, 'the concept of existence in physics.'

There are still those, of course, who hold that the physical objects such as electrons or quanta simply exist as anything exists and that the meaning of existence requires no special consideration. It is safe to say, however, that the majority of critical physicists do not. There are those who would deny them existence in this primitive sense and speak of them merely as 'dummies' in the physicist's mathematical equations, or as 'fables with which we deck our mathematical equations'. In view of these differences of opinion within the science itself it seems safest to say that physical constructs cannot be said either to exist or not exist—whether in the plain or the metaphysical sense of existence. The value of a construct in physics—'its functional value in description and explanation—bears absolutely no relation to its special mode of existence. The ontological status, in the more ultimate sense, has to be determined in accordance with a more elaborate analysis of existence than that which is germane to physics.' Which is, to be sure, simply another way of saying that, so far as physics as method is concerned, it is above realism and idealism, and that the genuine issues which this opposition presents can be understood, and ultimately solved, only by recourse to a larger context of thought than that supplied by the abstractions of physics—in other words, by recourse to that universe of discourse which we call metaphysics.

D

There is one aspect of the new scientific epistemology which has far reaching implications for this entire problem, namely, the status of space-time in modern physics. This seems to be the point at which it can be most significantly discussed, for 'the concept of physical existence' and its relation to the notion of existence in general is bound up with our notions of existence in space and time.

The background of the physics of the nineteenth century, with its exclusive realistic premises, was determined by the Newtonian concept of absolute space and time. What Newton did was to *presuppose* the independent existence of space, time and motion, and then merely use synonyms to describe them. 'Absolute space, by its own nature without relationship to anything external always remains like unto itself and immovable. Relative space is any measure or changing dimension of that space which is defined through our senses by its location with regard to bodies, and is commonly used in place of immovable space—thus the dimension of subterranean, aerial or celestial space is defined by its location in relation to the earth.'[1]

The essential of Newtonian physics from this point of view is that physical quantities are measurable and that this measurement takes place in terms of motion in space and time. But in modern physics the measurement of space and time becomes a problem and this measurement involves physical quantities. According to Eddington, the innovation made by Einstein in his relativity theory was that the physical quantities involved in the measurement of space and time were brought to observational or experimental test. The application of this principle led to the recognition of the dependence of these measurements upon the observer's motion, and this in turn to a new conception of space-time.

At first sight the theory of relativity seems to have penetrated beyond the relative and subjective aspect of phenomena and to have reached that which is objective and absolute. It showed that the usual separation of space and time is subjective, being dependent upon the observer's motion, and it substituted a four dimensional space-time independent of the observer. But this objectivity and absoluteness is only apparent. Relativity theory, as has been repeatedly pointed out, permits the removal of the subjective effects of the personal characteristics of the individual observer, but it does not remove the subjective effects of the generic characteristics common to all observers.[2] In other words, the independent existence of space and time, as presupposed by the Newtonian physics, is not implied in our present physical conceptions.

It is true, of course, that physics presupposes a mind-independent nature. Even simple awareness presupposes for its very existence an objective field, and this field, it would seem, has as its most fundamental features real independent space and time. How much more, then physical knowledge! And yet we must proceed with caution here. The objective field of the physicist has indeed as its fundamental feature space and time, but what he calls space and time is, as he constantly warns us, an abstract and an enigmatic scheme to which we cannot transfer the rules of ordinary spatial and temporal experience. Space and

---

[1] *Philosophiae naturalis principia mathematica*, Scholium to Definition Eight.

[2] A. S. Eddington, *The Philosophy of Physical Science*, p. 86.

time as we conceive them have shared the fate of the sensory qualities. Like them, such experience is a subjective phenomenon.

In any case—and this is the only point I wish to make here—modern physics does not necessarily imply, either in method or in theory, the independent existence of space and time. Professor Max Planck in fact argues quite the contrary. Indeed, he attributes some at least of the difficulties of modern physics to the 'erroneous assumption' that everything that exists, exists in space and time and that space and time are existents. 'Men,' he continues, 'must learn to regard space and time not as objective realities to which everything must conform, but as concepts which in the region of phenomena must now be transcended. They are not objective realities independent of our consciousness and perhaps none exist.'

If, then, a realistic view of nature implies, as is often maintained, the independent existence of space and time, science cannot be said to be necessarily realistic. On the other hand, it cannot be said to be necessarily idealistic in the philosophical sense. The question of the concept of existence in physics, of which we have previously spoken, involves in relation to space and time the same problems as in the case of other physical concepts or notions. If we are forced to an epistemological realism or idealism with regard to space and time it must be on other grounds than those of physical science.[1]

E

There seems, then, to be no doubt that there is a new scientific epistemology in physics—one which would scarcely have been understood by the Victorian physicist. This is, as I have said, the real ground for the idealistic tendencies in modern physics. Let us then summarize our conclusions by contrasting the new with the old.

On the older view, science was organized, or as sometimes expressed, glorified 'common sense.' Physical knowledge, it was supposed, starts necessarily from the world of everyday experience—'the furniture of earth,' the tables, the stars, air, water, wind and heat and light. It proceeds then to analyse these objects into certain constituents which are alleged to be in some

[1] This issue will be taken up again in chapter ix.

sense more fundamental than the world with which it starts. It is a postulate of everyday experience that the world of tables, stars, etc. exists independently of the mind that perceives them —this is a part of the natural realism of everyday experience— or of the animal faith which constitutes the first resistance of realism. It follows almost inevitably that this independence will be extended to the constituents into which the objects are analysed and which, to the physicist, are more fundamental than the objects of common sense themselves. It is but part of that same type of naïve or uncritical realism which says that the *sensa* are literally spatio-temporal parts of the object and that the spatio-temporal parts that are not manifested in sensation are of precisely the same nature as those which are manifested.[1] This conception, however, the new scientific epistemology makes it difficult to maintain, and it is for this reason primarily that the opposition between realism and idealism as formerly understood is now a thing of the past. Both the furniture of earth and the constituents into which they are ultimately analysed, no longer have the status which belonged to them in the older physics. The consequence of all this has been a significant alteration in the physicist's conceptions of appearance and reality in the physical world.

The distinction between appearance and reality has always been a necessary part of physical science to the extent that that science has been critical, and in this sense physics has always been philosophical. For the physics of the nineteenth century the furniture of earth was the appearance of which the constituents into which it was analysed were the reality; the rainbow was the 'phenomenon', the molecules of colourless matter the reality. For the physics of the twentieth century the constituents also, in so far as they are constructions, are appearances also. This was always well understood by many philosophers but, as Eddington says, 'it places a somewhat different complexion on the matter when this (the doctrine of appearance and reality) is not merely a philosophical doctrine to which intellectual assent might be given, but has become part of the scientific attitude of the day, illustrated in detail in the current scheme of physics.'[2]

[1] Chapter iii, p. 79.

[2] *The Nature of the Physical World*, p. 332.

IV

The Debate Between Idealism and Realism in Physics: Its Dialectical Character. The 'Facts of Physics' and the 'Facts of Epistemology.'

A

With this general view of the changing background of the philosophy of science and of the far reaching changes which the new scientific epistemology has brought with it, we are now in a position to take up the main theses of this chapter. These are (*a*) the thesis that neither realism nor idealism can be proved or disproved by the facts of physics; and (*b*) that the arguments for or in refutation of this idealism, while purporting to be in the realm of 'fact', are really in the realm of dialectic, with all the consequences which, we have already seen, follow from this situation.

The first of these theses constitutes the heart of our entire argument, for if it is valid it constitutes a confirmation, within the sphere of physical science itself, of the general thesis of Chapter IV. It is, accordingly, to be viewed as a special case under the general argument of that chapter, namely, that neither realism nor idealism can prove their positions or refute their opponents. But in order to see the force of this argument it is necessary to determine first the nature of the facts of physics.

It is often argued, as we have seen, as though the facts of physics were the tables, the stars and water and wind, etc. But that is precisely what they are not. They are such things as the length of a thread of mercury in a thermometer, the shift of a bright spot on a galvanometer scale, the displacement of a dark line in a spectrogram, etc.—in short, sense data and the similarities and differences of these sense data, determined by all the refinements of modern methods. It is upon observations of this sort, more especially refinements of measurement, that the 'theories' of physics with their inferences to unobservables depend.

These, then, are the 'facts' of physics, and from these facts only physical theories, never epistemological or metaphysical theories, can be inferred. Professor Stebbing insists that modern physics 'has brought forward no new facts that necessitate idealism,' and in this she is wholly right. Nor has it brought forward any facts that necessitate realism. It has brought forward no new facts, nor will it ever do so—for the simple reason that these facts are relevant only to physical theories, and these theories, as physical theories, are indifferent to the philosophical issue. The *value* of a physical construct or theory is wholly independent of its ontological status. Physical theory demonstrates, or makes probable, the 'existence' of its entities in its specific context or universe of discourse, but so far as physics itself is concerned there are no further implications as to existence in any 'metaphysical' sense. In this respect the logical positivist is wholly right, namely, in his general statement to the effect that there are no empirical facts relevant to the question of existence or reality in this metaphysical sense.[1] It is, therefore, wholly vain to suppose that a philosophical issue such as that between epistemological realism and idealism should ever be settled by reference to any 'new facts' of science.

But physicists do argue for both realism and idealism in this philosophical sense, and in doing so they often suppose that they are arguing from the facts of physics. In this they are, I am sure, wholly wrong. They are arguing from the nature of physical knowledge or, if you will, from the facts of epistemology. But, it will be asked, is not such a statement absurd on the face of it? Is it not precisely upon the facts of modern physics that the entire argument of Professor Eddington's book is based? Are not the main chapters of this book, 'Epistemology and Relativity Theory,' 'Epistemology and Quantum Theory?' Certainly they are, but it is upon the *epistemology* of these two theories—not the theories themselves—that the argument is based and, as I have said, this fact is specifically recognized by Eddington himself. It is this that marks this new work as a notable advance philosophically over his earlier writings.

From the facts of physics, then, no argument either for idealism or realism can logically be drawn. There are no new physical facts which necessitate idealism. But many physicists are idealists. What then is the nature of their argument? It is dialectical in character, proceeding not from the facts of physics but from the nature of physical knowledge, and, we shall maintain, any refutation of idealism, any argument for realism is, and must be, of the same general character. Let us look first at the argument for idealism.

An examination of the actual argument of the idealistic

[1] Chapter i, pp. 26 f.

physicists shows this to be the case. 'We reach then the position of the idealist, as opposed to the materialist philosophy. The purely objective world is the spiritual world; and the material world is subjective in the sense of selective subjectivism.'[1] This selective subjectivism, as an analysis of the preceding argument shows, is one based wholly upon an epistemological analysis of the procedures of science, not upon their results. We are even told that 'generalizations that can be reached epistemologically have a security which is denied to those that can only be reached empirically'—a clear indication of the change of venue involved in the argument. In its essentials it is the same argument from the nature of knowledge as we find in Kant's dialectical argument—in no sense significantly changed by factual changes in physical science but solely by our better understanding of the nature of physical knowledge. What has happened is merely that the same facts about knowledge which the idealist philosophers found in the analysis of knowledge in general, the physicist finds exemplified in the special methodology of modern physics. If he also comes to the conclusion that the purely objective world is the spiritual world, it is also an argument to presuppositions of the essentially Kantian type.

Now it is not a question here, we must again insist, of the cogency of this argument—that is another matter—but merely of the type of argument involved. The fact that the nature of the argument is clearly recognized is the significant fact. Thus when Eddington writes of the 'logical confusion' of his realistic critics, 'involving a switch over from the epistemological view of the universe as the theme of knowledge to an existential view of the universe of which we have to obtain knowledge,'[2] the nature of the argument is fully recognized. Such a logical confusion does, I believe, underlie the arguments of the realistic critics to whom reference is here made. The nature of that confusion will become obvious as we examine the dialectical refutations of idealism in physics by the realists. To the study of these refutations we shall now turn.

B

We have now seen in a general way the nature of the driving force of idealism as it has appeared again in modern physics.

[1] A. S. Eddington, *The Philosophy of Physical Science*, p. 69.
[2] *Op. cit.*, p. 150.

Against this driving force and its arguments, the resistance of realism has again appeared in the form of certain critical studies, the chief of which are those of C. E. M. Joad and L. Susan Stebbing. *Philosophical Aspects of Modern Science*, by the former, and *Philosophy and the Physicists* by the latter; both, in their several ways, represent this resistance.

Both critics deny that modern physics leads necessarily to idealism, but whereas Miss Stebbing's book is more general in character, raising the entire question of the philosophical implications of physics, Mr Joad's is more specifically a refutation of the idealism of the physicists and the formulation of a general realistic theory of knowledge. Both critics have, however, certain points in common, and before proceeding to the 'refutation' itself certain general comments will be in place.

In developing their counter argument both critics make two main points, although with different degrees of emphasis, concerning the nature and method of the idealistic argument. The first concerns the language of the idealizing physicists, the second their logic. Briefly, their language is confused and misleading, and their logic or dialectic self-contradictory, and although they do not use the expression, essentially muddle headed. Our primary concern is with the second of these points, although the first is by no means negligible and will be considered in the sequel. The essential thesis of the critics is that *in the very statement of their idealism, the philosophizing physicists presuppose the very realism which they deny;* in other words, their idealism refutes itself. The refutation, like the argument itself, thus becomes dialectical in character. It is in Mr Joad's criticism that this aspect of the situation becomes clearest, and it is, consequently, his argument that we shall have chiefly in mind at this point.

In developing his own argument he recognizes this character. On page 119, he tells us that the objection he is about to raise 'is directed against the dialectical process presupposed by the philosophers of the appearance and reality type, and applies, he thinks, with particular force to the particular views under discussion,' namely, those of Eddington. Evidently then, since the argument itself is dialectical, the criticism or refutation must be dialectical also. This we shall see to be the case.

There is, Mr Joad maintains, 'one criticism of a general type to which a number of current interpretations of the universe based upon modern science are exposed, and of these Eddington's interpretation is only a special form' (p. 45). 'Modern science starts, as it must needs do, from the world of everyday experience and proceeds to analyse the world into certain constituents which are alleged to be in some sense more fundamental than the world with which it starts. It then endeavours, on the basis of these constituents which it uses as raw materials to account for the emergence of the every-day world, or perhaps, I should say, for the appearance of the every-day world. In other words, the world of every-day experience is *presupposed* (italics mine) as the starting point of a process of analysis and construction which results in the world of every-day experience.' This procedure he exemplified in Professor Eddington's account of the universe, and such procedure he feels must be mistaken.

In the first place, the world of common experience is the datum from which the physicist starts and the criterion by which he determines the validity of the structure which he raises. It is, therefore, presupposed as real and objective throughout. In the second place ('the-world building of the ordinary man') the world of ordinary experience which for the idealistic physicists is also an appearance or construction, 'begins and proceeds from messages which reach his brain along the nerve fibres. These messages originate—I am taking, I think what is on the whole, Professor Eddington's main view—from the impact of something on his sense organs. This something appears to be the entities of discontinuous physics, atoms, quanta of energy, etc, and so forth. But how are the atoms or quanta reached? By a process of inference and deduction from the world which the physicist observes. No physicist has seen an atom; what he does see is the world of every-day experience, from which he infers atoms and quanta. Thus atoms and quanta are the results of a process of inference based upon the observation of the every-day world, while at the same time they originate a process which ends in the construction of the every-day world. Thus the every-day world must be presupposed before the process which results in the construction can take place.' In other words the realism of the every-day world is presupposed.

'If these considerations are valid,' writes Mr Joad, 'their moral seems to be first, that metaphysical reasoning' (in our terms dialectic) 'cannot be legitimately used to discredit the observations of the familiar world, or to suggest that such observation does not truly acquaint us with the nature of what objectively is. If it is sound it undermines its own foundations. Secondly, metaphysical reasoning, based on scientific results, cannot be legitimately employed to show that scientific reasoning which appears to be valid, in the sense that it is conducted according to the accepted laws of reasoning, is in fact invalid in the sense that it reaches misleading results. If so used the suspicion which it casts on the human reasoning faculty inevitably reflects upon itself. In other words, the metaphysical reasoning of modern scientists, in suggesting, as it does, that their reasoning as scientists did not reach true conclusions about the world, suggests also that it does not reach true conclusions about their reasoning as scientists.'[1]

This *seems* to be the moral of this effort at refutation—and many will doubtless accept it as such—but to me the moral seems quite other. For it is precisely at this point that the logical confusion of which Professor Eddington complains takes place—the shift, namely, from the epistemological view of the universe as the theme of knowledge to the existential view of the universe of which we have to obtain knowledge.' The moral seems to me in fact to be that we should recognize this shift and seek to avoid the confusion into which Joad and many others have unwittingly fallen—a confusion of two wholly different types of reasoning. We should learn to see that this refutation, like the idealism which it seeks to refute, has force only if we assume a logically unsupported judgment of value as to the nature of genuine knowledge. I am not arguing, of course, that Professor Joad is not justified in making this assumption; I am quite sure that he is. Some form, of critical realism is as much a requirement of significant or genuine knowledge as some form of critical idealism. I am merely arguing that his supposed refutation of Professor Eddington's idealism no more refutes it

[1] In a recent critical comment on Professor Eddington's *The Philosophy of Physical Science*, entitled 'Sir Arthur Eddington Philosophizes,' Professor Joad asks a number of questions among which is the following: 'If the world of physics is subjectively selected from the objective world, how are we to know that it is an objective world for the world of physics to be selected from?' Surely the answer is obvious. We don't know. We can only believe it, or have that sort of assurance which Locke thought deserved the name of knowledge. See the *Spectator*, December 8, 1939.

than any of the refutations of idealism which we examined in Chapter IV—and for the same reasons. The logical confusion involved in his attempt at refutation is really a confusion of two different universes of discourse—and therefore of two 'languages,' that of common sense and the quite different mathematical-physical language of physics.

This confusion of languages is, however, also brought against the idealistic physicists as well, and the strictures made by Miss Stebbing on the 'popularizing physicists,' Eddington and Jeans, although a subtle, are not an insignificant part of her criticism. The language in which these physicists write is, we are told, highly emotional and figurative. The argument is shot through with extrinsic appeals to value considerations and is figurative in the sense that it uses the language of common sense in the sphere of mathematical physics where it inevitably misrepresents the actual situation.

Something less than justice is, I fear, done to these physicists on both counts. I doubt very much whether these appeals are extrinsic in view of the issues involved, nor do I believe that anything very significant could be said on these issues without using the figurative idiom of common sense. Nevertheless, it still remains true that, as she says, 'both physicists and philosophers have drawn philosophical consequences from mixing up of the language appropriate to physics with the language appropriate to the familiar world, and these consequences stand in need of revision' (p. 274). Miss Stebbing seems to draw the inference that if these physicists would stick to their mathematical language no inference as to either realism or idealism would follow. With this I should not be expected to disagree, but I should also wish to point out that if they did stick solely to their mathematical language, they could say nothing on this or any other problem of human or philosophical interest.

The point at issue comes to a head in the senseless wrangle over the two tables, the familiar table of common sense and the quite strange and wholly unfamiliar table of the physicist. 'There are,' it is said on the one hand, 'not two tables, for there is actually for the physicist, as physicist, no table at all. The habit of talking as though there were, leads we are told, inevitably to confusion.'[1] But we are told, on the other hand,

---

[1] L. S. Stebbing, *op. cit.*, p. 54.

that there *is* a table for the physicist. 'If the physicist is not concerned with chairs and tables then the astrophysicists are not concerned with stars.'[1] This is, I repeat, a wholly senseless wrangle, for if it were not how could it eventuate in two such contradictory statements? The fact is that this is one of those cases in which both are in a measure right. They are both talking about the same thing but in very different universes of discourse, and in very different languages. In the context of common sense in which chairs are to sit upon, there are chairs for the physicist as well as for any one else. In the context of mathematical physics there are no chairs, for the facts from which the physicist starts are not chairs and tables, nor even stars, water and wind, but the length of a thread of mercury, the displacement of a dark line in a spectrogram, etc. These facts of physics can, as we have already seen, lead only to physical theories, not to theories of knowledge.

This, however, is merely one peculiarly annoying case of a larger issue, namely, the question of the two languages. It is true that the idealistic physicist often confuses the two languages, but so does the realistic physicist, as we have seen. If the physicist does actually stick to his mathematical language, no inference to idealism is possible, as Miss Stebbing rightly maintains, but neither is any inference to realism, which is precisely the position that I maintain. Perhaps the physicist should stick to his own language, but if he does it is certain that he can say nothing of significance on this or any other philosophical issue. As a physicist he should, perhaps, not wish to say anything on any such issue, but, as a man and a philosopher, he may, alas, find it very difficult always to hold his peace. If, however, he does allow himself to speak to men on these more ultimate subjects he will of necessity use a language understanded of the people, and if he wishes to speak to philosophers he will have to speak in their idiom also. In any case—and this is the point I chiefly wish to make—if he sticks to his own language the issue of realism and idealism does not enter into the question at all.

C

Of the three specific theses under our general theme, two have now been developed. We have shown, I think, that neither

[1] A. S. Eddington, *op. cit.*, pp. 189 ff.

realism nor idealism can be proved or disproved by the 'facts' of physics. We have shown, in the second place, that the arguments for idealism in modern physics and the arguments in refutation of that idealism, while purporting to be in the realm of facts are really in the realm of discourse and dialectic. Both the arguments for realism and idealism are dialectical and refutations of these arguments are dialectical also. We now come to the third thesis, namely, that modern physics, in both its methods and its results, is beyond realism and idealism.

In the sense that physical science is indifferent to the issue, many physicists would admit this thesis. 'Strictly speaking,' writes E. A. Milne, 'physics has no philosophy. It has method.'[1] Being merely method, the issue of realism and idealism is, for physics, as the positivist asserts, really meaningless, for it makes no difference to his facts. He has his methods for determining what is real or unreal in his world and that is all with which he is concerned. There is something to be said for Mr Broad's contention that the attitude of the modern physicist 'becomes more and more phenomenological, his objects being patterns like the patterns on the wall.' In which case we might, indeed, say that physical science is beyond realism and idealism in the sense that it is neither. And yet this cannot be quite the case. This may, indeed, be all there is to physics as method, but it can scarcely be all there is to knowledge of which physical science is a part. After all physics, to be genuine knowledge, cannot escape the presuppositions of knowledge as a whole. The significance of all knowledge, of whatever sort, rests we have seen, on two postulates neither of which can apparently be denied without loss of its 'peculiar significance'. The postulate of antecedent being or mind-independence and the postulate of intelligibility, or mind-dependence, are both necessary for any tenable theory of knowledge. From neither of these can any form of knowledge, including that of physics, cut itself loose without stultifying its very nature as knowledge.[2]

On my view, then, the thesis that physics, with its new scientific epistemology, is beyond realism and idealism must ultimately be interpreted in a second sense, in the sense, namely,

[1] E. A. Milne, F.R.S., *Some Points in the Philosophy of Physics*. An address before the British Institute of Philosophy, on October 17, 1933. *Philosophy*, Vol. IX, No. 33.

[2] Chapter v, pp. 142 f.

that it implies both. This I believe to be the true philosophical implication of the new scientific epistemology, and the one actually necessitated by the present situation. The best statement of this position is, I think, that of Hermann Weil. 'Science,' he tells us, 'proceeds realistically when it builds up an objective world in accordance with the demand—that the objective configuration is to contain all the factors necessary to account for the subjective appearance; no diversity in experience that is not founded on a corresponding objective diversity.' On the other hand, science 'concedes to idealism that this its objective world is not given but only propounded like a problem to be solved and that it can be constructed only by symbols.' Thus, as Weil says, 'the *Weltanschauliche* contrast of realism and idealism is reflected within science by two non-contradictory methological principles.'[1] In other words, modern science—in its very methodology and in its very symbolic form—implicitly contains both principles. But the point I wish to emphasize here is, as Weil rightly sees, that the two are non-contradictory. If this is true, as I believe it to be, we have within the methodology of physics itself a striking confirmation of the argument of Chapter V. Between a sufficiently critical realism and a sufficiently critical idealism there is no inconsistency—within science any more than in any form of knowledge.

V

The Philosophy of Nature. Metaphysical Perspectives.

A

With these conclusions the main theme of this chapter has been worked out and, in so far as its theses are validated, the main purpose of this chapter has been realized—namely, to show that the positions developed in the preceding chapters are confirmed by the nature and method of physical science. But for many 'philosophizing physicists' themselves the situation has more significance than this. One cannot make these concessions to idealism without apparently conceding a good deal more. It seems hardly conceivable that one should think of the 'objective world as a problem to be solved and to be constructed

[1] Hermann Weil, *Mind and Nature*, 1933, p. 38.

only by symbols,' without giving a privileged position to the mind that constructs them. Many physicists feel justified, therefore, in saying, 'we reach then the position of the idealist, as opposed to the materialist philosophy. The purely objective world is the spiritual world and the material world the subjective.'

The driving force of this metaphysical idealism derives, of course, from motives which transcend the realm of physics and physical science. When they tell us that they 'incline to the idealistic theory that consciousness is fundamental and that the material universe is derivative from consciousness,' we may be permitted to doubt that, as they further say, 'this inclination towards idealism is the outcome largely of modern scientific theories.' That these theories have had their weight is undoubted, although, as we have seen, as physical facts can lead only to physical theories not to philosophical, so these physical theories of themselves cannot lead to metaphysical theories. The actual driving forces, for the physicist as for other men, are what they have always been in the history of philosophy, namely, humanistic and axiological. The charges brought against these idealistic physicists—that the motivation of their thinking is often moral and religious, and thus extrinsic to the methodology of science, is partly true. But the philosophical physicists are men as well as scientists—not merely machines for registering pointer readings. If this is so it is inconceivable that they should not share the motives of men; indeed, if they did not they would not be philosophers. They can hardly be expected to be indifferent to those considerations which have always made the more ultimate problems of the philosopher also the fundamental problems of men.

B

The issue here hinges, I believe, on the question of the objective or aim of physical science. On this question there is considerable difference of opinion among physicists themselves. In the nineteenth century it was the common idea that physical science 'is a systematic effort to observe and then to explain the phenomena of nature. The progress of science is thus the gradual acquirement of a clearer and more comprehensive discernment

of the truth behind phenomena in so far as it can be apprehended by rational inference from phenomena themselves.'
This idea is, however, many physicists now inform us, 'quite
false'—that is to say, 'it does not correspond to what science
actually is, whatever we think it should be.' It consists solely
in 'finding and establishing rational relations between phenomena.'[1]

I should not wish to dispute this conception of the objective
of science *as method*—indeed, it is my own view, as has been
apparent all along. I should wholly agree with Professor Dingle
that the electron is 'not an object like a stone or a star,' but is
rather a 'concept formed to account for certain phenomena
which are many and various, and its existence and character
alike are ascribed to it not from observation but solely in
obedience to the necessity of making it account for these phenomena.' That is, indeed, the import of my entire treatment of
symbolism in science. I should agree with him also that 'where
physicists differ is not the question whether the electron is a
concept but on the question of whether it is merely a concept,'
although that is, of course, a significant difference. So far as
scientific method is concerned the electron, like any other
physical construct, functions solely as a means of establishing
relations between phenomena. 'Intelligibility in science consists,' as Miss Stebbing says, 'exclusively in necessary relations
The fact is no longer isolated and it is therefore intelligible.'[2]

All this is true, then, so far as physics is a method and not a
philosophy. The real question is rather whether a genuine
understanding of it as method does not in the end compel a
philosophy also—whether a science of nature does not involve
ultimately a philosophy of nature. I am quite sure that it does.
However, *qua* physicist, one may confine himself merely to
establishing rational relations between phenomena, as a man
the scientist will inevitably seek some understanding of the
'nature' which is the object of his concern. There are metaphysical perspectives even to physical science and it is these that
I should now like to suggest.

The method of natural science inevitably eventuates in a

---

[1] See on this point Professor Herbert Dingle in 'A Current Misconception of
Science,' *The Hibbert Journal*, October 1939.

[2] L. S. Stebbing, *A Modern Introduction to Logic*, p. 392.

scientific concept of nature, and it is this concept rather than the particular theories of science which, for the philosopher, is the significant thing. I think there is little doubt as to what that concept is and what its implications for the philosopher are. In his *The Concept of Nature* Whitehead rightly tells us that 'the homogenity of method,' arising out of the nature of science already described, eventuates in a concept which excludes all reference to values. But he also tells us, equally truly, that it is precisely these values, thus excluded, that constitute the 'clue to metaphysical synthesis.' In other words, despite their exclusion by scientific method, the values are still there and thus is opened up, even for the physicist who excludes them, metaphysical perspectives which their presence demands and which the physicist, in so far as he is a philosopher, will also wish to explore. Not however, until, as a man, he not only acknowledges these values, but has also fully realized what their existence and nature really presuppose, is any such metaphysical synthesis possible.

It is understandable, to be sure, that many, like Jeans, should suppose that merely as physicists, and from a purely scientific concept of nature, they have 'reached the position of an idealistic as opposed to a materialistic philosophy,' but in this, they would, I think, be mistaken. At most they could say that science, properly understood, does not imply materialism. It is understandable that, like Eddington, they should suppose that the methods of physics themselves lead to an objective world of spirit into which physical methods and symbols are not fitted to penetrate, but in this they would also be mistaken. At most, they could say what these methods, when properly understood, far from denying a world of values and spirit, actually make us quite sure that it is there. To this extent then, even physical science itself opens up metaphysical perspectives, although by the very nature of its methods and symbols it cannot explore them. The clue to any such metaphysical synthesis is in the values which the homogeneity of scientific method excludes. To the following up of this clue the next chapter will be partly devoted.

Chapter VIII

Realism, Idealism and 'The Philosophy of Spirit.' The World of Values.

I — A

THE THESIS of the preceding chapter is that the philosophy of nature or of science is beyond epistemological idealism and realism. This may be stated in several ways. From the developments of modern physics, the basal science of nature, no inference can be drawn either way—that is for an exclusive idealism or an exclusive realism. On the other hand, modern physics concedes something to both positions and must so concede. In both these senses physical knowledge is beyond realism and idealism.

So much then for the world of physical objects. But there is another world which, in contrast with nature, we may call the world of spirit. When we enter this world, and consider man's attempt to know and understand the human spirit, the situation seems at first wholly different. It is here that we should expect idealism in its multiform phases to celebrate its chief victories and to be given the privileged position in the interpretation of the world. The implications of this world we should expect to be wholly idealistic.

This is, indeed, the view generally held. Idealism from Plato to Hegel has been primarily a humanistic movement. So long as it deals with the human, the social and the historical—with mind subjective or objective—it seems to be at home. It is when it deals with physical objects, and the sciences concerned with these objects, that its inadequacy displays itself. This view is held alike by idealists and realists. It was, according to both, because of Hegel's power of interpretation of 'mind' that his philosophy had its extraordinary vogue; it was because of its failure to explain nature that it broke down. In other words, the implications of the humanities are idealistic.

The situation is, however, by no means as simple as this. Modern thought is full of paradoxes and one of the paradoxes of the present situation is precisely this—that while there is a strong tendency in physics towards idealism, the sciences of mind and of society have in recent times tended, on the whole, more and more towards naturalism and realism. The motives under-lying this tendency are, of course, many. There is the prevailing assumption of the nineteenth century that naturalistic realism is an essential part of the structure of science and of the scientific method, and that if there are any sciences of life and mind they must follow this model. In the second place, however, there is a deep-seated revolt against a certain element of 'rationalism' that has been inherent in idealism from the beginning. The increasing sense of the meaninglessness of life, and of the world in which our life is lived, makes all idealism repugnant to the modern mind. In the sphere of the human, realism is, it seems, almost identical with irrationalism. In contrast to Hegel's, 'the real is the rational and the rational is the real,' for the modern, it might almost be said, the real is the irrational and the rational always a 'rationalization'.

This then is in part the truth. 'The Crisis in Idealism,' as A. Liebert has called it, is precisely this—the fact of its betrayal in the house of its friends. It is the anti-idealistic tendencies in the various *Geisteswissenschaften*, which he pictures with such significant detail, which, rather than any developments in the physical sciences, constitute the real driving force of present-day naturalistic realism. But while this is true it is only half of the picture. On the other hand, there are powerful forces within these sciences, some of which we shall consider later, leading to a reconsideration of this attitude. Self-criticism of their methods and assumptions, on the part of the so-called social sciences themselves, is bringing about a revision of their epistemology which is no less significant than the revision in the epistemology of physical science. Here also there is a 'resurgence of idealism' which must be taken into account in any view of the situation as a whole.

This crisis in the *Geisteswissenschaften* or 'social' sciences raises the entire question of the possibility of a science of the human. The notion of such sciences is in the main a recent development and dates primarily from the application of the concept of naturalistic evolution to the human and the social. Formerly, men spoke of natural philosophy and moral philosophy, and the moral philosophy of which they spoke rested upon wholly different presuppositions from those which determine the humanistic sciences today. The possibility of a science of the human, in the sense understood today, would have been denied outright by these moral philosophers.

Now there is no question, of course, of 'science' of the human in the general sense of science as knowledge, but there is every reason to question whether there is science of the human in the narrow sense of science as understood by the naturalism of the nineteenth century. Indeed, as we shall see, it is precisely this issue which has come to the fore in recent thought and which constitutes one of the most important elements in the changing backgrounds against which the problem of idealism and realism must be viewed. In any case the situation within the humanities themselves—and in the so-called sciences which deal with the human—is highly ambiguous. The assumption of the unity of science, and of the similarity of method in all the sciences, which dominated the nineteenth century is now seriously questioned. The crisis within the 'social sciences,' of which their practitioners are more or less aware, raises the question whether these sciences are really science at all. Whatever we may say on this point, there is undoubtedly knowledge of the human and the social, and this knowledge is more or less organized, sufficiently organized, we may suppose, to deserve the name of science. In any case we shall assume that it is and shall use the term humanistic sciences as our equivalent for the general notion of *Geisteswissenschaften*.[1]

B

The theme of this chapter corresponds then, *mutatis mutandis*, with that of the preceding chapter. Broadly stated, it is the implications of the humanities, and the knowledge of the human, for our problem of realism and idealism. Here also, to the question whether the humanities and humanistic sciences are realistic or idealistic, we shall answer neither, exclusively, that they too are beyond the opposition and include elements of both. This chapter may be looked upon also as an application to a specific sphere of the position and principles of the study as a whole and as, therefore, further confirmation of our general thesis.

[1] It is unfortunate that the only term in English for the notion of the *Geisteswissenschaften* is the social sciences. The *differentia* of these sciences is not sociality which is at best but a secondary aspect of their material and character. The fundamental *differentia* is the 'human' and we shall accordingly speak of the humanistic sciences.

Nevertheless, while the theme is in general the same, its development must, for obvious reasons, take a somewhat different course from that followed in the preceding chapter. The different situation in the sphere of the philosophy of spirit requires that the issue shall be presented in a somewhat different way. It is generally recognized that the issue here is primarily between idealism and naturalism, and when we use the term realism here we shall have in mind the naturalistic realism of which we have already spoken. The issue is then, in a sense, different from that of the preceding chapter. There the problem concerned the concessions which modern scientific epistemology must make to idealism; here the question is what concessions the humanities and the humanistic sciences, primarily idealistic in temper, must make to naturalism.

This general theme and its development will also include certain specific theses which we shall attempt to 'prove'. We shall attempt to show, in the first place, that the philosophy of the humanistic sciences implies neither epistemological idealism nor realism, but that, in fact, there has been a meeting of extremes in this field which makes their methodology in a very real sense beyond realism and idealism. We shall attempt to show, secondly, that in this sphere also there is no proof or disproof of either position; that here also the arguments on both sides are dialectical, and that when the nature of the human, and of knowledge of the human, is understood, that knowledge cannot be made intelligible on either idealistic or realistic assumptions alone. Finally, we shall attempt to show that while the humanistic sciences are beyond realism and idealism in the sense defined, the issue raised by the opposition of idealism and naturalism is of a different character and requires for its solution considerations which go beyond questions of epistemology and involve a philosophy of spirit.

II

The Changing Backgrounds of the Controversy. Evolutionary Naturalism. Matter, Life, Mind, Value.

I — A

The changing backgrounds of the controversy in the sphere of physical science have already been noted. It seems scarcely an exaggeration to say that 'the opposition between realism and idealism, as formerly understood is now a thing of the past.' Scarcely less significant is this general change in background against which the problem of the humanities must be viewed. Perhaps we may be able to say that in this sphere also the opposition between realism and idealism as formerly understood is now a thing of the past.

The development of this part of our argument is much more difficult, for the reason that it concerns general notions of life and mind, and in this sphere the situation is not so clearly defined as in the sphere of physical science. The two poles about which the issues of realism and idealism have always revolved are those of matter and mind. In both spheres fundamental changes have taken place in our concepts which have vitally affected the issue. But whereas in the sphere of the physical sciences the changes in our concepts of matter, as described, are relatively clear, and their effect on the philosophical problem definitely understood, the same cannot be said of mind and spirit. 'Matter' may have become elusive, but mind has become still more so—so much in fact that it is sometimes denied that there is any such thing at all, that in psychology, the science of mind, all that remains is but a name. The so-called crisis in psychology which makes it possible for such diametrically opposite positions as those of Behaviourism and Gestalt psychology to suppose themselves to be forms of the same science, shows how utterly ambiguous the entire notion has become.

One thing may, however, be said with reasonable certainty. The background of nineteenth-century naturalism and realism in the humanities and humanistic sciences is to be found in evolutionary naturalism and the notions of life and mind connected with that philosophy. The concept of evolution, first developed for the science of living things, was then extended to the realm of mind and spirit. With respect to the human, for the first time it was felt that knowledge here would finally be placed upon a scientific basis, and this scientific basis involved naturalism and realism. Extended first to the instincts and emotions which man obviously shares with animal forms of life, it was gradually extended to include his morals and his knowledge—to the 'naturalization' of the entire spirit of man.

13

B

This was then, in the most general terms, the background of nineteenth-century naturalism and realism in the sphere of the human and of the humanistic sciences. It was, however, when this temper and attitude were strongest that the background itself began to change, and with it corresponding changes in our notions of mind and spirit began to appear. The changes which have taken place in this sphere have also not been brought about by any demonstrative proofs, but rather by a series of flank movements—namely, first, gradual and almost insensible changes in the conception of evolution itself and, secondly, changes in our conceptions of the methodology of the sciences of life and mind.

The concept of evolution itself has gradually undergone significant changes, due partly to new factual elements in the sciences of life and mind, due partly to considerations of a philosophical nature. The classical conception of evolution, known as the Darwinian-Spencerian, has suffered changes as great perhaps as the classical Newtonian physics. Its conceptions of life and mind have been modified as significantly as the Newtonian conception of matter. The general effect of this movement has been to give us new views of mind which have made it increasingly difficult to 'naturalize' it in the sense of earlier conceptions of evolution.

These changes have given rise to new names, the chief of which are Creative Evolution and Emergent Evolution. It is not within the range of our present purpose to discuss in detail either the factual grounds for these new conceptions or the philosophical reasons which have led gradually to the abandonment of earlier notions—these in their essentials are common knowledge—but rather to note the changes in 'intellectual climate,' which constitute the background of our present notions of life and mind. These may best be brought out by comment on the two notions, creative and emergent.

Both terms register, in different ways, changes in our conceptions of life and mind, as significant for our present purposes as the changes in our conceptions of matter brought about by the development of modern physics. The notion of emergence is, perhaps, in one way of primary significance. It tells us that while life and mind have 'emerged' in a process of evolution in time, and are, therefore, conditioned by elementary processes of the physical and chemical type, they cannot be explained by them in the sense of reductionism. The autonomy of both life and mind from the standpoint of knowledge and explanation is the cardinal notion. The notion of creative, although in one sense not so primary, is even more significant in a philosophical sense. It tells us that the evolutionary process itself, in which these forms or levels have emerged, cannot be understood as a 'mechanical' rearrangement of unchanging elements but rather as itself creative of novelties.

These changes in our concepts of evolution have given rise to a new type of naturalism, and with it has come a decided change in the intellectual climate in which the sciences of the human are prosecuted. Men speak of a 'new naturalism' and contrast it with the 'past-naturalism' of the nineteenth century. Of this new naturalism as such we shall speak more at length in a later context;[1] here we are concerned wholly with the notion of mind and of the 'place of mind in nature' which these changes have brought about. The notion of mind being ultimately inseparable from that of life, the notion of life demands our first consideration.

The important change here is the notion of the autonomy of life from the standpoint of knowledge and understanding. In the sphere of the living the 'organism' appears to be a more genuine embodiment of unity than the more mechanical conceptions envisaged, and has in itself a self-preservative tendency such as gives rise to the 'struggle for existence.' The very nomenclature of biology, as J. S. Haldane writes, 'embodies the conception that life, in whatever form it may occur, occurs as a specific whole in which the parts and actions are essentially related to one another and cannot be isolated without destroying that nature.' In the same context he makes it clear that 'the very essence of these wholes is to be self-regulative.'[2] It is true that within the biological sciences themselves there is difference of emphasis—'the embryogenists and naturalists,' as Bergson maintains, 'believe much less readily in the physico-chemical character of vital actions than do the physiologists—' but the dominant tendency, and that alone with which we are here

[1] Chapter ix.

[2] *The Sciences and Philosophy* [Gifford Lectures], p. 92.

concerned, is in the direction of these changes in our notions of life. The revival of vitalistic conceptions is one aspect of this change, but no theory of vital control or of 'entelechy' can, of course, explain the type of unity which the living thing possesses. At best the neo-vitalist position 'can only be formulated as being that the unity of the organism is its fundamental characteristic and that it has to be taken account of if any complete or approximately complete explanation is to be given of the processes which occurring within it, serve to maintain it in existence.' But even so, merely in its negative function, vitalism is significant.

In the setting of our changing concepts of life still more significant changes have taken place in our notions of mind and of its place in nature. As the autonomy of the living is becoming the postulate of the biological universe of discourse, so also is the autonomy of the mental the postulate of the psychological. Here too, it may be truthfully said, the mind appears to be a more genuine and more unique embodiment of unity than the atomistic psychologies of the nineteenth century had envisaged. As we may speak of a criterion of the living—and find it in the notion of living wholes that are self-regulative—so we may speak of a criterion of the mental and describe it as intentionality or meaning. Intentionality, meaning, are all-pervasive aspects of mind as we understand it, and it is these aspects which determine its autonomy and its unique place in nature.

This changing background of the humanistic sciences has brought about a crisis similar to that which appears in the opposition of mechanism and vitalism in biology, expressing itself in a deep-seated divergence both as to the object and the methods of the sciences of mind. This divergence appears in its sharpest form in the contrast between Behaviourism and Gestalt psychology, and while the divergence appears at many points it is sharpest, perhaps, on the question of meaning. Meaning, intentionality, are all-pervasive in mind as we understand it, of the very *essence* of mind, and many psychologists recognize that, without these fundamental categories, knowledge of mind is *ipso facto* impossible. Behaviourism, being atomistic in principle, cannot cope with meanings and, in its most exteme and consistent forms, excludes the problem as non-psychological. Gestalt psychology, on the other hand, recognizing meaning as the very criterion of mind, and insisting that meaning is bound up with totalities or wholes, also holds that the method of the study of mind must be determined by the fact. In further insisting upon the principle of non-correspondence between stimulus and meaning, it maintains that there can be no understanding of mind by any method that seeks to build up meaning out of the summation of sense elements, conditioned reflexes, or what not. In sum, the insistence upon the uniqueness and autonomy of mind, characteristic of some at least of the tendencies in present-day psychology, is symptomatic of our changing conceptions of mind and of its place in nature.

It was one of the main assumptions of the nineteenth century that psychology constituted the basal science for those studies known as *Geisteswissenschaften*. It became evident, however, that psychologies of the elementaristic type were incapable of fulfilling this function. The modern mind was therefore faced with a dilemma. Either it could hold fast to the conception of psychology as a science which actually gives us knowledge and understanding of mind, as intentional and characterized by meaning, or, accepting the notion of psychology as a natural science in the accepted sense, deny its function as the exclusive source of the knowledge or understanding of mind, and turn to other cultural sciences in forming our conceptions of mind. It is the second alternative that, in the last decades, has in the main, been chosen.[1]

It is no part of our purpose to enter into the specific problems of mind, but merely to record the changing concepts correlated with our changing concepts of evolution—changes which condition more or less the character of the issue of realism and idealism as it appears in the humanistic sciences. Not only is the emerging conception of mind different in fundamental ways from that of the naturalism of the nineteenth century, but with it has come also a change in our conception of the place of mind in nature, giving rise to what we have already referred to as the new naturalism. Of the significance of these changes we shall have more to say later.

[1] These issues are treated in greater detail in my chapter in *Contemporary Idealism in America*, entitled, 'The Philosophy of Spirit: Idealism and the Philosophy of Value.'

C

Two things stand out, I think, with reasonable clearness. The first is the gradual emergence of a new conception of mind and of its place in nature; the second is a corresponding revision of our conceptions of knowledge of mind, and consequently, of the methodology of the humanistic sciences.

There are few thinkers, of any philosophical sect whatsoever, who would not be wary of reducing meaning and value, which belong to the level of mind or spirit, to any lower levels of being. The wide acceptance of the negative aspect of the doctrine of Emergent Evolution registers this wariness. It has also a bearing on our problem of realism and idealism in the humanistic sciences. In interpreting the significance of this theory Professor R. B. Perry has wisely said that, 'by employing this notion it has been thought possible to reconcile the essentially realistic insistence on the priority, from a genetic and explanatory point of view, of processes of the elementary type such as those of physics and chemistry, with the essentially idealistic insistence on the genuine uniqueness and in a sense privileged character of the cultural processes of a higher and more complex type.'

In saying this much one has said a great deal—something which has all along been one of the major contentions of an idealistic philosophy of mind. And in saying this much, one is compelled, I think, to say a great deal more. The next step—and one not so very far off—is to recognize a fundamental difference between the methodology of the natural sciences and that of the humanistic sciences of mind and spirit. The recognition of this difference is one of the outsanding features of the present situation. To show the stages of its development is our next task.

III

The New Epistemology in the Humanistic Sciences. The Limits of Natural Science. The Realism of Values.

A

It goes without saying that these changes in our notions of mind have not been without their influence on the methodology of the 'social sciences'. Just as the conceptions of nineteenth-century evolutionism seemed necessarily to involve, not only the realistic temper, but a certain philosophical naturalism, so the changes which we have described have insensibly had their effect upon the present status of these sciences. But after all, the problem of epistemological realism and idealism is an epistemological problem and here, as in the case of the physical sciences, it is problems of knowledge growing out of the methodology of the sciences which are determinative. Here then, as in the former case, we may note changes in our views of knowledge of the human which may also be characterized as a new epistemology.

This change is indicated, and may indeed be more or less symbolized, by an epoch-making pronouncement of Dilthey. 'Things we explain, the soul we understand.' Eunciated in opposition to the physiological and mechanistic psychology of his day, it became the rallying cry for certain movements in the humanistic sciences[1] (*Geisteswissenschaften*) which, if they have not changed completely the standpoint of these sciences, have certainly brought with them consequences of great significance —consequences, moreover, which have a direct bearing on our problem of realism and idealism. The contrast of understanding with explanation in Dilthey's statement suggests the main issues between the new epistemology and the old. Knowledge of the human—to be genuine knowledge—involves a kind of understanding which is not necessary in the knowledge of 'things'. This understanding, moreover, involves an appreciation and acknowledgment of the values which determine human activity. The problem of the knowledge of values thus becomes part of the problem of knowledge in the social or humanistic sciences.

This new epistemology contains a number of elements but we shall select two for special consideration in the present context. These we shall describe: (*a*) as the notion that the humanistic sciences have a unique object and a unique method; this involves the further conception of the limits of the natural sciences. Secondly, (*b*) the important conception that knowledge in this sphere is understanding and that understanding involves

---

[1] This statement in German reads: 'Die Naturrklaären wir; das Seelenleben verstehen wir.' It occurs in the famous dispute between Dilthey and Ebbinghaus over the nature of psychology.

cognition of values—in short, these sciences are value sciences.

B

The first element in the new epistemology is, then, the notion of the uniqueness of the object of the humanistic sciences. The general movement of which this is a phase may be described as a tendency towards the decentralization of the sciences.

The most distinctive characteristic of nineteenth-century thought from this angle was its absolute confidence in the unity of science. That is, that all the 'sciences', whether physical, biological or social, would prove to be continuous and all exemplifications of one elementary method. There were pronounced difficulties in biology, and still more in the sciences of mind, for life and mind could not be brought without certain distortions into the primary mechanistic scheme, yet it seemed eminently reasonable to suppose that this must be due, not to any difficulty inherent in the principle, but rather to defects in our factual knowledge. The recognition of the delusive character of this ideal is, however, one of the outstanding characters of the present situation.

The change has come about in two ways. In the first place, it has arisen directly out of the self-critical reflections within the specific humanistic sciences themselves. 'More intelligent intercourse with the objects of these sciences,' to use a phrase of Ernst Troeltsch, forced a critical revision of this dogma. While the belief in the fundamental homogeneity of science was quite generally accepted in the nineteenth century, actually the various sciences made their way as best they could independently of this dogma. As their intercourse with their objects became more intelligent, the frank recognition was forced upon them of the internal diversity of reality, and consequently, of the necessity of a corresponding diversity of methods of knowing and understanding. To this was added also a specifically epistemological movement, the full influence of which on the humanistic sciences has not yet been appreciated.

The decentralization of the sciences took place then, in the first instance, in a purely empirical fashion. The physicist and the historian might, for instance, suppose that they were doing the same thing—and concerned with the same kind of objects (and in most cases they probably did so believe)—but they were able to say this only because in most cases neither knew actually what he was really doing. Physical science was, as we have seen, the first to become thus self-conscious, but the humanistic sciences could not long escape. It was only when they came to interpret their own cognitive activity and became aware of problems of method, that they realized that they were doing quite different things and concerned with quite different objects.

Physical science, as Poincaré pointed out, found that it was interested only in repeated phenomena—in uniformities and universals. It might find out, on more critical reflection, that these uniformities or laws are not, as first supposed, things in nature, but rather statistical in character; but, however conceived, these alone are the objects of its interest and knowledge. On the other hand, the historian (the term historian being used in the broad sense of the term) found that he was interested primarily in unique and individual events and with the meaning of these events. The historian may, in deed, speak of historical laws, but he has come increasingly to understand that they are not laws in the sense of those of physics. This distinction has been stated by numerous historians and philosophers of history, but may be considered as epitomized for our purpose in Rickert's *Die Grenzen der naturwissenschaftlichen Bergriffsbildung.*

C

This notion of the limits of the natural sciences and of their methods, marks at once the acceptance of the important principle of the decentralization of the sciences and the development of a new notion, namely, that the humanistic sciences are value sciences, or *Wertwissenschaften.* It is partly against the background of this changed conception that the problem of realism and idealism must be viewed.

The notion, as is well known, was first clearly developed in connection with the 'science' of history. It was realized, first of all, that knowledge in this sphere could not be subsumed forthwith under the current conception. The notion of knowledge which identifies it with the beholding or grasping of wholly independent and self-sufficient objects reaches an *impasse* when it comes to deal with historical science in contrast with physics.

But it was also realized that the mind-dependence of the his-historical object includes dependence of a special kind—namely, dependence upon values for its understanding. The notion of history as *Wertwissenschaft* is an essential part of the present methodology of history, and has been expressed in many forms, but the essential point in all is the recognition of the fact that the *material* of history is itself 'value-charged', so to speak, and that this character of the material determines the character of the method.

The material of history is, of course, 'facts'—but they are facts of a unique order, namely, *artifacts*. To a large extent the material of history is the artifacts of various kinds with which the anthropologist and the archeologist deal—the various products of the hand and brain of man. But, properly understood, the term includes much more; not only monuments but documents, not only works of art, but works of culture, such as economic and political institutions. All these, in the first instance at least, constitute the sources of historical knowledge. It is the understanding of what really was—what these meant to those who made them—that constitutes historical reconstruction. This understanding is, however, possible only through recognition of the purposes and values of those who made the artifacts. Many historians ignore this aspect, and, consequently, deceive both themselves and us. They suppose themselves to be understanding what really was, when they have merely produced what they call the 'factual past', apparently quite unaware that mere physical events in time are not historical facts at all, but become historical only through interpretation.

This view has, of course, been grossly misunderstood. There is a sense in which history, like any other 'science', starts with facts of experience and develops theories to explain the facts. There is a sense also in which it develops rules of evidence for the confirmation and verification of facts. But that is not the issue. The issue concerns the nature of the facts and these, it is now generally understood, are of the kind above described. There are constant attempts to show that history deals with value-free events, as does natural science; but all such attempts have, I think, failed.

The notion of value science, when once applied to history, involves necessarily its ultimate extension to all the so-called social sciences. Not only is any social or political theory inevitably a philosophy of history, but the social and political sciences are made up of both factual and value propositions. It is obvious, of course, that these sciences contain matters of fact, independent of any judgments of value. We may compare forms of the family, styles of art, and political institutions such as the State, with one another as impartially and objectively as we can compare two minerals, or two forms of anatomic structure, such as the vertebrates and invertebrates, but who is naïve enough to suppose that we can form the *notions* of the family, of a style of art, or the concept of the State, without reference to values? Values are here part of the material of the sciences themselves. The very categories employed are meaningless without this reference to values.

It is, to be sure, entirely possible to say that the idea of a value science is a misnomer, if not actually a contradiction in terms—that any limits set to the categories of natural science are limits to the scientific method itself. A strong case can be made out for this contention. Certainly when we speak of political science, or of history as science, we cannot mean quite the same thing as when we speak of physical science. This is in a sense a question of definition, namely, whether we shall use the word science in the classical sense of *scientia*, or all knowledge, or in the restricted modern sense of sensationalistic empiricism. Certainly the so-called humanistic or social sciences give us knowledge, but equally certainly it is impossible to understand the higher cultural processes with which they deal except in terms of the values which give them meaning. If then, in addition to the realistic insistence on the priority, from a genetic or explanatory point of view, of the elementary processes of physics and chemistry, we also insist upon the idealistic principle of the uniqueness and privileged character of the cultural process of a higher and more complex type—and call the knowledge of the latter science, we may speak of value sciences, for it is only through the values embodied in these cultural processes that their nature and meaning can be known.[1]

[1] For a more detailed treatment of this general subject, see my article *Science and Value: Fact and Value in the Social Sciences, Ethics*, April 1941 [Vol. LI, No. 3].

IV

Realism and Idealism in the Theory of Value. The Reality of Ideals and the Objectivity of Values.

A

Our examination both of the changing backgrounds of the humanities and of the new epistemology which has emerged as a result—has made it clear that the problems of this chapter centre about problems of value. The recognition of this general situation instead of simplifying our problem, appears, at first sight at least, to complicate it and to confuse the issues. For the dispute between idealism and realism is carried into the sphere of values itself.

Realism in this sphere has two meanings, even among the realists themselves—to the confusion of all clear thinking. A realistic theory of value means for many a purely naturalistic theory. What we call values are merely the functional relation between natural tendencies, wants, desires or interests, and the objects which fulfill or satisfy them. On the other hand, for other realists the realism of values means the exact opposite. There is, we have seen, a form of Neo-realism for which realism of values means that values have objective being, independent of the organism or mind which conditions their experience or realization. Realists of this school are, as we have seen, 'outraged' by those who would reduce this realm of subsistences to subjective states, whether this is done by professed idealists or by those who call themselves realists. Which of these views shall be called true realism in the theory of value? For reasons which we shall now develop we shall call the latter 'realism in value theory.'

Notwithstanding the confusion thus indicated, the development of modern value theory has been characterized by a continuous and ever increasing movement towards realism of values in this latter sense. This movement has been most pronounced in the sphere of ethical studies but its influence has extended to all the humanistic sciences. The same movement which distinguishes the new realisms of British and American philosophy is embodied in the Phenomenological movement on the continent.

The argument of the realist for the mind-independent character of values is in principle the same as that for the independence of *sensa* or sense data. The distinction between the sensation of blue and the *datum* blue is no more and no less significant for him than the distinction between the feeling of value and the value datum of which we become aware through that feeling. As the realist insists that there is no question of how we get out of the circle of our sensations—merely to have a sensation is to get out of that circle; so likewise he insists that there is no question of how we get outside the circle of our feelings and ideas of value—to be aware of these values is already to be outside that circle.

The force of this argument is to my mind no more and no less than the argument against subjectivity which was met by the distinction between sensation and sense datum. As the former does not constitute an empirical refutation of mentalism, neither does the latter. It is again a dialectical argument. But parallel to this positive argument for the objectivity of values there has been a constant critique of subjectivism and naturalism in value theory. Idealists, realists, and even pragmatists, join in seeking to show that the generic concept of value cannot be expressed in terms of desire or interest. These arguments are familiar to all and need not be rehearsed in the present context.[1] The important point for our consideration here is that actually the net result of these arguments, both positive and negative, has been an ever increasing movement towards the objectivity of values, as I have shown in a recent account of the present situation in value theory,[2] and that this movement has had a significant effect upon our present controversy.

This, then, is the value realism which we have been at pains to make clear. It is significant that Mr Joad, whose criticisms of the idealistic tendency in physical science we examined in the preceding chapter, holds this view of the realism of values. For several reasons it is desirable to state it in his form of words.

'I myself believe,' he writes, 'that the world of which we are aware in æsthetic and religious experience is objective and that in knowing it we discover and do not create what we know. It

[1] An especially cogent form of this criticism is found in John Laird's *The Idea of Value*.

[2] *The Present Situation in Axiology*, Revue Internationale de Philosophie, July 1939.

is for this reason among others that I am anxious to maintain that the worlds revealed to us in everyday experience and in scientific research are also objective. It is, indeed, partly because the subjective attitude towards the world of science favoured by modern physics seems to me to be prejudicial to the objective status of the world of value that I have tried to show that this attitude is mistaken.'[1] It is, I repeat, significant that the realism of values is so important for Joad that, by his own confession, it constitutes the deeper source of his resistance to idealism. But that is not the point that I wish to emphasize here. It is rather that, just as the argument for realism in science, so the argument for the realism of values, is essentially dialectical in character. It is assumed that the significance of values, like the significance of knowledge, depends upon the acknowledgment of their objective status and it is this, in the last analysis, which is determinative. The argument of Joad, that it is because a subjective attitude towards the world of physical science favoured by many physicists, would be prejudicial to the objective status of the world of values and should, therefore, be opposed, brings out the point clearly. In neither case does it make any difference to the facts whether they are interpreted subjectively or objectively—theory can never destroy facts, they are simply there—but theory can make a great difference in the significance of the facts, and it is with a question of significance that we are here concerned. As the argument for opposing a subjective attitude in physical science is dialectical, so also is it dialectical in the present case.

The problem which has been engaging us all along is the bearing of this movement to objectivity—this realism of values —on the issue of realism and idealism in the philosophy of spirit. One thing at least stands out clearly thus far, namely, that this movement represents the acceptance of one principle which has always been an essential part of historic metaphysical idealism, namely, the objectivity of the Good or value. Thus by one of the dialectical movements of history, of which we spoke in the introduction, realism has come to include an element which hitherto had been almost the exclusive property of idealism.

This fact is recognized by Professor J. H. Muirhead, who

[1] *Philosophical Aspects of Modern Science*, p. 264.

states it in the following way. 'In this matter of values,' he tell, us, there has been, among English philosophers at least, a broadening of view, a widening of outlook, shared by idealist and realist alike. It has come to be recognized that, as there are trans-individual values, so there may be, and are, trans-social values. Whatever the origin of values, or more concretely, of the sense of duty of devotion to truth or love or beauty, these objects, once apprehended, mean not only an *addendum* to existence, but a source of insight into the nature of the world of which they are a product or expression. They thus acquire a status and value of their own by which our conceptions of being are extended and enriched.'[1] What Professor Muirhead finds characteristic of present British philosophy is also true of German thought, of which it may be said that this is a basal insight, cutting across all divisons of realism and idealism.[2]

[1] *Introduction to Contemporary British Philosophy*, Vol. II.

[2] No account of the movement to realism in value theory would be complete without reference to what is called the deontological theory of morals, represented especially by H. A. Prichard and Sir W. D. Ross, a theory which may, perhaps, be said to have found its full expression in the latter's *The Right and the Good* and his Gifford Lectures, the *Foundations of Ethics*.

This movement, although raising issues of importance in the sphere of Ethics itself, is only secondarily significant with respect to the epistemological problem here involved. Although it bases morality largely on a realism of duty, as opposed to a realism of values, it is still realistic with respect to both.

So far as this issue is concerned, the criticism of subjectivist theories of the grounds of rightness and duty parallels in many respects similar criticisms of subjectivist theories of the good. The arguments against naturalistic and subjectivist theories of the right do not differ in principle from similar arguments with respect to value. (*Foundations of Ethics*, pp. 59 ff.). So far as concerns our present problem then, the only issues of significance are whether right and duty are separable from the good or value and whether the theory of the good in Deontology is subjective or objective, for the good or value must have some place in any theory of ethics.

With respect to the first question, I think we may admit that, in so far as their intuitive meaning is concerned, the right and the good are *sui generis* and that neither is resolvable into the other without a remainder, and still maintain that, as attributes of actions and things, they can be understood only as standing in organic relations the one to the other. 'It would be a mistake,' Ross tells us, 'to suppose that there has ever been an ethics of duty which did not include a recognition of intrinsic goods or an ethics of ends which did not include a recognition of duties.' (*Foundations of Ethics*, p. 4). The reason for this is, I think, that ultimately the one cannot be thought without the other. From our present standpoint the entire issue, it seems to me, is one of priority or primacy. This primacy belongs to value for the reason, as I have long maintained, that there is a synthetic relation between them, such that there is a judgment of an 'ought-to-be' implicit in all acknowledgment of value—(this ought-to-be being part of the meaning of the

V

The Philosophy of Spirit. Metaphysical Perspectives.

A

With this the main theme of this chapter has been worked out. We have shown that the methodology of the humanistic sciences is neither exclusively realistic nor exclusively idealistic —that any adequate theory of knowledge in this sphere must include both elements. In the second place, we have shown that the philosophy of value itself, so closely bound up with the humanistic sciences, is beyond the distinction of realism-idealism. The sharing in large part, by realist and idealist alike, of the notion of objectivity of values marks this transcendence. We may say here, also with a show of reason, that the opposition between realism and idealism as formerly understood is now largely a thing of the past.

---

concept), the ought-to-do of moral agents being secondary and derived from this acknowledgment. This view I share with the phenomenological movement of Germany, although developed independently of it.

The *a priori* character of this relation, it seems to me, cannot be seriously challenged. But it also has a further aspect. That the better ought to be chosen rather than the worse, the greater rather than the lesser good, seems to me self-evident and to constitute, I should agree with Brentano, the one and only absolutely evident moral law, and therefore the ultimate sanction of morality.

With respect to the second point—the place of value in Deontology—it is maintained by the latter that while the promotion of the good has nothing to do with the rightness of acts, it is nevertheless one of the main factors in determining it. Now I shall not ask here how this is possible—how, if it is one of the main factors in determining the rightness of the act, its promotion can have nothing to do with that rightness. I shall simply make the point that if it is one of the main factors in determining that rightness (I believe it to be the ultimate factor) even this relation implies the objectivity or realism of values. A realism of duty, however we may view it, implies a realism of values, and thus the main point of this note has been made.

I have appended this note to the paragraph from Muirhead on the meeting of realism and idealism in value theory. It would seem only appropriate to refer to his little book, *Rule and End in Morals*, published, to be sure, before the appearance of the *Foundations of Ethics*, but which treats Deontology, with its revived intuitionism of duty, in the same eirenic spirit manifested in this paragraph. I should, I think, agree wholly in principle with both his criticisms of this movement and also with his last chapter, 'Towards Revision and Synthesis,' in which a statement of the relation of the Right to the Good is attempted.

The parallel between this and the preceding chapter holds then up to a certain point, but there is one important difference. Whereas in the physical sciences realism seems to be primary and the question is one of concessions to idealism, in the humanistic sphere the idealistic insistence is primary, and the question is one of concessions to realism. The fact that, in the humanistic sciences, the priority and privileged character of the idealistic insistence must, it seems, be maintained, raises further questions as to the meaning and implications of this methodological fact. Does not this fact require an idealistic interpretation of reality as a whole? Does not the fact—of the reality of ideals and of the objectivity of values in the sphere of the human— require also a similar reality and objectivity of these values in the cosmos—in short, metaphysical idealism? This is the basal issue of the philosophy of spirit as distinguished from the 'sciences' of the spirit, and with the issue here presented we come to the more metaphysical issue of the opposition of idealism to naturalism, as distinguished from the epistemological issue of realism and idealism, for in recent times realism has become largely identified with naturalism.

Idealism has always been the humanistic philosophy *par excellence*. It has constantly maintained a value realism, but it has always maintained that the objective reality of values is bound up with a spiritualistic metaphysic, and that they lose their significance if the rational basis for such a metaphysic is denied. Naturalistic humanism, on the other hand, denies this contention. It maintains that the human significance of values is wholly independent of this cosmic background and that, indeed, so it is maintained by some, to give them cosmic significance is to destroy their human significance. It may be described as an attempt to synthesize a humanistic idealism with a scientific naturalism—an attempt which, as we shall later see, is one of the outstanding characteristics of present-day philosophy. The issue has been presented by Nicolai Hartmann under the heading, 'metaphysical perspectives', and it is under this caption that we shall attempt to discuss it.

B

The idealistic argument at this point has been uniformly and consistently that the validity and objectivity of values in human experience *presuppose* their objectivity in a cosmic sense—that they are 'part of antecedent being'—and that this fact, when properly interpreted, means that nature contains 'a spiritual principle'. It is, we must insist, the same argument in principle, whether it be put in the traditional form of Kant's postulate of a moral world order as the condition or presupposition of the validity of morals; or in the form of T. H. Green's argument for a 'spiritual principle in nature'. The essence of the idealist's insistence is, not merely that man, to be man, must live by values higher than any deducible from 'nature', but that these values by which he lives, to retain their vitality and significance, must be effective not only in man but in the cosmos also. This we found to be the driving force back of epistemological idealism and to have finally found its most adequate expression in the formula of axiological idealism. We cannot, so it is there maintained, ultimately take nature as existing *per se;* it has to be taken as an element in a whole which cannot be expressed except in terms of conscious values. . . . Familiar with values in our own experience, we feel it impossible to conceive anything devoid of value (such as an unconscious material system would be) as ultimately real and self-subsistent—in other words, as a whole, as *res completa*. It is, we finally agreed, 'this moral impossibility of a world unperceived or unthought of' that is the driving power of this form of the idealistic argument. Moral impossibility, however, as here understood, since it means intelligibility, cannot be ultimately separated from speculative impossibility, also rightly understood.

This then is the metaphysical perspective—the cosmic significance of values—which an adequate philosophy of values seems to open up. But to this naturalism, as opposed to idealism, has an answer both clear and definite. On the one hand, it insists that the human significance of our values is wholly independent of their cosmic significance, or of any scientific concept of nature we may hold. On the contrary, it is further maintained that to give our values cosmic significance really destroys their human significance that, as it has been said, the 'humanizing of the cosmos' means the 'moral annulment of man.'

Humanistic naturalism is in no doubt as to what science has actually done to this spiritualistic metaphysics. Gone, clean gone, we are told, is the entire magnificent scheme of thought with which our values have hitherto been bound up. The acids of modern science have not only eaten God out of the cosmos, but also the values for which in man's childhood, the name of God had stood. But—and this is a most important but—the realities or values by which this scheme of thought had life, are found to persist. The values are there. Even science in taking stock of the world is brought up against the existence of values and must acknowledge them.

The values are there—undoubtedly. But the real question is *how* they are there. It may be said that, as in the case of knowledge, we simply have them 'like the measles'. This sounds plausible, but actually it represents a complete *ignorantia elenchi*. Certainly no theory can destroy facts, but it can denature them, take all the meaning out of them. A subjective attitude towards values denatures them just as certainly as such an attitude towards the objects of science denatures them. But so also does an attitude which views them merely as essences which have no existence in the world of cosmic reality. It really makes little difference, from this standpoint at least, whether our values evaporate into subjectivity or into mere essentiality, whether we relegate them to the human mind or to that no-man's land which is neither human nor cosmic.

Naturalistic humanism not only denies the cosmic significance of values, but often goes so far as to assert that such a notion is in some fashion inimical to human values themselves. Not only are they there and fully real irrespective of any question of their existence or non-existence in the cosmos, but actually they are real and valid only if this cosmic significance is denied. The humanization of the cosmos means the moral annulment of man.

This sounds impressive as it is epigrammatic, and we are not surprised to hear it asserted in one form or another, in the most unexpected places. It is but an echo, of course, of the old cry that to give glory to God is to deny glory to man. But it ceases to be impressive when we examine the supposed grounds for such an assertion. It is widely held, of course, that beliefs such as these inhibit practical activities in the direction of the realization of human good, but actually quite the contrary is the case. For it is precisely those who believe most deeply that the values they aim to realize in life are 'transcendentals', and grounded in ultimate being, who are freeest from the sense of futility and whose spiritual initiatives are most powerful.

Nor is this view any more impressive when we examine the theoretical grounds for the assertion. In the first place, the thesis that to assert the cosmic significances of values is to humanize the cosmos, is itself the very opposite of the truth. For while our values are human, they are, as objective, more than human. We do not read our values into the cosmos, we find them there. In any case, a cosmic teleology is no more anthropomorphic in a dyslogistic sense than is cosmic mechanism. Anthropomorphism for anthropomorphism, who shall say, except on the basis of an anterior prejudice, which is the more ultimate and more valid? Nor is it at all clear why such a cosmic teleology should be inimical to human values and constitute the moral annulment of man. It is admitted that teleology, or axiological determination, is a fundamental character of the human; why then, we may well ask, should belief in a moral world order of which we are a part, annul our belief in our own human moral order? The source of this paradox of paradoxes is, of course, the supposed ultimate opposition between teleology and axiological determination in man and a supposedly merely casual and mechanical teleology when applied to the cosmos. This assumes, however, that there are only two possibilities here, axiological determination and casual determination, whereas there is actually a third possibility, namely, an immanent free teleology which involves no determinism which would be inimical to human freedom. This is the situation envisaged by Kant in his solution of the antinomy of freedom and determinism, the full significance of which is not always seen.

The arguments brought against cosmic teleology, while at first sight impressive, cannot it would seem, in the end be maintained. On the other hand, such a teleology far from meaning the moral annulment of man, seems to be a necessary presupposition of the human. It is admitted that teleology or axiological determination is a necessary criterion of the human, but in order to be really possible what does human teleology presuppose? The essence of human purpose is the actualization of ends, and of the values they presuppose. But surely, unless these values, when actualized and enhanced, were also conserved, human teleology would have no ultimate significance. The labours of Sisyphus, the drawing of water in a sieve and the rolling of the stone up the hill only to have it roll back again, have a metaphysical significance which cannot be gainsaid by any amount of modern sophistication. Unless values have cosmic significance, the actualizing of values demanded by man as a moral being is, in a larger world perspective, as though it had never been. It is, of course, possible to conceive a world as wholly devoid of value, at least intellectually, but morally it is not, and this the metaphysical idealist has always seen.

C

In the preceding chapter we spoke of the philosophy of nature which inevitably arises out of the methodology of the physical sciences. Just as surely does a philosophy of spirit inevitably arise out of the sciences which deal with the human. The homogeneity of thought about nature excludes any reference to values, although the values are there and are the clue to any metaphysical synthesis. The homogeneity of thought about the human, on the other hand, far from excluding reference to values, makes precisely this reference the essential of its method. Whatever we may say of nature, as conceived by physical science, what is said of human nature, as conceived by the humanities, is something very different. What then is the philosophy of spirit which apparently emerges from this method?

Does not, so we asked the question earlier, the idealistic insistence upon the priority and privileged character of values in the understanding and interpretation of the human, also require, in the end, an idealistic interpretation of reality as a whole, and therefore an idealistic or spiritualistic metaphysic?

I doubt whether we can go quite this far, but it is, I think, of the utmost importance to determine just how far we may—and indeed must—go. Certainly we may say that a philosophy of spirit must be idealistic in the sense that such a philosophy must postulate that the values, reference to which constitutes the very essence of its method, to be significant for the human, must operate on a more than human scale also and thus have cosmic significance. Certainly we may also deny that nature with which the philosophy of physical science is concerned is something existing *per se* as a *res completa*. Even for science it cannot, as we have seen, be so conceived. This, however, is to go a considerable way on the road of metaphysical synthesis. If we cannot say that an adequate philosophy of spirit requires an idealistic interpretation of reality as a whole, we can at least say that any such interpretation of the whole must include the philosophy of spirit as well as the philosophy of nature. Any such a philosophy must be to this extent idealistic, even if it is 'along realistic lines.' This is the topic of the next chapter.

Chapter IX

An Idealistic Philosophy on Realistic Lines: The Synthesis of Idealism and Naturalism.

I — A

'No sane philosophy,' wrote Samuel Alexander, 'has ever been exclusively realistic or idealistic.' If the arguments of the preceding chapters are sound we should now be ready to give to this assertion our full and cordial assent. What Alexander means is that no sane philosophy has ever failed to include in some form the fundamental motives of both realism and idealism—has failed to acknowledge the driving force of idealism or to recognize the significance of the resistance of realism. The minimum of each which has shown itself to be irrefutable must find its place in any significant and lasting philosophy.

The expression 'sane' is in a sense a question begging epithet and yet we can, I think, fully appreciate what it means. If life itself which, as we have seen, contains these two motives also reconciles them, then a philosophy which shall not be inimical to life, and in this sense sane, must find a way to reconcile them also. There are, to be sure, logical minds—logical in the sense that the insane man is logical, to use Chesterton's terms—who insist upon being exclusively one or the other. But this 'all or nothing' type of thought consorts ill with the real motives and objectives of a significant philosophy.

Alexander is himself an illustration of his own dictum and of that essential soundness of mind which is the *desideratum* of the great philosopher. When in his *Space, Time and Deity* he approaches the levels of life, mind and values, his work becomes increasingly idealistic both in spirit and method. And somewhat the same may be said of other philosophers of this type. It is undoubtedly partly the desire to do justice to life, mind and values which leads Whitehead to seek 'to transform some of the main ideas of objective idealism unto a realistic basis.' It is also the ground for the expression of the opinion, on the part of many philosophers who have grown up in the naturalistic tradition, that the next stage in philosophy must be a 'fusion of

idealism and naturalism.' I am not saying, of course, that pro-
posals such as these are either possible or impossible of realization but merely seeking to indicate the significance of the
dictum.[1]

If then Alexander's dictum is sound—certain consequences
follow with reasonable clarity. If no sane philosophy is ever
exclusively realistic or idealistic, it is high time, is it not, that
we should cease trying to construct philosophies which are
exclusively one or the other. Still more is it high time that we
should consciously try to formulate a philosophy which is exclusively neither but, in our terms, beyond realism and idealism.
It is because I believe that such an enterprise is both possible
and reasonable that I undertook the labours of this book.

In any case, some of the materials for such a structure are
already in our possession. By an examination of this debate we
have come to see that a sufficiently critical idealism and a sufficiently critical realism are 'separated from each other only by
a word.' By an examination of physical science we have seen
that there is nothing in the latest concepts of these sciences that
forces us to either an exclusive realism or an exclusive idealism.
On the contrary, they make the antithesis of idealism and
realism, as formerly understood, largely a thing of the past, and
seem to suggest that the methodology of science is really beyond
this distinction and includes elements of both. A similar examination of the humanistic sciences in their present form showed
that here too neither an exclusive idealism nor an exclusive
realism will suffice. The further development of these notions
should conceivably lead to the desired end.

B

The difficulties in the way of such an enterprise are not to be
minimized. There are the difficulties due to the extrinsic appeals
to emotion and habit which constitute the hidden sources of the
driving force of idealism and of the resistance of realism, and
which are the real forces lying back of the exclusive logics of the
two positions. There are the difficulties which arise out of the

[1] During a memorable week-end spent with Professor Alexander at his home in
Manchester, I had the opportunity to ask him what he meant by this epigram.
I am sure I am not misrepresenting his answer when I say that it expressed the
spirit, if not the letter, of what I have here written.

instability of all apparently eclectic positions which find it difficult to maintain themselves. But the chief difficulty is the
tyranny of names. There is nothing so embarrassing to the
'magnanimous' philosopher as to find himself immediately
labelled by one of these exclusive and question-begging epithets.
Bosanquet felt this difficulty so intensely that he even proposed
to drop the terms entirely. The meeting of extremes in modern
philosophy had, on his view, made this opposition, as ordinarily
understood, largely a thing of the past and transferred the
significant oppositions in modern thought to other issues. We
need new names, but new names are hard to find and still
harder to have accepted. In the face of this difficulty many have
proposed combinations of realism and idealism with the accent,
now on one, now on the other, of the two terms in the combination. Thus Marxians often claim to set forth a *Real-idealismus*, a
synthesis of realism and idealism with realism supreme.
Followers of objective idealism, on the other hand, have proposed an *Ideal-realismus* which, while making idealism dominant,
seeks to do justice to the demands of realism and naturalism.
The difficulty with such terms is that of all hyphenated words—
namely, their artificiality. In addition they represent divided
loyalties, whether in citizenship or in philosophy, a loyalty
which is not only eclectic and artificial, but which also creates
the suspicion of insincerity.

Instead, therefore, of seeking a new name for the position I
shall attempt to develop in this chapter, I shall choose rather a
descriptive phrase taken from Kemp Smith, namely, 'the
development of an idealistic philosophy on realistic lines'—a
phrase which represents more or less adequately the idea I have
in mind, namely, that a sane philosophy—and with it an
adequate epistemology—must contain both elements. I choose
this phrase all the more readily for the reason that the position
which it describes represents in some measure at least the position which I should like to maintain.

In his *Prolegomena to an Idealistic Theory of Knowledge*, Kemp
Smith endeavours, as he says, to carry out an enterprise he has
long had in mind. He is convinced that idealism and realism,
properly understood, are compatible. An idealist philosophy, in
the broadest and most generally accepted sense, seems to him not
only possible but also the necessary *desideratum* of any significant

philosophy; but he holds it to be equally true that such an idealism, to be valid, must be along realistic lines, realism again being used in its broadest and historically most significant sense. With this general thesis I am in complete agreement. The enterprise seems to me not only possible but, if carried out, of great significance for philosophy. In taking his formula as the starting point of our final study it is not so much the solution itself, although that too up to a point we shall accept, but chiefly the idea which we wish to make our own. Indeed, while accepting the general thesis of the compatibility of idealism and realism, there are important points, both in his statement of the problem and in the form of the solution, with which we will have to take issue.

II

An Idealism on Realistic Lines: The Argument.

A

Before entering upon the statement of the problem as conceived by Kemp Smith, I must, however, take issue with an evaluation of this position offered by Dr Rudolf Metz. 'The title of this work,' he tells us, 'should not lead us astray.' For in fact his doctrine belongs entirely to the New Realist school and that which in this case is called 'Idealist' is rather an emotional background in the form of a belief in a world of spiritual values, than a theory immediately connected with his epistemological views or resulting from them. It is nearer the truth when Smith, in the course of his argument, frequently emphasizes his 'truly realistic standpoint.'[1]

This, I hold, is seriously to misrepresent Kemp Smith's position. The background is not merely emotional and his doctrine is not entirely new-realist. The idealistic position he maintains goes far beyond any mere emotional attitude or mere belief in a world of spiritual values; it represents a dialectical argument which corresponds, in modern form, to the main arguments of historic idealism. The realistic element in his philosophy does not belong entirely to new realism, as ordinarily understood, but contains a strong ingredient of Kantian thought which gives it its own character. But let us proceed with a statement of his position.

[1] *A Hundred Years of British Philosophy*, p. 686.

B

Kemp Smith recognizes that the terms idealism and realism have 'such numerous and conflicting meanings' that both must be taken in a very broad sense. The essential point of his contention is, however, that the significant opposition today is between idealism and naturalism. 'I shall contend,' he maintains, 'that what is truly distinctive of idealism is its contention "that spiritual values can be credited with operating on a more than planetary plane, that is on a cosmic scale".' 'Should,' he believes, 'this contention have to be given up, the only sort of idealism that would then remain would no longer be distinguishable from at least some naturalistic philosophies.' It is, then, idealism in this metaphysical sense which he believes to be entirely compatible with a realistic epistemology, properly understood, and ultimately with certain necessary elements in naturalism.

The entire argument for the compatibility of idealism and realism depends obviously upon two points: (a) upon the adequacy of his conception of idealism and (b) upon the possibility of the implied separation of realism from naturalism. It is obviously futile to attempt any reconciliation of idealism and realism unless we are quite sure that we have true and adequate conceptions of the two philosophical positions which we seek to combine.

It requires no further argument to show that idealism as here defined is, indeed, idealism in the historic sense. This has not only been the ultimate driving force of historic idealism, but the source of its continuity of epistemological intention throughout its manifold changes. Even Berkeley's argument was directed primarily against the materialism of his day, which was the form in which naturalism then expressed itself. The critical idealism of Kant, although it contains a strong realistic ingredient, and might equally well be described as critical realism, is motivated primarily by its opposition to naturalistic scepticism, by the attempt to reinstate the objectivity of values, and to give a privileged position to mind or spirit in the ultimate interpretation of the world. Objective idealism, in both its logical and axiological forms, is motivated primarily by its opposition to naturalism, and when the latter finds the ultimate driving force of idealism is the moral impossibility of separating value and being, it is merely expressing consciously what was always the driving force of idealism. Kemp Smith is then, I think, wholly right in finding the essentials of idealism where he does. The real question at issue, and it is a very important question, is whether this idealism, when examined, does not imply something more—whether, in fact, it does not presuppose at least the minimum of *epistemological* idealism which we found to be included in all forms of historic idealism as described in Chapter II.

'Idealists,' we are told, 'have tended in the main to believe that the establishment of their contention demands very much more than it really does.' As a result, 'they have been apt to overreach themselves and to weaken the force of their better arguments by attempting to prove very much more than the available data can justly be expected to yield.' Under this partial condemnation fall, in Kemp Smith's view, all forms of modern epistemological idealism, the mentalism of Berkeley, the transcendental idealism of Kant (at least as usually interpreted), and objective idealism, especially in its logical form. These various idealisms differ in the extent of their demands. There is the uncompromising Berkeleyan thesis that material nature is mind dependent. There is, however, a more moderate form which has more or less displaced it. Initially, at least, it is more modest, although usually much less definite, the claim namely, that mind and nature stand in relations of mutual implication. In one of its formulations, mind is organic to the world but the world is also organic to mind.

According to Kemp Smith, none of these epistemological positions is required by idealism as defined—none constitutes the indispensable *minimum* of an intelligible theory of knowledge. Now it is extremely doubtful whether one can go that far. It is possible, and indeed necessary, to make many concessions to realism, as we have seen in the preceding chapter, although, as we have also seen, the nature of physical knowledge also makes it necessary to make concessions to idealism. Certainly the uncompromising character of many forms of historic idealism is unnecessary. But it seems to me something more is necessary to define the idealistic *minimum* as required by metaphysical idealism. If our argument of the preceding chapters is valid, apparently it does. Actually, the 'more moderate form' of epistemological idealism, namely, that mind and nature stand in relations of mutual implication—is, I think, when properly understood, indispensable to any form of metaphysical idealism. It is also, as I have attempted to show, when properly understood, actually beyond realism and idealism in any exclusive sense.[1]

C

With these modifications, then, we may consider that the essential idealistic contention is rightly stated. Let us see then the 'realistic lines' along which it is conceived that such an idealism may be developed.

Kemp Smith is persuaded that in an adequate philosophy values must have cosmic significance, and to that extent his idealism, far from being a mere emotion, is a philosophical conviction. But he sees rightly that values can scarcely be given cosmic significance unless *the cosmos itself has a significance quite independent of our minds*. He is anxious to oppose the claims of mere naturalism, but that cannot be done unless the element of truth in naturalism is itself recognized. It is meaningless to insist that values have more than human significance unless the world in which they are thus significant is also mind-independent in some sense and in some degree.

I think we must recognize the general truth of this contention, and that the lines along which a tenable idealism could be developed must involve at least this *minimum*. This general position was indeed implied in the arguments of the preceding chapter. The real issue of course is the determination of just what such a realistic *minimum* must include. Here, too, as we shall see, I do not find his formula wholly satisfactory. As he concedes too little to historical idealism, so, I believe, he concedes too much to contemporary naturalistic realism.

Briefly stated, this realistic requirement is the mind-independent character of nature. The important question then is what 'nature' includes. For him it involves the mind-independent character of the entire spatio-temporal world—more technically stated, the mind independent character of space, time and the categories—and, as we shall see, of values. In other words, 'nature,' while not quite the natural world view which Berkeley

[1] Chapter v.

found so strange, is yet that modified natural view which the critical realist has found it necessary to put in its place. Let us examine then the type of critical realism which he believes to be required both by the 'facts' of knowledge and by the demands of a metaphysical idealism, properly understood.

For Kemp Smith, as for most modern philosophers, the primacy of the physical object for knowledge is assumed and the problem of sense perception thus stands in the foreground. Of what kind are the *sensa* which form the content of our acts of perception? According to naïve realism, they are qualities of external things and exist in these themselves. As such they are objective and public. According to representative perception, they are pure data of consciousness, and therefore, subjective and private. According to Kemp Smith, who rejects both views, they are events which are conditioned by physical, physiological and possibly also by psychical factors. They are not accessible to a number of percipients, but to one only. He calls them, therefore, 'objective and private.' 'Nothing that we experience,' he holds, 'exists independently in precisely the form in which we experience it.' So far we can agree with the subjectivist theory and the thesis which it propounds. 'If what we experience is in any degree public and not private, independently real and not subjective, then the sense data, although the private possession of the percipient, are not necessarily in the mind or "mental" states, but objective occurrences which belong integrally to the system of the physical world and appear within the spatio-temporal continuum.'[1] Thus the *sensa* are mind-independent, but for the critical realism here under discussion they have an independence which does not exclude mind-dependence.

An important part of the development of his realism is his critique of representative perception and of the type of realism which it involves. His criticism of this form of realism is in principle not different from those with which we are already familiar,[2] but it is modified in certain significant ways by evolutionary conceptions which in general play a large part in his entire theory. The chief source of error in this theory is, of course, the failure to distinguish between sensations and sense data. But equally important is an illegitimate assumption which

[1] *Op. cit.*, p. 227.

[2] Chapter iii, pp. 86 f.

underlies this type of realism, namely, that sense perception gives us absolute, not relative knowledge; and a still more deep-lying assumption, namely, that the sense organs were made primarily for knowledge, when actually they were made for adaptation and practice, and only later became the organs of knowledge for its own sake. Both of these assumptions modern evolutionary studies have, he holds, shown to be false,[1] and no form of realism which is based upon them can stand.

These two modifications in the older forms of critical realism are not only important in themselves but significant for the later developments of his theory. Relativity of knowledge, both with respect to sense perception and to the biological purposes of perception, must therefore enter into any modern realism. But even more significant is the fact that, as a result of these ele-ments in his realism, he makes extensive concessions to natural-ism and its account of knowledge which raise important questions as to the satisfactoriness of his solution of the main problem.

Sensa form, then, the content factor of our experience, but no less important for the existence of knowledge are the formal and uniform factors, the categorical relations and the intuitional forms of space and time. These are not contents but *a priori* forms for the organization of variable sensory material. But these also are 'objective.' Awareness presupposes for its very existence as objective field and this field, he holds, has for its most funda-mental features real and independent space and time. Space and time do not reveal themselves to us except in terms of *sensa*, but they themselves are not objects of sensation. 'They disclose themselves directly to mind, and in so doing they prescribe certain categories which equip the mind for discerning those ideals which constrain the mind to the pursuit of science and philosophy.'

With this we come to the aspect of Kemp Smith's realism which has special significance in the present context. That the idealistic position, as defined by him, involves the independent reality of nature in some sense we have already admitted. The sole issue now is the question as to what nature includes—more specifically, whether the independence of nature involves the independent reality of space-time as here maintained. The

[1] *Op. cit.*, p. 65.

grounds for belief that it does can, I think, be only of two kinds, namely (a) that realism of this type is necessitated by the 'concept of nature' of modern physical science; and (b) that it is demanded by the notion of the objective or cosmic significance of values, in other words, by the metaphysical idealism of which Kemp Smith is the protagonist. Let us examine both reasons.

This view is, I believe, neither necessitated nor justified by the situation in modern physical science. It seems to me that if there is anything that can be said with certainty here it is that the notion of the independence of nature, in so far as it is postulated by physical science, does not necessarily require this conception of space and time. The new scientific epistemology indicates quite the contrary. The space and time of physical science are not entities but constructions. They are not unchanging frame works, as they were for Newton, and in his own special way, for Kant also. Space and time in the Newtonian sense have shared the fate of the sensory qualities. What the modern physicist calls space and time is an abstraction to which we cannot transfer the rules of spatial and temporal existences. We have no right, I think, to demand as part of our realism any more than modern physics makes necessary, for it is on the notion of the primacy of the physical object for knowledge that the main source of the resistance of realism depends. To make my point here it is not necessary to repeat the arguments of the idealists in physics—important as they are—but merely to insist, with Planck, that 'the notion that they are objective realities independent of consciousness' is not necessary for physics.[1]

Nor can it be contended that such a view is necessitated by the cosmic significance of values. The contention that it is being the dialectical nerve of Kemp Smith's argument, it becomes a very important part of his position as a whole. It may be admitted that idealism involves the objectivity of values. It may be admitted also, that this objectivity, to be significant, must be cosmic. But it does not at all follow that the independence of nature or of the cosmos, thus required, involves this doctrine of space and time.

Human action, no less than human knowledge, presupposes, of course, an objective field for its significance. Since human life is bound up with physical existence, our values are closely con-

[1] Chapter vii, pp. 173 f.

nected with the physical world. We are faced with the struggle for existence and with the competitive problem due to the limited amount of physical goods. This involves the reality of the space-time world; space and time are part of the very nature of economic goods as such. Moreover, *all* our experiences of value, ethical and æsthetic no less than economic, derive their significance from the fact that spatial and temporal relations are fundamental characters of this objective field. All our plans depend for their meaning upon the empirical reality of the 'here' and 'there,' of present, past and future. If for them be substituted a purely spaceless and timeless order, our purposes and values seem to become unmeaning. Teleology is a necessary character of the human as such, and in so far as the finalistic nexus presupposes for its very meaning and reality the causal nexus, it presupposes the reality of the space-time frame work; the relation of means to ends is the 'time-form of value'. All this is true, and if we further argue that human teleology, in order to be significant, presupposes cosmic teleology in some sense, then the independence of nature, in so far as it is involved in action and values, seems to involve also the mind-independence of the spatial temporal field.

This is the argument—dialectical in character—which we have now to consider. Taken in a certain sense, this conclusion would scarcely be denied by any one. Traditional idealism, even in its most mystical forms, has always taken time seriously, has always insisted that the external world, as viewed spatially and temporally, is an essential part of reality. But it does not at all follow that the objective field, which is necessarily presupposed by intelligible action no less than in intelligible knowledge, presupposes the *absoluteness* of space and time as a fundamental character of that field. All that is necessary is what Kant called their 'empirical reality.' What is fundamentally significant in this objective field, as the necessary condition of intelligible finality, is an objective order of values (value realism), including the principle of order or scale. To these 'spiritual realities' the forms of space and time do not apply; indeed, in the nature of the case cannot apply. The notion that space and time are not ultimate but are somehow phenomenal of value in its ultimate sense—that they are necessary forms in which values are realized, in both man and nature, but yet transcend these forms

15

—is an imperishable element in traditional philosophy. The mind-independence of nature, so far as it is presupposed by a value realism, does not require the doctrine of absolute space and time.[1] The importance of this will become apparent as we seek later to distinguish between realism and naturalism.

Notwithstanding these criticisms of the type of realism which Kemp Smith maintains, we are not disposed to find fault with the main point of his argument—namely, that idealism, in the sense of the cosmic significance of values, does necessitate the notion of the mind-independent character of the cosmos in which the values are realized. The issue concerns solely what this independence implies. We are not disposed to question the necessity of concessions of idealism to realism, but solely how far these concessions should go. The realistic requirements of an intelligible theory of knowledge do not go as far as Kemp Smith maintains, as our examination of the realistic *minimum* has shown. Nor do the requirements of idealism in the sense of his definition extend to the independence of 'nature' in the sense above maintained. But in principle his contention is sound and any valid idealistic philosophy must be 'along realistic lines.'

As we do not question the validity of this part of his general argument, neither do we question the further development of his argument, namely, that as a valid idealism requires some form of realism, so also a realism, one that shall be a genuine realism, also implies or requires idealism—in other words, the mutual implication of the two positions. To this phase of the argument we shall now turn.

D

We have seen what is the 'idealistic philosophy' which Kemp Smith seeks to maintain and also the 'realistic lines' along which he thinks it may be developed. These two positions are in his mind perfectly consistent with each other. Nay more, they *require* one another. 'Is not,' he asks, 'this the idealist's view alone truly realistic? Do not the two positions require one another?' His answer to both questions is in the affirmative.

In developing his argument he starts with what he calls the

[1] This position has been developed in more detail in *The Intelligible World*, chapter vii, 'Space, Time and Value,' especially pp. 245 ff. See on this point also N. O. Lossky, *Value and Existence*, pp. 204 ff.

realistic view of nature, including the 'naturalistic account' of mind and knowledge, the truth of which he would accept so far as it goes. Speaking this language he proceeds as follows: 'Nature in determining the character of the animal organism, of its sense organs and nervous system generally, has had, apparently, in view primarily only the self-preservation of the species. Yet in following this path she has also made possible the acquiring of knowledge. In preparing such knowledge as is of aid in survival—allowing no more knowledge than is indispensable for the purpose—she has in man brought into existence, or at least liberated, a type of sense experience which, when reinforced by instruments of precision . . . yields data sufficient for the attaining of scientific insight. What has been evolved under the apparently exclusive domination of purely practical needs, turns out in the end to subserve, with amazing adequacy, the requirements of the disinterested seeker after truth.' But there is more to it than this. 'All along,' we are told, 'Nature has seemingly been intent upon providing her creatures in their conscious experience with an adequate instrument of practical adaptation. And now we find that, while successfully doing this she has at the same time, *as it were inadvertently* (italics mine), provided the last-born of her children with the means of setting aside these practical purposes. . . . Discerning truth, beauty and goodness he (this last-born) adopts the attitude of contemplation and in view of these absolute values, organizes even his practical life on a different plane.'[1]

Kemp Smith accepts the naturalistic account of mind and knowledge *so far as it goes*, but after all, he finds that it does not go very far. 'Can Nature's proceedings,' he asks, 'be so purely accidental as the preceding account would suggest? Is not this a perverse and unnecessary view? Is not Nature here revealing herself as Super-Nature and can she be synoptically envisaged save as when so conceived?' For are not these intrinsic values which appear in the course of evolution in space and time characters of the cosmos itself, and does not this make the idealist view alone truly realistic? So far so good. If, however, he envisages nature in this fashion, can he really accept the naturalistic view of mind and knowledge as far as he does? For in so doing has he not really abandoned the scientific concept

[1] *Op. cit.*, p. 231.

of nature from which he started? It is natural to want to accept the grandiose picture of evolutionary naturalism at its face value, but it is doubtful whether this can be done and the essence of idealism retained. Of this we shall speak more fully presently; here we are alone concerned with his concilience of idealism and realism.

The idealistic view, as thus defined, is, however, for Kemp Smith the only truly realistic, and in this I think he is right. But he further asks, do not the two positions really require one another? This also he answers in the affirmative, and in this also he is, I think, right. As any genuine realism requires the idealistic thesis of the objectivity of values, so any genuine idealism, with its thesis of the cosmic significance of values, requires the mind-independent character of the cosmos. In other words, the two positions are perfectly consistent with one another. Between a sufficiently critical idealism and a sufficiently critical realism there is not only no ultimate conflict, but in so far as they are critical, they presuppose one another.

This, then, is the argument, and the nerve of the argument is, as already indicated, dialectical, as all such arguments are. It is, in principle, the same kind of argument employed in Chapter V, by which we tried to show that idealism and realism, far from being inconsistent with each other, mutually imply one another. In principle, then, we accept the argument, and it was for this reason that we proposed to take it as our model. We accepted the enterprise as legitimate and praiseworthy, but suggested that there were certain difficulties in this particular solution. An idealism to be significant does, indeed, demand a realistic basis, but it does not at all follow that the realism required includes the concessions to naturalism he thinks necessary. On the other hand—and this is the point I wish now to make—he also concedes too little to historic idealism. I am quite sure that an idealism such as he desiderates involves more of a concession to epistemological idealism than he is willing to admit and which the new scientific epistemology actually allows. It requires, I believe, a form of idealism in which mind and nature mutually imply one another and which holds that, while mind is certainly organic to the world, it is equally true that the world is organic to mind.

Of this view, Kemp Smith says that, while it is more moderate than the earlier forms of idealism, it is still much more ambitious than the needs of the idealist orientation towards life and the universe would seem to demand; that the representatives of the position have never been able to prove their point. By such conceptions 'they restrict themselves to considerations of logical implication whereby self and not-self, subject and object, mind and nature are supposed to demonstrate their inseparable mutual implication.' By such methods they have 'never yet succeeded in giving, in terms of their own standpoint, any satisfactory account of that other, very different, and yet surely no less important type of connection, in which physical existences exhibit causal efficacy.' This is undoubtedly true. Idealists have never been able to prove their point if this is the point they have to prove, and if they thought so they were grievously mistaken. They have never been able to deduce nature from mind or to explain causal relations in terms of logical relations, and we should be in serious error if we supposed that they should. We should be guilty of the confusion already noted, involved in switching over from the epistemological view of the universe as the theme of knowledge to the existential view of a universe of which we have to obtain knowledge. I cannot help feeling that Kemp Smith is guilty of this confusion also. On the other hand, it is equally true that if we cannot deduce nature from mind, just as little can we derive mind from nature. Concessions to naturalism, such as he proposes, end necessarily in a conception of the derivative character of mind, and with this conception no genuine idealism is consistent. To show this is the task of the following section.

III

The 'Synthesis of Idealism and Naturalism.' The Limits of Naturalism.

A

It is plain from the preceding that we have been dealing not only with an effort to conciliate realism and idealism, but, by implication, with a much more fundamental enterprise, namely, that which has been described as the synthesis of idealism and naturalism. While recognizing that the real conflict in philosophy today is between idealism and naturalism, there are those who hold that this conflict is also unnecessary, and that if the essential elements of both are made clear a synthesis is possible.

The two problems, while not identical are yet closely related, for, as we have seen, realism and naturalism tend to be identified in the modern world. When we penetrate beneath all its technical disguises, modern realism does appear to 'consist in the contention that reality is prior to knowledge and that *consequently* (italics mine) mind has a status which is derivative and not pivotal.' The derivative status of mind is the characteristic feature of all forms of naturalism. Any proposed synthesis with idealism requires the acceptance of this notion as its initial premise.

The attempt to combine the 'truth' of both positions has arisen, in the first instance, out of the belief that there has been such a significant revision of our notion of nature itself, and, therefore, of naturalism, that the essence of idealism, properly understood, is no longer inconsistent with such notions.

For nineteenth-century science, we are told, naturalism meant something quite different from our present conceptions. As nature then was simply our name for the mechanical system of matter and motion to which, it was assumed, all things could in principle ultimately be reduced, so naturalism was the name for the philosophy which believed solely in this system and in the methodology of the science by which the system was built up. In contrast with this 'past-naturalism,' as Sellars calls it, modern naturalism has discarded both mechanism and reductionism. 'An up-to-date naturalism,' as he further insists, 'is not a reductive naturalism. The old naturalism ignored novelty and evolutionary synthesis. An adequate naturalism must not make this mistake.'[1] It must not make the error of supposing that because naturalism insists upon the priority, from the genetic and explanatory point of view, of processes of the elementary type such as those of physics or chemistry, it thereby excludes the equally fundamental insistence on the privileged character of other categories in the interpretation of cultural processes, still less of reducing the latter to the former.

As the notion of naturalism has undergone revision, so also, it is held, has our conception of idealism and of an idealistic philosophy, properly understood. The essential of idealism,

[1] *Evolutionary Naturalism.*

according to this view, is humanism, and idealism in this sense does not require the metaphysical basis of historic idealism. For the latter, the cosmic significance of values is essential. Modern humanism, associating itself with naturalism, believes that it can retain the essentials of idealism and yet deny this thesis—that it is possible to retain the values of idealism without the metaphysical structure with which these values have hitherto been bound up, their human significance without their cosmic significance. Past idealism, if we may coin a corresponding term, thought that in order to be humanly significant, values must operate on a more than human plane. A present-day idealism will not make this mistake. It will see that 'all that is significant in idealism' is retained if we recognize human teleology with its axiological determination. It will also see that to project values into the cosmos is to humanize it, and that such 'anthropomorphism' is not only out of tune with a scientific concept of nature, but is no longer needed by the developed human spirit.

B

Seen against the background of these revisions it is possible to understand the attempts at synthesis which have characterized recent thought. There is a wide spread popular movement in this direction which is represented by two books which may perhaps be taken as indicative both of the general mood and of the character of the synthesis proposed.[1]

There seems to be, first of all, a large measure of agreement as to what naturalism, as now understood, involves. It has three general characters. First, nature now means merely the 'totality of all that is' and naturalism merely 'the empirical study of all that is.' In the second place, naturalism does not necessarily mean mechanism or materialism; in fact present-day naturalism is quite the opposite, explicitly denying this. Naturalism, in the third place, when thus viewed, makes a place for whatever we wish to put into nature. Immanent teleology is recognized as part of nature and 'all that is significant of idealism' is retained in its world picture.

For these thinkers, then, 'Naturalism is simply a faith in the

[1] James Bissett Pratt, *Naturalism*, Yale University Press, 1940; Irwin Edman, *Four Ways of Philosophy*, 1938, chapter iv.

unity of nature or substance of which all life is a derivation, upon which all action is posited, and within which the structure of mechanism is seen to be simply a systematized technique of practice and of economical understanding. Naturalism is far from being dependent on the picture, almost as mythical as the teleological one, of the billiard ball physics of the nineteenth century.' And again, 'it is only by calling the whole of nature mechanical that it is possible to deny ideality to it.'[1]

In this last sentence we have, I think, the key to all these more popular forms of synthesis. Reduce idealism to the vague 'ideality' of modern humanism; remove the mechanical element from nature—(a removal apparently justified by modern science); reduce the notion of nature to the vague 'totality of all that is,' and all opposition between the two notions disappears. And indeed it does. But one wonders whether it is quite as simple as all this. One wonders, in fact, whether both concepts —of idealism and naturalism alike—have not been so watered down as to have become as useless as they are harmless. One wonders whether naturalism in the hands of these moderns has not taken over so much that was formerly idealism that the retention of the name is not somewhat strained; whether, on the other hand, idealism in their hands has not taken over so much of pure naturalism as to make the retention of that term little more than an expression of emotion and sentiment.

My own feeling is that this is so. As a matter of fact, attempts at synthesis of this type are rarely long successful. They are not viable, for they are in a state of unstable equilibrium and, when subjected to strain, tend inevitably to fall back into the older form of naturalism to which they have, often unconsciously, been committed from the beginning.

This unstable equilibrium is actually manifest in the ranks of the new naturalism itself. When the strain comes, its varied representatives tend to fall apart and their positions become almost as diverse as the idealism and naturalism they seek to fuse. There seems to be only one plank in their platform upon which all can agree, and that is the identification of naturalism with the primacy of the scientific method. As nature is simply their name for the 'totality of all that is,' so naturalism is but a name for the 'empirical study of all that is.' When, however,

---

[1] Edman, *op. cit.*, p. 297.

this empirical study is further defined, it seems to be nothing else than the application of scientific method to all things whether in heaven or earth. Everything turns then, on the nature of scientific method and the 'concept of nature' which eventuates from its application. The concept of nature, however, which follows from the homogeneity of that method is much more limited than that which the new naturalism presupposes. This naturalism then finds itself in the dilemma of choosing between the notion of nature as the totality of all that is, or, assuming the primacy of science, of identifying it with the 'nature' of physical science—a dilemma for which I have never found any of its representatives proposing any adequate solution.

The point I am making is, I believe, of the utmost importance, for it concerns a fundamental ambiguity in the concept of nature which the so-called new naturalisms have exploited 'to the limit.' On the one hand, naturalism is defined in terms of scientific method, and thus is secured all the prestige which comes from such identification. On the other hand, when the new naturalists wish to display their humanity, and to prove that naturalism is friendly to all forms of the human spirit, sometimes including even religion itself, they soft pedal, even if they do not abandon outright, this scientific concept of nature and include in their *omnitudo realitatis* all those things which such a concept, by its very nature, necessarily excludes. Here we have a sort of double talk, or double book-keeping, which to all critical minds must appear, if not downright disingenuous, at least fatal to the formulation of any adequate philosophy.[1]

I am well aware, of course, that there are much more profound philosophies which might be, and indeed have been, described as syntheses of idealism and naturalism. I have in mind those of S. Alexander and Whitehead. Even more than the former are they to be welcomed as significant attempts to overcome the dualism of thought and feeling of the modern man, but as the problem is more profoundly conceived, so are the difficulties inherent in its solution the more clearly displayed.

Their more profound conception of the problem appears in the fact that both see the main task of philosophy to be the over-

---

[1] This fundamental ambiguity runs throughout the entire length of a recent volume of essays entitled *Naturalism and the Human Spirit*, Columbia University Press, 1944, and it is upon this mainly that its appeal rests.

coming of the isolation between natural science and values. Both in different ways acknowledge the objectivity of values. Alexander maintains that value, 'in its elementary, non-human form is a universal feature of the interconnection of things' a restatement of course of his position in Space, Time and Deity.[1] Like Alexander, Whitehead also in *Process and Reality*, reads value down into the elementary constituents of the universe. But this more profound envisagement of the problem serves but to emphasize the difficulties of such a synthesis, difficulties which I believe are to be found at the same place as in the more popular formulations. In the former the concepts of both idealism and naturalism are so watered down as to become as innocuous as they are useless. In these latter philosophies the notion of value is so watered down or, as I have elsewhere expressed it, so redesigned, as to make it compatible with almost any concept of the elementary constituents of the universe— short of brute material entities. In any case, one could scarcely claim to have transformed the main ideas of objective realism unto a realistic basis, for the ideas of value here employed are no longer those of any historic form of idealism.

No less serious are the difficulties presented by the realism with which the idealism would be synthesized. In both cases the realistic basis turns out to be a pure naturalism in which mind is wholly derivative. We understand this perfectly in the case Alexander's realism, which makes space-time primary and all other categories, including that of Deity itself, secondary and derivative. But no less naturalistic in this sense is a theory such as that of Whitehead, which makes 'events' primary (even though space and spatialized time are considered secondary). The primacy of the physical, non-mental categories in the categorical scheme is the essential of both philosophies, and this is the primary criterion of naturalism for it involves the derivative character of mind and knowledge.

It is true that with respect to Whitehead we must proceed with caution. That he differs in important ways from Alexander, and that he does not *intend* a mere naturalism in the sense defined, I am entirely ready to admit. But I cannot escape the

[1] *The Objectivity of Values*, Travaux du IXe Congrès International de Philosophie, Paris, 1937. See my comment on this paper in *The Present Situation in Axiologie*, Revue Internationale de Philosophie, 15 Juillet, 1939.

conviction that in the end his 'realistic basis' differs in no significant way from that of Alexander. It may be argued, as indeed it has been by some, including Professor Hoernlé, that 'the attribution of subjective immediacy to actual entities aligns him with the idealists and that Whitehead calls his doctrine realistic because, while thus attributing subjective immediacy he holds them to be devoid of consciousness.' But the notion of mind involved, as in the case of the notion of value already commented upon, is such as is not compatible with any form of idealism, objective or otherwise.[1]

C

The main issue then, from which this entire discussion started, and which is involved in the modern identification of realism with naturalism, is the contention that, since reality is prior to knowledge, mind must *consequently* (italics mine) have a status which is derivative and not pivotal. Why this, consequently, should ever have entered into modern thinking I am at a loss to see. It does not at all follow that, because the principle of being, or the postulate of antecedent reality, is dialectically necessary for an intelligible theory of knowledge, the mind that knows is causally derivative from this antecedent, being conceived as nature in the sense of modern science. This derivative status of mind and knowledge does not follow from the epistemological postulate of realism but is rather an inference, whether rightly or wrongly made, from a specific scientific theory, namely, that of Darwinian evolutionism.

It is natural to want to take the evolutionary picture at its face value, with all that it involves for human knowledge. But we have seen that this naturalistic account does not go very far, and that, when pressed too far, tends to become something 'perverse—' for it, denatures mind and with it the knowledge which it is the minds function to achieve. Such an account makes of the Sermon on the Mount as much of an accident as

[1] It can, I think, only confuse the issues to place Whitehead among the idealists, as does R. F. Alfred Hoernlé in his article 'The Revival of Idealism in the United States' in *Contemporary Idealism in America*. The reasons for my belief, as well as for the above account of Whitehead's position, are developed more fully in my article 'Elements of Unintelligibility in Whitehead's Metaphysics,' *The Journal of Philosophy*, Vol. XXXV, No. 23.

the Ninth Symphony and of Newton's *Principia* an even greater anomaly, perhaps, than both.

To the 'transcendentalists' who demur at this perverseness it is pointed out that, after all, it is simply a matter of historical fact that thinking and reasoning man did evolve by natural processes from anthropoid ancestors, a fact not disputed even by those whose deepest feelings are opposed to the admission. But so long as mystery surrounds the manner of the evolution there will always be the refuge of ignorance for the transcendentalists. To me this seems clearly a case of *ignoratio elenchi*. The issue here is not one of historical fact, although even on this count the phrases 'historical fact' and 'evolve by natural processes' are both too ambiguous to say whether the above proposition is or is not disputed; in some interpretations it certainly is. The issue is not whether man actually evolved; the question at issue is whether natural processes, in the sense conceived by natural science, can account for mind and intelligence as presupposed by natural science itself. We have here that same logical confusion characteristic of all naturalistic accounts of knowledge. First, various natural sciences are taken as premises for the conclusion that the objects or contents of consciousness occur within the organism as part of the response to stimulation by physical objects other than it. Then we are told that these intra-organic contents have a cognitive function. But how ascribe to these mere contents functions which, by their very nature, they are patently incapable of discharging? This is the *pons assinorum* which no purely naturalistic account of mind has been able to cross. Or, making use of a figure often employed in this connection, by this supposed 'scientific' account of knowledge, the scientist himself cuts off the very limb upon which he sits. For in thus deriving mind and knowledge from nature, as science conceives it, he must assume that his own account of nature is true. But on his premises, the truth of this account, like that of any other bit of knowledge, is merely the function of the adjustment of the organism to its environment, and thus has no more significance than any other adjustment. Its sole value is its survival value. This entire conception of knowledge refutes itself and is, therefore, *widersinnig*. The fact that so many modern minds do not feel difficulties of this sort is one of the things I have never been able to understand. I can only surmise that our devotion to so-called empiricism has robbed us of all sense of logicality, or what I should call the finer inner harmonies of thought—in short, the sense for philosophical intelligibility.

As to the transcendentalists, their belief in the transcendental character of mind is not the refuge of ignorance, but rather the result of their realization of the peculiarly vicious circle involved in all naturalistic accounts of knowledge. It is not their feelings that are outraged but their intellects.

There remain then the 'limits of naturalism' of which nineteenth-century philosophy constantly spoke, and these limits are precisely where they have always been, namely, when scientific method seeks to deal with knowledge and value. To say that nature is merely the totality of all that is, and naturalism merely the scientific study of all that is, are statements which have a pleasing sound, but when they are examined they are found to be either meaningless, or, if meaningful, imply conceptions which themselves set limits to naturalism. If we include in nature all that really is, we have made of nature something which is no longer recognizable as the nature of scientific method or of any critical philosophy that man has ever known—in short, that monstrosity which Kemp Smith described as supernature. Such conceptions can, however, serve only to introduce confusion into our thinking. How much better to abandon these mythologies of nature and to fall back upon the scientific concept, frankly recognizing that what goes beyond nature in this sense is no longer nature and that no philosophy which hopes to deal adequately with the totality of all that is, will call itself naturalism?

This is, however, not the main theme of this chapter, which is rather the synthesis of idealism and realism. In order, however, that it might be shown that a genuine idealism could be developed along realistic lines, it was necessary to dissolve the unholy alliance between realism and naturalism which has become the chief characteristic of modern thought. That this consistency of idealism with realism is possible has, I think, now been shown. That the postulates of both are not only consistent but actually require one another in any intelligible theory of knowledge was shown in an earlier chapter. This conclusion was, apparently, further confirmed by a more concrete study of the physical and humanistic sciences. The manner in which an idealistic philosophy could then be developed along realistic lines is the theme of the present chapter. Throughout the entire argument one of the main contentions has been that this synthesis of idealism and realism is present at least implicitly, throughout the entire great tradition of European philosophy. This contention, already stated in a preliminary way in the introductory chapter, is the specific theme of the concluding study.

Chapter X

Realism, Idealism and Philosophia Perennis. Epilogue.

I — A

THE theme, Beyond Realism and Idealism, has now been developed through the various stages of the argument as outlined in our introductory statement of the problem. Whether the general argument is convincing or the more specific attempt at a conciliation of realism and idealism of the preceding chapter is found tenable must be left for the reader to decide. In any case, nothing more can be added to the argument itself. There is, however, still a question that may significantly be raised. Granted that the case has been made out with some degree of convincingness, what is its meaning for philosophy and for the general culture of which philosophy is always the epitome?

That significance, I am bold enough to believe, would be very great. In the first place, if this position could be maintained, it would, as I have already suggested, free philosophy from many of the inhibitions from which it is now suffering and release its energies for the genuine problems of speculative thought which it has so long suppressed. In the second place, it would re-unite philosophy with the great stream of *philosophia perennis* from which it has been so long estranged. Since I believe both of these to be fundamental *desiderata* of our present culture this epilogue becomes an important part of our general study.

B

The arrest of spiritual initiative is an outstanding fact of our modern culture. The sources of our inhibitions are many and varied, but underlying them all is, I believe, the deep-seated feeling that there is no answer to the demand—as fundamental as life itself—we must know! Positivism in its various forms has sought to meet this depression by telling us that the problems generated by this demand are not genuine problems at all, but the human mind knows that this is not true. If these problems are meaningless, so also is life itself, for science as a human

239

enterprise demands a valour which science as a negation of ultimate meaning cannot give.

Not the least of these problems is this recurrent opposition of idealism and realism which, as I have maintained, has, for a long time arrested the energies of metaphysical thought. Is it strange that many have deprecated the constant revolving of our thought around this 'fruitless issue' and have sought to find a way out of the *impasse* by calling the whole problem meaningless. So far as the technical aspect of this issue is concerned all that is necessary has already been said. Still less is the problem meaningless from the standpoint of the cultural life of man. It represents, as we have seen, two irrefutable tendencies of life—two 'life forms' of thought, both of which are equally necessary. Denial of either can result only in arrest of the life of reason and ultimately in a fundamental dissociation of life and thought. Recognition of mere necessity, either psychological or social, is, however, as depressing as scepticism. It is only when they are seen to be reconcilable, not only in life but in thought and reason also, that the issue becomes significant; and with the recognition of its significance the energies of men can be turned to the fundamental problems—the very problems which not only interest philosophers but are profoundly significant for all thinking men.

C

The freeing of philosophy's energies for the genuine problems of speculative thought is, then, the first result which might legitimately be expected to follow from the transcendence of this opposition. But there is a second result, equally significant for modern culture, namely, the reuniting of our thought with the great stream of traditional philosophy from which we have long been estranged.

That this estrangement is the source of much of our present social and political ill is felt by many, and a return is advocated in many quarters. The doubtful wisdom of some forms of this reaction need not be denied, but the feeling that has motivated them is wholly sound. It is gradually coming home to many minds that our cultural and spiritual values are indeed bound up with a fundamental metaphysical structure and that estrangement from these ways of thinking means estrangement from the values themselves. It is increasingly realized that the foundations of our culture are Hellenism and Christianity, and it is this, more than anything else, that has led men to rethink the more ancient ways of thought.

The more general conditions of such a return to *philosophia perennis* I have discussed elsewhere,[1] but certainly among them is the solution of the epistemological problems which the modern conceptions of the physiology of knowledge have generated. I have no wish to exaggerate the importance in culture, either of the problem of knowledge itself or of the specific problem with which our discussion has been engaged, but he would be blind indeed who did not recognize that scepticism regarding human reason and knowledge is the root, acknowledged or unacknowledged, of scepticism in morals and religion. The conditions which created the modern epistemological problem are the same which have cut us off from traditional philosophy, and the confusions which this problem has engendered have led to a deep-seated confusion regarding the fundamental issues of philosophy. It is above all the senseless opposition of realism and idealism which has closed our eyes to the more fundamental issues which have made *philosophia perennis* what it is. It is only when we shall have freed ourselves from this senseless conflict that our eyes will again be opened to what these ultimate issues really are. That the rapidly changing cultural and intellectual *mileu* is itself relegating this conflict to the background is fortunately true, but it is still a disease of philosophy which philosophy itself alone can ultimately cure.

With this we are brought to the final stage of our argument, namely, the demonstration of the thesis, propounded in the introduction, that this entire European tradition in philosophy, with which our culture it bound up, is beyond the issue of epistemological realism and idealism; or, in terms of the preceding chapter, constitutes a synthesis of the cognitive values of both, and contains elements of both positions as necessary parts of its structure.

The development of this phase of the argument involves three stages: (*a*) the justification of the idea of a *philosophia perennis;* (*b*) the development of the cognitive presuppositions of this philosophy; (*c*) the relating of these presuppositions to the modern epistemological contrast of idealism and realism.

[1] *The Intelligible World*, chapter v, entitled 'The Return to Perennial Philosophy.'

II

The Idea of a Philosophia Perennis: 'The Unity of Philosophical Experience.'

A

The idea of a *philosophia perennis*, so long the object of neglect, and even of contempt, is again coming into prominence. So long as men lived in the afterglow of the Renaissance called the Enlightenment it seemed only natural to think that precisely this glow—and still more the colder light of reason which followed—marked a complete break with the 'dark ages' in which the natural light of reason was obscured by the clouds of superstition and obscurantism. Nothing, we now know, is further from the truth. The break with this philosophy did not occur in the Renaissance. The great stream of European rationalism not only continues this tradition, but carries along, in new forms, all the basal presuppositions of this philosophy.

We are now seeing European philosophy in a new perspective, and it is chiefly the experiences of modern Darwinian naturalism which have changed the point of view. We now see that the real break came with Locke's 'physiology of knowledge,' a naturalization of the intelligence which found its culmination and final form in the evolutionary naturalism which followed upon Darwin. In contrast with this naturalism, and its corresponding naturalization of the entire spirit of man, all that precedes takes on a significant unity and continuity, both of intention and of fundamental presuppositions.

The unity and continuity of the entire European tradition is the outstanding insight of the history of philosophy of the present. The continuance of this tradition with its *corpus philosophicum*—not the least part of which was the rational proofs for the existence of God—is the outstanding fact of the entire rationalistic movement from Descartes to Kant and Hegel. This continuity in one of its important aspects has already been made clear in earlier chapters. The significant point here is that it constituted the one 'comprehensive and magnificent scheme of thought which dominated European culture for a thousand years,' and with which all its values were bound up. This is the outward aspect of the tradition, but if one looks below the surface it becomes clear that that which determined both the unity and the continuity of this *philosophia perennis* were certain common presuppositions of intelligibility and intelligible thought which dominated the entire period, and which were first seriously challenged by modern sensationalism and naturalism. It is these, rather than the particular content of the *corpus philosophicum*, which determined both its character and its form. It is these that made it the perennial philosophy which it is.

B

It is true that the character of this *philosophia perennis* is often more narrowly conceived, namely, as identical with scholasticism. They are, however, far from identical. Scholasticism, as a unitary closed system, has never existed. True, there was a philosophy of the scholastics, but this philosophy appears quite different in the early scholasticism, the classical period and late scholasticism. The philosophy of an Erigina is another from that of an Anselm and an Abelard. St. Thomas carries on his battle on two fronts—against Augustinianism and Platonism, on the one side, and the Aristoteleanism of Averroes on the other. The basal question of the relation of knowledge to faith is differently solved in the early scholasticism of Anselm in the classical period by Albert and Thomas, and in the late scholasticism by Duns Scotus the William of Occam. At one point in particular the differences within the general movement of scholasticism become especially significant for our present purpose. The idealistic motive, with its so-called ontologism, to which perhaps St. Thomas himself made significant concessions, is as much a part of this perennial philosophy as the Aristotelean realistic motive. But while scholasticism has never existed as a closed system, it has existed as a form of thought determined by certain universally accepted presuppositions, which we shall examine presently. In this sense it represents not only a necessary part of *philosophia perennis*, but a part which is in a sense symptomatic of the whole.

St. Thomas was himself far removed from identifying his own system with the *philosophia perennis*, or conceiving it as a final stage of philosophy. He valued rightly the limited contributions of the individual to this stream of philosophy. The knowledge of truth is not a matter of the individual, but a common enterprise. As the present stands on the shoulders of the past and its tradition, so is it also the basis for progress in the future. Above all, St. Thomas knew that knowledge of a thing does not mean complete knowledge. This is a root principle of his thought. His thesis concerning the knowledge of being, namely, that our understanding is by nature directed to being, is meant only in the sense of an ideal programme. As he did not exclude from *philosophia perennis* his predecessors and compatriots, no more would he have excluded his philosophical successors who should carry on in the spirit of the Great Tradition. In this general movement St. Thomas is, however, an all-important figure. He was not only the great architect and systematizer of philosophy, raising it to a self-sufficient and independent 'science', but he, more than anyone else, became fully conscious of the presuppositions of this philosophy. In this respect he is the outstanding figure and it is, accordingly, about his thought that much of the succeeding discussion must revolve.

C

This idea of a *philosophia perennis* underlies Étienne Gilson's recent book, *The Unity of Philosophical Experience*. Philosophy is perennial in the sense, first of all, that, as he says, 'it always buries its undertakers.' But it is perennial in a second and more fundamental sense; it exhibits a unity and continuity which is essentially dialectical, although, for understandable reasons, he does not use the term.

It is dialectical in the sense that while philosophizing depends for its activity, in the first instance, upon individual philosophers, and is never found separate from them, it has in a certain sense its own independent life. Philosophy consists in 'the concepts of philosophy taken in the naked impersonal necessity of their own content and relations.' 'The constant recurrence of definite philosophical attitudes should suggest to the mind,' he holds, 'the presence of an abstract philosophical necessity. Granted that there is no such thing as historical determinism, it still remains true that history contains a metaphysical determinism. In each instance of philosophical thinking, both the philosopher and his particular doctrine are ruled from above by an impersonal necessity. Philosophers are free to lay down their own set of principles, but once this is done, they no longer think as they wish—they think as they can.' In the second place, it seems to result from the facts under discussion that any attempt on the part of the philosopher to shun the consequences of his own position is doomed to failure. 'What he declines to say will be said by his disciples, if he has any; if he has none, it will remain eternally unsaid, but it is there, and anyone going back to the same principles, be it several centuries later, will have to face the same conclusions.'[1]

The unity and continuity of philosophical experience is thus dialectical in character, and it is this which constitutes *philosophia perennis* in the second and more fundamental sense. '*Philosophia perennis*' is thus for Gilson, as he rightly says, 'not an honorary title for any particular form of philosophical thinking, but a necessary designation of philosophy itself, almost a tautology. That which is philosophical is also perennial in its own right.'[2] With this, one must in the main agree. *Philosophia perennis* should not be applied as an honorary title to scholasticism, however important in the history of thought the scholastic movement may be. But we cannot agree that it is merely a necessary designation for philosophy itself—almost a tautology. In fact, it is this expression, 'almost', that we find significant. If it is not a complete tautology, then there must be elements in *philosophia perennis* which are not characteristic of all philosophizing; there must be some types of philosophizing which are not in the movement of *philosophia perennis* and are contrary to its very spirit. In fact, it is only in a very limited sense that philosophers are free to lay down their own set of principles. Even in philosophy there is a difference between freedom and license, and an uncharted freedom—one which violates the conditions of intelligibility and intelligible expression—not only tires us but very properly serves only to call out our indifference if not contempt.

There is, then, a narrower sense in which the term *philosophia perennis* has been and, as I believe, must be used. As ordinarily used, the term has been employed to characterize certain elements in philosophical thinking that have persisted amid all the changes which have been brought about by historical and social

---

[1] *Op. cit.*, p. 302.   [2] *Op. cit.*, p. 318.

conditions. These elements may be described as the necessary presuppositions of intelligible thought. Philosophy not only buries its undertakers; it also, by its own inherent logic or dialectic, refutes and reduces to futility those forms of philosophizing which violate the conditions of philosophical intelligibility as such. Philosophy also buries some of its own practitioners. In other contexts, I have developed both the conditions of philosophic intelligibility and the form of an intelligible world which have been developed and established in the dialectic of European thought.[1] In the present context we are concerned with only one aspect—namely, the presuppositions of *philosophia perennis* as they concern the problem of knowledge —those presuppositions without which an intelligible theory of knowledge is impossible. This study involves the relation of these presuppositions to the issue set by realism and idealism.

III

The Cognitive Presuppositions of Philosophia Perennis. Their Relation to Idealism and Realism.

A

The unity of philosophical experience in the sense in which we have defined it, is very real and is, indeed, the outstanding fact of the entire Greek and Christian tradition. This unity is determined not so much by continuity of specific philosophical beliefs—although such continuity is there—as by the fundamental presuppositions that underlie the movement. It is these, rather than specific metaphysical beliefs, that distinguish it fundamentally from what I have called modernism in philosophy.

The presuppositions of such a *philosophia perennis* are twofold. On the one hand, there is the assumption of antecedent being; being is uniformly and necessarily a first principle of this philosophy. On the other hand, there is an equally fundamental assumption or first principle, namely, that *ratio est capabilis*, in other words, that there is such a relation between mind or reason and being that being can be known. This we may describe as the double cognitive presupposition underlying

---

[1] *The Intelligible World*, chapters v and vi; *Language and Reality*, chapter xiv.

traditional philosophy. Without either an intelligible theory of knowledge is impossible.

The first of these presuppositions, as the scholastics have always rightly seen, is the *sine qua non* of philosophy as such; the first metaphysical principle is being. This presupposition or postulate is quite independent of distinctions of idealism and realism within the European tradition, and was never denied prior to modern naturalism and pragmatism. This principle of antecedent being is itself not provable. It is, in Fichte's terms, an underivable first principle. The only sense in which it may be said to have any ground or reason is that with its denial the peculiar significance of knowledge is lost, or, as Maritain says, the denial of this first principle 'strikes at the very roots of the intelligence itself.'

The second of these necessary presuppositions is that *ratio est capabilis*, the assumption, namely, that the human spirit possesses the power to apprehend or understand being in ever-increasing measure. The rationality of being (the meaningfulness of the given) and the possibility of translating this rationality into the categories of human experience and knowledge, are the necessary presuppositions of the whole of traditional philosophy. They represent the idealistic ingredient in perennial philosophy. This second principle is no more provable than the first. The validity of the intellect—and of its primary ideas and principles—cannot, as for instance St. Thomas admits, be directly proven. We can only show that the denial of this validity leads to self-contradiction and unintelligibility. Its denial also strikes at the very roots of intelligence, and with such denial also the peculiar significance of knowledge is lost. The transcendence of mind, in this sense, is as much a presupposition of this philosophy as the transcendence of being.

This is the double epistemological presupposition underlying perennial philosophy, and its presence may be used as a touchstone to differentiate traditional from modernistic forms of thought. But there is a third element or presupposition, closely related to these primary principles and without which they themselves would scarcely be understandable, namely, the inseparability of value and being. This is the axiom of intelligibility which constitutes the underlying presupposition, and ultimately the driving force, of the entire Greco-Christian tradition. In so far as this is true, the driving force of this tradition is idealistic in the more fundamental and metaphysical sense, although, as we shall see, the position is beyond idealism and realism in the epistemological sense.

This characteristic presupposition of all traditional philosophy is a fact which Dewey also recognizes in his account of traditional European philosophy. An essential part of that philosophy, as he rightly sees, is its conception of the relation of values to antecedent reality.[1] In this tradition 'idealist' and 'realist' alike agree that ultimately being and value are inseparable—that the validity of our values rests upon the fact that they are grounded in being, while the significance of being rests upon the fact that being includes values as part of its nature.

This was technically expressed in the famous doctrine of the 'transcendentals'. Whatever is, in so far as it is or has being, is at the same time, and for this very reason, also true, good and beautiful. 'The humblest form of existence exhibits the inseparable privileges of being, which are truth, goodness and beauty.' These transcendentals are not predicates in the ordinary sense that being might have them or have them not; rather are they inseparable from being as such. This is the axiom of intelligibility—the inseparability of being and value—which underlies *philosophia perennis* in all its forms and expressions.

In this third, and basal, presupposition is included already the double presupposition of which we have spoken. By this very doctrine it has already placed itself beyond realism and idealism in the narrow modern sense, for it includes in it the motives of both. It is true that in the Thomistic version of *philosophia perennis* substance is first in the order of knowledge, but this does not mean that it is first in the order of being. From this more ultimate point of view being and value are equally primal. These 'modes', as St. Thomas calls them, do not add anything to being. They are aspects of being as such. All reality, therefore, has meaning, is intelligible. It is this basal assumption which, while beyond realism and idealism in the epistemological sense, is the very essence of metaphysical idealism as we have come to understand it.'[2]

[1] John Dewey, *The Quest for Certainty*.

[2] See on this question of the 'transcendentals,' Fulton J. Sheen, *The Philosophy of Science*, p. 137 ff.

B

These, then, are the necessary presuppositions of *philosophia perennis* in the sense in which we have used the term. The universal acknowledgment of these underivable first principles, whether merely tacit or explicit, constitutes the unity and continuity of philosophical experience which is the outstanding character of European thought. It is now necessary to examine the relations of these presuppositions to idealism and realism in the epistemological sense.

As the character of *philosophia perennis* itself is often too narrowly conceived, so also are its epistemological presuppositions. Scholastics frequently identify it with the Aristotelean and Thomistic strain in traditional philosophy and characterize this philosophy as realistic in the modern sense. I agree, however, with Hans Meyer that 'realistic epistemology in the sense of the idealism realism controversy, is wholly secondary to the concept of *philosophia perennis*.'[1] This I shall attempt to show and, in so showing, shall hope to make good the thesis that *philosophia perennis* is above realism and idealism in the epistemological sense.

I consider it one of the fatalities of modern thought that so frequently the issues are confused by this identification of the realism of the scholastics with realism in the modern sense. One might almost speak of a 'modern perversion' of the notion of realism, for realism in the sense of the postulate of antecedent being is as much a part of historic idealism as of realism. Certainly, as our historical sketch has shown, realism for scholasticism had almost an opposite meaning from that which it has today.

Realism, as understood in the scholastic philosophy, has as its opposite not idealism but nominalism. Realism, whether extreme or moderate, presupposes that the ultimate object of knowledge is the *idea* or *essence*, whether that idea is *ante rem* or *in re*. Knowledge is ultimately of the idea; only that which is ideal is intelligible. The ground of truth lies in its being independent of the knower, but only because reality itself is the realization of a spiritual content or idea. Only so do things possess a meaning and a sense; only so are they knowable. Further, the *logos* or idea in the real is understandable only because of the

[1] Hans Meyer, *Die Philosophie*, 1936, p. 179.

highest logos or divine spirit. It is true that there is an element in scholasticism—at least in the Thomistic version—which seems to justify to an extent the identification of this realism with modern naturalistic realism. For St. Thomas the only objects immediately known are physical objects. Knowledge of mind, both of the self and the other, and knowledge of God are possible only by inference. The physical object thus becomes the starting point and the norm of all knowledge, and in this sense constitutes a common ground for modern and mediaeval realism. It is probably true that this notion of the physical object as the object of knowledge *par excellence* has, through a long period of time, sufficed to give this object a privileged position in modern thought. But granted this, it still remains true that the Aristo-telean epistemology is not a necessary part of *philosophia perennis*. It is not necessarily involved in the primary principle of ante-cedent being and is at least secondary in this philosophy. More-over, even in the realism of St. Thomas, the physical object is not the physical object as understood by modern naturalistic realism; for him realism does not in the least imply naturalism. For whatever is, is, by its very being, also good, true and beautiful. This not only separates it completely from the naturalism bound up with modern realism, but embodies the very essence of all metaphysical idealism, namely, the cosmic significance of values.

Philosophia perennis is of course realistic—in the sense that any sane philosophy is realistic. For it every truth is *veritas ontologica*. The ground of truth lies in an antecedent reality; but only—and this is a most important *but*—because reality itself is the realiza-tion of a spiritual content or 'idea'. Only so do things possess a meaning and a sense. Further, the *logos* or idea in the real is understandable only because of the highest *logos* or divine spirit. A realistic epistemology, in the sense of the reality of ideas, is, of course, a necessary presupposition of this philosophy—as it is of its teleological world view, and of the absoluteness of our knowledge as well as of our values and norms. But realism in the narrow sense of modern epistemological discussion is not a necessary presupposition. I do not mean that many of the representatives of this tradition have not been realistic in this modern sense also, or at least may be made to appear so. That is, of course, a fact. What I do mean is that many have not.

Thus realism in this second sense is, I repeat, not a primary presupposition of *philosophia perennis*, but at best a secondary character of some aspects of it.

C

The necessary presuppositions of traditional European philosophy are then, when examined, seen to be beyond realism and idealism in the modern epistemological sense. But more than this is true. Both realistic and idealistic presuppositions, as we have defined them, are necessary and complementary parts of this philosophy; it really represents a genuine synthesis of the two—of the driving force of idealism and the resistance of realism. This we shall now attempt to show.

'The most tempting of all the false first principles,' writes Gilson, 'is that thought, not being, is involved in all my representations. Here lies the initial option between realism and idealism which will settle once and for all the future course of our philosophy and make it a failure or success. Are we to encompass being with thought, or thought with being? In other words, are we to include the whole in one of its parts or one of the parts in its whole? If intellectual evidence is not enough to dictate our choice, history is there to remind us that no one ever regains the whole of reality after locking himself up in one of its parts. Man is not a mind that thinks, but a being who knows other beings as true, who loves them as good and who enjoys them as beautiful. For all that which is, down to the humblest form of existence, exhibits the inseparable privileges of being, which are truth, goodness or beauty.'[1]

With much of this we can fully sympathize—especially with the last sentences which, as we have maintained, contain the very essence of the Great Tradition. But so far as the problem of realism and idealism is concerned, it represents, I believe, a serious misunderstanding and states the issue falsely.

First of all, I should maintain, the initial option of philosophy is itself wrongly stated. There *is* an initial option but it is found elsewhere. It is an option which lies far deeper than any choice between being and thought; it is the option between the inseparability of being and value, which is the underlying principle or presupposition of *philosophia perennis* in all its forms,

[1] *Op. cit.*, p. 316.

and the divorce of being and value which is the root principle of modern naturalistic realism. If this ultimate principle is rejected, if the cosmic significance of values is denied, then, as we have already seen, there is no significant difference between epistemological realism and idealism so far at least as fundamental issues are concerned.[1] The initial option which determines our entire philosophy is embodied in the doctrine of the 'transcendentals'. In comparison with this the option between 'thought and being' is wholly secondary. This cannot, I think, be too much emphasized. So far as the major issues of philosophy are concerned, a metaphysical idealism based upon this principle is closer to traditional philosophy than a realism which denies it.

In the second place, the principle of being is not the initial option in the sense that its choice *excludes* the second primary and underivable principle. A large part of our study has been devoted to showing that the realistic and idealistic presuppositions are not contradictory but mutually supplement each other. But since Gilson makes so much of the exclusive primacy of the principle of being we must examine the issue again.

Now that antecedent being is a fundamental notion of all philosophy or metaphysics is beyond question. Anyone who denies it (as for instance Dewey, if he really does) really abandons the philosophical enterprise as it has been understood. For, as Gilson says, 'Our mind is so made that it cannot formulate a single proposition without relating it to some being. We cannot speak about that which is not.' This is the primary element in all analyses of knowledge, realistic and idealistic alike. 'But if it is true,' Gilson continues, 'that human thought is always about being, it follows that the understanding of being is the first to be attained, the last into which all knowledge is ultimately resolved and *the only one* to be included in all our apprehensions. What is first, last and always in human knowledge is its first principle, and its constant point of reference. . . . We can safely conclude that since being is the first principle of all human knowledge it is *a fortiori*, the first principle of metaphysics.'[2]

Now I do not, for a moment, deny that being *is* an underivable first principle and that this principle is first, last and always in human knowledge. I merely deny that it is the *only* first

---

[1] Chapter ix.   [2] *Op. cit.*, p. 312.

principle. From the fact that we cannot formulate a single proposition without relating it to being, it does not at all follow that we can formulate it wholly by this relation. It does not follow that being is the only principle to be included in our apprehensions. As a matter of fact it is neither true that any metaphysics can be developed from this first principle alone nor that traditional philosophy has ever worked with this as its sole initial principle.

The classical objection to Gilson's position is, as he recognizes, that from such a vague idea as that of being alone, no distinct knowledge can be developed or deduced . . . (This is the basal argument of all those who, from Hegel on, have insisted that in order that knowledge should be possible, not only must mind be organic to being, but being must be organic to mind.) It is true, Gilson holds, that from the mere idea of being no knowledge can be deduced, but he also holds that it is not really an objection. 'To describe being as the principle of knowledge does not mean that all subsequent knowledge can be analytically deduced from it, but rather that being is the first knowledge, through which all subsequent knowledge can be progressively acquired. As soon as it comes into touch with sensible experience, the human intellect elicits the immediate intuition of being, X is, or exists; but from the intuition that something is, the knowledge of what it is, beyond the fact that it is something, cannot be deduced, nor is it the task of the intellect to deduce it. The intellect does not deduce, it intuits, it sees, and in the light of the intellectual intuition, the discursive power of reason slowly builds up from experience a determinate knowledge of concrete reality.'[1]

I do not think that the notion of an immediate intuition of being constitutes an answer to this classical objection. First of all, it seems clear to me that the belief in the mind-independent character of being is not part of the sense intuition itself. That much modern epistemological analysis, from Locke on, has made clear. It is doubtless an 'assurance that deserves the name of knowledge,' but it is itself not knowledge in the sense of intuition. It is a faith, a postulate, what you will, but not sense experience. But perhaps this intuition of antecedent being is an 'intellectual' intuition. If it is so conceived, the difficulty is

[1] *Op. cit.*, p. 313.

increased rather than diminished. For an intellectual intuition can be only of ideas or essences, and this is the very heart of idealism in the traditional sense; only an ideal world is ultimately intelligible. But Gilson's answer to this classical objection contains still another difficulty. This lies in the fact that 'the discursive power of reason,' which, according to him, 'builds up from experience a determinate kind of concrete reality' is itself wholly unintelligible unless this very reason is in some way organic to a principle of mind or reason in the world itself. For knowledge to be possible, not only must mind be organic to the world, but the world must be organic to mind.

Actually, as I have already maintained, traditional philosophy has never worked with the principle of being alone. It has always had a second equally fundamental and underivable principle, namely, the rationality of being, the meaningfulness of the given and the possibility of translating this rationality or ideality into the categories of human experience and knowledge. This is just as much an underivable principle as the first; no more provable than the first and no less certain. Indeed, these two principles mutually imply each other. For without the second the first is empty—the emptiest notion the mind can conceive—in itself it contains by no means all the flower and fruit of knowledge which Gilson supposes. Without the first principle the second is not less empty—can indeed be nothing more than the spinning of empty ideas in the inane. Each requires the other—as much as the notion of a valley requires the notion of a mountain, or the inside of a curve requires the outside. Any theory of knowledge which works with either, alone, is not sane in the meaning of the term given to it by Alexander, and *philosophia perennis* is, above all things, sane.

D

Philosophia perennis, as we have come to understand it, constitutes, then, a genuine synthesis of the two primary motives or first principles which we have characterized as realism and idealism. It is for this reason that it is equally possible to describe it as idealism or realism, according to the perspective in which it is viewed. It is possible to say with Willmann in his *Geschichte des Idealismus*, that this is the true idealism in contrast to the false which arose from starting exclusively from the subject. In contrast to this false idealism, it is possible to say that it is realism and to emphasize the realistic elements in the position. *But in the actual life of European philosophy they are held together in a genuine synthesis.* I call it a genuine synthesis for it is not merely an arbitrary union, attempting by some merely logical formula to combine cognitive values which are themselves metalogical, but a natural synthesis deeply grounded in the life of reason itself.

Philosophia perennis is the natural metaphysic of the human mind, and therefore, pre-eminently a sane philosophy—close to earth with all the furniture of earth, and close to Heaven with its celestial choirs. Arising out of life in all its fullness, it shares the fundamental initiatives of life itself, and, therefore, quite naturally presents in theory a reconciliation of these two tendencies which are equally indigenous to life. But the synthesis is really ultimately genuine because it takes as its initial option the axiom of all intelligibility—namely, the inseparability of value and being—an axiom incapable of 'proof', to be sure, but for that reason no less part of the natural light of reason itself. In this initial option is presupposed from the beginning the transcendence of realism and idealism.

IV

The Return to Perennial Philosophy: The Modern Era in a New Perspective.

A

So much then for the main thesis—that the great stream of European thought is above the opposition of realism and idealism in the modern epistemological sense. Recognition of that fact should enable us to transcend the opposition in our own thought and thus again make connections with those more fundamental ways of thought from which we have been long estranged.

Whether such a return is either desirable or possible, is of course, a debatable question and much in the forefront of philosophy today. It may not be desirable. It may be that not only an irreligion of the future, but also a purely positivistic and anti-metaphysical culture is the ultimate ideal of man. But even if a return were desirable, it might now be no longer possible. It may be that Western civilization, having passed through the stages of creative religious faith and the philosophical culture that developed from it, has now reached the stage of mere civilization, with its techniques—a stage in which only positivism and anti-metaphysical attitudes are possible. These are, indeed, debatable questions, answers to which can ultimately be little more than expressions of philosophic faith. Nevertheless, a word on these points may be in place.

Of the desirability—even imperative necessity—enough has perhaps been said. The pathetic attempts of modern man to retain his values without the rational structure with which they have been bound up, and to graft them upon an evolutionary naturalism with which they are wholly incompatible, constitutes the intellectual scandal of modern thought. A case could, indeed, be made out for the abandonment of these ideals themselves. I am myself not insensible to the force of the Nietzschean argument which, starting with the assumption that this structure is gone, and proceeding from the premises of evolutionary naturalism, concludes that all our values, moral, cognitive and metaphysical, must be transvalued. That seems to me to be perfectly logical and coherent. It is possible that our attempts to retain them, despite their absurdity in the light of the reigning naturalistic premises, is itself a weakness; that these very ideals themselves are 'ghosts' which in the light of a more scientific day will vanish away.

The possibility of such a return is even more a matter of doubt. There is a certain sense in which it is impossible to turn back the clock, even if it were desirable. For better or for worse, modern man has gone through certain experiences which have made him what he is and he cannot be other. Perhaps a positivistic and wholly anti-metaphysical culture is, even if not desirable, at least inevitable.

Signs are not wanting that this may be so. One need not accept the metaphysics of Spengler's philosophy of history in order to admit to an unhappy feeling that our culture is going very much the way that he describes. One need not bow to such notions as fate and destiny in order to recognize that the tide in the affairs of men has set in this direction, and to recognize also that there is little that can be done until the tide turns. It may be that it will never turn, or it may be that it is turning now; who shall say? But unless—and until—it does turn, all argument will be of little avail.

Whether then such a return is possible or desirable is a question which turns on such large issues, both cultural and philosophical, that answers to it, whether positive or negative, can be little more than matters of philosophic faith. Into this region I shall not seek to press further. Instead, I shall attempt to illuminate my main thesis by giving an account of what seems to me the present situation in philosophy as seen against the background of traditional thought. I shall characterize it as 'the modern era seen in a new perspective.'

B

I cannot escape the conviction that we have been viewing the modern era in large part in a false perspective. It is ordinarily assumed, almost without question, that 'the break with traditional philosophy' began with Descartes. This I believe to be a fundamental misunderstanding. Despite his method of doubt and his *cogito ergo sum*, which is thought by many to contain the germs of subjectivism, actually he continued the main motives of *philosophia perennis*, as indeed did the entire rationalistic movement of the continent. In the *corpus philosophicum* of this movement was included not only the entire theistic argument but the conception of reason upon which that argument was based. The break began rather with Locke's physiology of knowledge which Kant recognized for what it was. It implied already a naturalization of the intelligence which needed only to be confirmed by Darwinism, to be extended to the entire spirit of man. The key to the understanding of the nineteenth and twentieth centuries is then the fight of idealism with naturalism or, in its epistemological form, of transcendentalism with sensationalism. Modernism, as distinguished from the modern era in philosophy, is the story of the triumph of naturalism and positivism in every form of human life and culture.

Assuming the truth of this thesis recent European philosophy first becomes understandable. The story of this philosophy really concerns the nature and significance of the modern idealistic

17

movement for it is about it that all the issues of recent philosophy centre. As an inveterate enemy of naturalism, it alone, I shall maintain, has attempted to keep the faith of perennial philosophy and, however unsuccessful the attempt, to state its essential elements in a new form. It is opposition to this movement that has generated modernistic forms of philosophy, and this opposition has logically led to the 'destruction' of traditional philosophy itself.

Seen in this perspective, Kant's critical philosophy, despite its negative elements, takes on a positive form. His understanding of man as more than empirical and natural, and as linked with supernatural values, is a reaffirmation, in opposition to sensationalistic naturalism, of the driving force of the entire European tradition. It is true, he denied the mediaeval doctrine of the transcendentals with his lips, but he accepted it fully in his heart. Kant attempted valiantly to stem the tide of naturalism, already implied in Locke's physiology of knowledge, and thus the epistemological problem becomes central. For Kant knowledge is not possible, *i.e.* intelligible, except on the basis of the presupposition of transcendental mind; and values are not possible (or intelligible) except on the assumption of a transcendental free subject. Indeed, knowledge itself, including the distinction between truth and falsity, is possible only on the presupposition and postulate of freedom, for reason in all its forms is oriented towards the good.[1] It is, however, his position regarding realism and idealism which is from this point of view most significant. The ambiguity of Kant on this point, his attempt to combine an empirical realism with a transcendental idealism, is really his way of expressing the double presupposition of *philosophia perennis*. That it does not express it satisfactorily, either for the realists of that tradition, or for the still more exclusive naturalistic realists of the modern era, does not in the least affect either its intention or its significance. It is precisely because of this attempt at combination, however unsatisfactorily he may have expressed it, that he is still the philosopher that has most to say, not only to the critical philosopher, but to the critical scientist also.[2]

[1] For a fuller development of this interpretation of Kant, see my article entitled 'Kant and Modern Axiology,' published in *The Heritage of Kant*, The Princeton University Press, 1939.
[2] Chapter vi, p. 168.

The objective idealism, following upon Kant, is a continuation of the attempt to restore traditional philosophy in a new form. It may almost be said (*pace* the Neo-scholastics) to restore the scholasticism of the middle ages. It takes God, not man, as its starting point, being, not sensation, as its initial option. God, or the absolute reason, becomes again the centre of the world and the subjectivism which followed from starting with man, and the physiology of his knowledge, was transcended in a conception which again connected the human and the divine *logos*. This is the essential of the movement and in any attempt to evaluate it, it must be given first place.

In so far as the particular epistemological opposition is concerned, this too was an attempt to express the double presupposition of *philosophia perennis* in a new form. For the 'either —or' of the exclusive realist or idealist, Hegel is constantly saying 'both—and.' That he does not express it satisfactorily, either for the exclusive realists of that tradition or the still more exclusive realists of modern naturalism, does not, again, affect either his intention or its significance. His attempted synthesis of the two may fail to convince, but Royce is wholly right in maintaining that objective idealism is an attempt to effect just such a synthesis.[1]

It was, I suppose, recognition of the general truth of this interpretation which, partly at least, led Whitehead to hope that his own philosophy would be viewed as a transformation of the main ideas of objective idealism unto a realistic basis. That these ideas, expressed in the idiom of objective idealism failed to convince, is a matter of history. The reasons for this failure are many and varied. Internal logical weaknesses of its own, doubtless contributed to this downfall, weaknesses too well known to require mention here. Failure to recognize the relative autonomy of science and rightly to evaluate the empirical element in knowledge—above all, a certain over-intellectualization at the hands of narrow logicians led to a far-reaching reaction to the pragmatic or 'life' philosophies. A progressive subjectification of its originally objective character, especially on the part of the English idealists, led to a justified revolt which gave rise to modern forms of logical realism. Doubtless, too, idealism in the main 'tended to overreach itself' and

[1] Chapter iv, pp. 112 f.

weakened the force of its more fundamental arguments by attempting to prove too much. All this may be admitted, but these internal weakness would in themselves not have been sufficient. It was evolutionary naturalism which gave it its final *coup de grâce*. It was one of those cases in which the Time-Spirit did not change its mind but woke up to find its mind changed.

Seen in this larger perspective, the meaning of typical movements in present-day philosophy first really becomes clear. The essential irrationalism which characterizes them all, whether that of pragmatism or that of the still more fundamental existential philosophy of the continent, all stem from the reaction against objective idealism. But as the movement proceeded it became ever clearer that it is not merely this idealism which is attacked, but the entire rationalistic European tradition. Kierkegaard, the father of much of this irrationalism in Europe, was the first, so we are told, 'to break with the philosophy of essence which continued from the Greeks to Hegel,' and in a sense this is doubtless true. For this reason Heidegger, influenced by Kierkegaard, proposes in his *Sein and Zeit* the 'destruction' of all philosophy (meaning thereby the Greco-Christian tradition) as the propædeutic to his own modern philosophy of existentialism. John Dewey's attack on this tradition is part of the same movement. In all this we have, however, a confirmation of our main thesis, that this idealism is a continuation of the essentials of that tradition and that modern naturalism is the common enemy of both. It is little wonder that this same existential philosophy has already become in many quarters an expression of post-war disillusionment and irrationalism, and still less that Catholic philosophers find it more inimical than the scientific rationalism and positivism of preceding decades.

C

This interpretation of modern philosophy does not mean that I am arguing for a return to this idealism. The preceding account recognizes not only its internal weaknesses but also the fact that this particular formulation of perennial philosophy was conditioned by cultural and scientific factors which belong to the past also. It does mean, however, that I am arguing for a truer and saner evaluation of the movement in the entire story of European philosophy. In saying this I do not have in mind those childish attacks on Kant and Hegel arising out of the passions and prejudices of war, which would charge them with responsibility for all the ideas which we dislike in our enemies—with such things no really responsible or critical philosopher is for a moment concerned. What I have in mind is something much more fundamental, namely, the recognition of the fact that, however disguised at times, the 'main ideas' of this idealism constitute a continuation of the European tradition—and that which is more important in this context, when once modern naturalism with its physiology of knowledge and its naturalization of the intelligence, was inaugurated, these same main ideas could be expressed only in the form of this transcendentalism, and that therefore, seen in this perspective, this idealism has a permanently significant place in European thought.

If, however, I am not arguing for a return to objective idealism, just as little am I arguing for a return to *philosophia perennis* in any of its specific ancient forms. It is doubtless tempting to try to reinstate such ancient forms literally—and there are those who have yielded to the temptation—but this is surely to try to turn back the clock. Even in scholasticism, as we have seen, a *philosophia perennis* as a unitary and closed system never existed, and St. Thomas himself was far from identifying his own system with such a philosophy. These ancient formulations, magnificent as they are, had their local conditioning also, and this makes it necessary to separate the spirit from the letter. What then, it may properly be asked, perhaps impatiently, do you really mean by traditional philosophy and by advocating a return to its principles?

Tradition in philosophy, no more than in any other sphere of culture, is a literal repetition of dead concepts; it is life, movement and perpetual reinterpretation. But the reinterpretation which is necessary for life and movement, is always limited by the bounds of certain necessary presuppositions within which life and thought themselves must move if they are to be meaningful and intelligible. There are certain conditions of intelligibility and it is the recognition and acknowledgment of these presuppositions which alone makes philosophy perennial.

First of all, it is my contention that philosophers are really not free to lay down their own first principles. This is true of individuals and epochs alike. Even in thought, free as it must necessarily be, there is a difference between freedom and license. Philosophy is sometimes defined as thinking without prejudices or presuppositions, but this is true only in a limited sense. The philosopher does, indeed, seek to free himself from certain prejudices—of temperament, of time and of race—but precisely in that he does so he brings to light certain hidden presuppositions and postulates from which he cannot free himself and remain a philosopher. In fact, it is only in the light of these more fundamental presuppositions that he is able to recognize and eliminate his particular prejudices. These more ultimate presuppositions he cannot transcend. To do so is to court the irony of self-refutation, either in his own time or later. For there are conditions of philosophical intelligibility which cannot be gainsaid. It is my contention also that it is the acknowledgment, either explicitly or implicitly, of these necessary presuppositions, rather than the presence of particular doctrines, which constitutes the essence of *philosophia perennis*.

It is of the utmost importance that this position should not be misunderstood. To contend that there is a philosophy, however perennial, that remains unchanged and unchangeable despite the development of knowledge in the sciences, is precisely the dogmatism which it is the task of critical philosophy in all stages of its history to expose and transcend. Again, to maintain that this philosophy, however perennial, is final in the sense that it is completely coherent and intelligible, is to claim for it the status of a divine revelation rather than the product of fallible human thought. But neither of these impossible positions would any philosopher in his right senses for a moment maintain. Far reaching changes, not only in our knowledge of facts but in our categories of knowledge, such as our notions of space, time and causality, affect the form of statement of a metaphysical position. But no such changes, however vast, can affect in the slightest degree the ultimate demands of rationality and intelligibility. This is what I mean by *philosophia perennis* and whatever elements in this traditional philosophy time, and the knowledge of things in time, may change, there is that in its basal presuppositions, its initial options, which is, I believe, timeless and in principle irrefutable. What particular forms this philosophy may take in the future we cannot know. But of one thing we may be assured —if one form is refuted, it will immediately take another.

These general reflections apply with special force to the specific problem which constitutes the theme of this book. Here too, in the problem of human knowledge, the philosopher is not free to lay down his first principles. He is not free to choose to be either an exclusive idealist or an exclusive realist. Both realistic and idealistic postulates are necessary to an intelligible theory of knowledge; both realism and idealism are necessary parts of the natural metaphysic of the human mind and, therefore, of *philosophia perennis*. Both have undergone endless transmutations; but both are in the end irrefutable. It is for this reason that no sane philosopher has ever been exclusively realistic or idealistic and that every philosophy that has endured has really been beyond the opposition, at least in spirit if not in the letter. When we penetrate beneath the letter, with which naïve and literal minds ever seek to fetter the human spirit, we shall find that on the supreme issues, the great minds, whether we call them realists or idealists, are really one. Thus it is that, not only in their understanding of the issues but in the main ideas in which they have expressed their solutions, they are beyond realism and idealism.

INDEX OF NAMES

INDEX OF SUBJECTS